www.wadsworth.com

wadsworth.com is the World Wide Web site for Wadsworth Publishing
Company and is your direct source to dozens of online resources.

At *wadsworth.com* you can find out about supplements,
demonstration software, and student resources. You can also
send e-mail to many of our authors and preview new publications
and exciting new technologies.

wadsworth.com
Changing the way the world learns®

The Wadsworth College Success Series

Campbell, *The Power to Learn: Helping Yourself to College Success,* 2nd Ed. (1997). ISBN: 0-534-26352-6

Corey, *Living and Learning* (1997). ISBN: 0-534-50500-7

Holkeboer and Walker, *Right from the Start: Taking Charge of Your College Success,* 3rd Ed. (1999). ISBN: 0-534-56412-7

Petrie and Denson, *A Student Athlete's Guide to College Success: Peak Performance in Class and in Life* (1999). ISBN: 0-534-54792-3

Santrock and Halonen, *Your Guide to College Success: Strategies for Achieving Your Goals* Media Edition, 2nd Ed. (2002). ISBN: 0-534-57205-7

Van Blerkom, *Orientation to College Learning,* 3rd Ed. (2002). ISBN: 0-534-57269-3

Wahlstrom and Williams, *Learning Success: Being Your Best at College & Life* Media Edition, 3rd Ed. (2002). ISBN: 0-534-57314-2

The Freshman Year Experience™ Series

Gardner and Jewler, *Your College Experience: Strategies for Success* Media Edition, 4th Ed. (2001). ISBN: 0-534-53423-6

   Concise Media Edition, 4th Ed. (2001). ISBN: 0-534-55053-3

   Expanded Reader Edition (1997). ISBN: 0-534-51898-2

   Expanded Workbook Edition (1997). ISBN: 0-534-51897-4

Study Skills/Critical Thinking

Kurland, *I Know What It Says... What Does It Mean? Critical Skills for Critical Reading* (1995). ISBN: 0-534-24486-6

Longman and Atkinson, *CLASS: College Learning and Study Skills,* 6th Ed. (2002). ISBN: 0-534-56962-5

Longman and Atkinson, *SMART: Study Methods and Reading Techniques,* 2nd Ed. (1999). ISBN: 0-534-54981-0

Smith, Knudsvig, and Walter, *Critical Thinking: Building the Basics* (1998). ISBN: 0-534-19284-X

Sotiriou, *Integrating College Study Skills: Reasoning in Reading, Listening, and Writing,* 6th Ed. (2002). ISBN: 0-534-57297-9

Van Blerkom, *College Study Skills: Becoming a Strategic Learner,* 3rd Ed. (2000). ISBN: 0-534-56394-5

Watson, *Learning Skills for College and Life* (2001). ISBN: 0-534-56161-6

Student Assessment Tool

Hallberg, *College Success Factors Index,* http://success.wadsworth.com

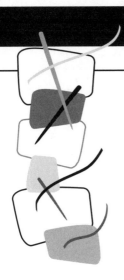

Foundations

A Reader for New College Students

SECOND EDITION

VIRGINIA N. GORDON
THE OHIO STATE UNIVERSITY

THOMAS L. MINNICK
THE OHIO STATE UNIVERSITY

WADSWORTH

™

THOMSON LEARNING

Australia • Canada • Mexico • Singapore • Spain • United Kingdom • United States

WADSWORTH

THOMSON LEARNING

Executive Manager, College Success: *Elana Dolberg*
Assistant Editor: *MJ Wright*
Project Manager, Editorial Production: *Trudy Brown*
Print/Media Buyer: *April Vanderbilt*
Permissions Editor: *Bob Kauser*
Production Service: *Scratchgravel Publishing
    Services*

Text Designer: *Paula Goldstein*
Copy Editor: *Carol Lombardi*
Cover Designer: *John Walker*
Cover Image: *IT Stock International, PictureQuest*
Compositor: *Scratchgravel Publishing Services*
Text and Cover Printer: *Webcom, Ltd.*

Printed in Canada
1 2 3 4 5 6 7 05 04 03 02 01

Wadsworth/Thomson Learning
10 Davis Drive
Belmont, CA 94002-3098
USA

For more information about our products, contact us:
Thomson Learning Academic Resource Center
1-800-423-0563
http://www.wadsworth.com

International Headquarters
Thomson Learning
International Division
290 Harbor Drive, 2nd Floor
Stamford, CT 06902-7477
USA

UK/Europe/Middle East/South Africa
Thomson Learning
Berkshire House
168-173 High Holborn
London WC1V 7AA
United Kingdom

Asia
Thomson Learning
60 Albert Street, #15-01
Albert Complex
Singapore 189969

Canada
Nelson Thomson Learning
1120 Birchmount Road
Toronto, Ontario M1K 5G4
Canada

Library of Congress Cataloging-in-Publication Data

Foundations : a reader for new college students / [edited by] Virginia N. Gordon, Thomas L. Minnick. — 2nd ed.
    p. cm. — (The Wadsworth college success series)
    Includes bibliographical references and index.
    ISBN 0-534-52430-3 (alk. paper)
    1. College student orientation—United States.   2. College freshmen—United States.
    3. College readers   I. Gordon, Virginia N.   II. Minnick, Thomas L.   III. Series.
LB2343.32 .F68   2002
378.1'98—dc21
                                                                    2001026019

Brief Contents

Contents

UNIT 4
How Should I Expect to Learn?   105
. . . .

UNIT 5
What About Technology?   143
. . . .

UNIT 6
What Should I Know About Careers?   179
. . . .

UNIT 7
What Are My Rights and Responsibilities as a Student?   211
• •

UNIT 8
What Is Diversity and Why Is It Important to Me?   233
• •

UNIT 9
Life After College: Future Success or Future Shock?   275
• •

Preface

Students entering college face many important decisions involving academic, career, and personal life choices. The purpose of this anthology is to stimulate the thinking of first-year college students about issues they will likely confront during their college years. We hope that, by reflecting on the ideas and insights provided by the writers included, students will recognize—and perhaps be comforted by—the universal character of the issues they face and will be better prepared to address and resolve them.

This anthology is designed to serve courses that help orient students to college life. In some colleges this text may also be suitable as a reader in first-year composition, and some high schools might find it useful in courses that introduce college issues to prospective college students. In compiling these essays, we have sought to incorporate topics in higher education about which entering college students should have some knowledge as they begin their journey to graduation.

The reader format provides a diversity of opinions and perspectives on a variety of topics. Consequently, it encourages dialogue among different points of view. Because such dialogue is essential to a learning community, students are encouraged to participate in the exploration of ideas, which is how their journey toward knowledge and self-knowledge can best proceed. Instructors are also encouraged to participate in the dialogue, because students will benefit from their example.

The topics are drawn from the common experiences of entering college students. Unit 1 examines the value of a college education by raising such questions as "How is college different from high school?" and "Is a college education an investment for the future or an end in itself?" Unit 2 focuses on what you can reasonably expect of college work and how you are likely to change during your college experience: Among the questions discussed are "What kinds of pressures will college work expose you to?" and "How can you deal with them effectively, not only as a maturing individual but also as a developing scholar?" Unit 3 takes up very practical topics—such as using the library, selecting your major, attending classes, and turning in assignments on time—that relate to the general question of "How can you succeed academically?"

Because the act of learning is such an integral part of student life, the writings in Unit 4 offer a variety of perspectives on this important process. Included are practical matters such as how to understand your own learning style and how to take an active role in shaping how you learn. New forms of learning that have taken root on many campuses—service-learning and distance learning—are also discussed in Unit 4.

Unit 5 complements Unit 4 by raising issues about technology—namely, how it can and will affect how we think, learn, and associate with others. The readings in Unit 5 cover different aspects of technology's influence that now permeate our academic, work, and personal lives. From a historical perspective on how technology has evolved to a futuristic view of tomorrow's workplace, the writers in this unit offer a fascinating picture of where we have been and where we might be headed. The essays in Unit 6 will help students better understand how their professional lives are likely to develop and, therefore, how best to prepare for careers in the changing world of the twenty-first century.

Unit 7 introduces the idea of college as a special kind of community, one defined by the common mission of its members—the search for knowledge and truth. Academic freedom (the freedom to express any point of view so that it can be studied and evaluated) is the essential condition of the college community. Because the search for truth is at the heart of the academic experience, certain kinds of behavior are intolerable within it, including, for example, cheating or plagiarism. Unit 8 discusses the value of diversity in a college setting: The dialogue essential to discovering truth places a high value on diversity because, through their diverse opinions and experiences, the members of an academic community enrich that dialogue and make it likelier to uncover many truths. Behavior that limits or undervalues diversity, especially discrimination against individuals based on minority group status, weakens an academic community and its ability to serve its primary mission.

Unit 9 looks forward to life after graduation. We believe that post–high school education needs to prepare students for lifelong learning. The essays in Unit 9 encourage you to think about the future, so that even in your first year of college, you begin to lay the foundation for the days after graduation.

In compiling this anthology we have been helped by many students, colleagues, and friends, and we thank them. Dr. Mac A. Stewart, dean of University College at The Ohio State University, supported us through his encouragement and by making time and resources available to us. Mary Ellen Jenkins, assistant dean of the Colleges of the Arts and Sciences, undertook the essential task of securing permissions for reprinting material under copyright and contributed important biographical information about the authors included here. Kristin M. Anderson, Augsburg College; Betsy Barefoot, University of South Carolina; Marvin Druker, Lewiston-Auburn College University of Southern Maine; Bruce Janasiewicz, Florida State University; and Margaret Turner, Coppin State University, reviewed drafts of the first edition manuscript and contributed invaluable counsel. The following responded to a survey that greatly helped us in making revisions for this second edition: Charles F. Aust, Kennesaw State University; Michael Chron, Eastern Illinois University; John L. Coffey, Eastern Illinois University; Jeanette DeJong, Curry College; Jackie Donath, California State University; Nate Hosley, Lock Haven University; Mark May, Eastern Illinois University; Kip L. McGilliard, Eastern Illinois University; Kelly Miller, Eastern Illinois University;

Michael Redd, Kennesaw College; Carrie Sharago, Eastern Illinois University; Wahfeek S. Wahby, Eastern Illinois University; Jan Wencel, Curry College; Margaret Willen, Eastern New Mexico University; and Rose Zhang, Eastern Illinois University. Natalie Wathen patiently typed and retyped the manuscript and helped us when our efforts at word processing threatened to go awry. Finally, we want to acknowledge the lessons we have learned from generations of colleagues and students in University College at Ohio State who enrolled in and taught University Survey, a course we have been associated with for more than 25 years that has, in that time, introduced more than 250,000 first-year students to the values and challenges of living and learning in an academic community.

Virginia N. Gordon
Thomas L. Minnick

The Value of a College Education: Why Am I in College?

S tudents attend college for many reasons. In a national survey by Alexander Astin of UCLA, who has studied each class of first-year students for many years, the largest number of entering students (73 percent) indicated they were coming to college to prepare for a better job. Other common reasons that students gave were to make more money, find a philosophy of life, become a more cultured person, or satisfy their parents' wishes.

Examining your reasons for enrolling in higher education can help you determine what you can realistically hope to accomplish as a student. Because new students may find it difficult to set tentative educational and occupational goals, they usually find it helpful to understand what the college experience is intended to, and can, provide. Such an understanding establishes a foundation on which to shape your personal expectations.

College will open for you an unbelievable range of opportunities to explore diverse fields of knowledge, along with a variety of activities that will help you grow personally

Enter to grow in wisdom. Depart to serve better thy country and mankind.

—Inscription on the 1890 Gate to Harvard Yard

and socially. Although you could educate yourself outside the college environment, it is much more expedient and satisfying to learn with other students and from teachers who are committed to creating an environment that supports learning.

In college you will have the time and freedom to delve into many areas of interest that you may not have explored. You will also be exposed to areas of the human experience that you did not know existed. Imagine! In a four-year (now often longer) span of time, you can acquaint yourself with a wide range of human knowledge and experience. Even in a two-year institution, these same opportunities exist, although they will be more focused.

At no other time in your life will you have such a concentrated opportunity for learning. In high school, most of the courses you took were prescribed for you by others. In college, although some majors are more rigidly structured than others, you have more freedom to pursue your personal interests. You are in control of your own learning.

On the other hand, if one of your reasons for being in college is to obtain a job, consider what college can offer you in preparing for your future career. A U.S. Department of Labor study, done with the American Society for Training and Development, identified the following seven basic skills that workers in the future must possess if they are to be successful: learning to learn, competence, communication, personal management, adaptability, group effectiveness, and influence. Many people feel that you will be able to acquire and perfect these basic skills through your college experience. Consciously working to acquire these skills in the classroom, in campus activities, and in social and other contacts will enhance your effectiveness with them by the time you graduate.

The readings in this unit are intended to stimulate your thinking about why you are in college and what you expect from it. The essays present a broad perspective on higher education and its value to the individual, not only intellectually but also as the beginning of a lifelong pursuit of learning. The first three essays in this unit (those by Bennett, Meiland, and Cicarelli) attempt in various ways to reconcile the notion of learning for its own sake with a practical question about careers that students frequently and justifiably ask: "But what can I do with a major in _____?" Gardner tackles the same question in a different way, by defending the (to him) universal value of liberal learning. Halverson briefly summarizes the history of American higher education in an essay included here because, when you want to know where you are, it can be helpful to know where you have been. These readings can help you compare your reasons for enrolling in college with some of the goals and objectives of higher education in general. You might also want to discuss with faculty, administrators, and other students your institution's mission and goals for preparing its students for the future.

The Lure of Learning

William J. Bennett

William J. Bennett is an accomplished scholar, teacher, and academic administrator. He was chairman of the National Endowment for the Humanities in the early 1980s, Secretary of Education in the Reagan administration, and the nation's "Drug Czar" in the Bush administration. Since leaving government service, Bennett has remained an active commentator on cultural issues, publishing more than a dozen books. He has stated that students should be taught "patriotism, self-discipline, thrift, honesty, and respect for elders." He received a Ph.D. in philosophy from the University of Texas and a law degree from Harvard.

This essay reflects Bennett's strong belief in the value of college teaching and its effect on students' learning. His career as an outstanding professor was obviously influenced by those who taught him and brought life to the subjects.

When I arrived at college as a freshman some time ago, I had definite ideas about how I wanted to use my four years of higher education. I wanted to major in English because I wanted to become *sophisticated*.[1] I wanted to become sophisticated because I wanted to land a good job and make big money.

But because of my college's course requirements, I found myself in an introductory philosophy class, confronted by Plato's *Republic* and a remarkable professor who knew how to make the text come alive. It seemed to me and many of my fellow classmates as if we had come face to face with a reincarnation of Socrates himself. Before we knew it, we were ensnared by the power of a 2,000-year-old dialogue.

In our posture of youthful cynicism and arrogance, we at first resisted the idea that the question of justice should really occupy our time. But something happened to us that semester as we fought our way through the *Republic*, arguing about notions of right and wrong. Along the way, our insides were shaken up a little bit. Without quite knowing it, we had committed ourselves to the serious enterprise of raising and wrestling with questions. And once caught up in that enterprise, there was no turning back. We had met up with a great text and a great teacher; they had taken us, and we were theirs.

Every student is entitled to that kind of experience at college. And if I could make one request of future undergraduates, it would be that they open the door to that possibility. College should shake you up a little, get you breathing, quicken your senses and animate a conscious examination of life's enduring questions. Know thyself, Socrates said. Higher education worthy of the name aspires to nothing less than the wisdom of that *dictum*.

---

[1]Vocabulary words are italicized in each essay—ED.

These are lofty ambitions. What do they mean in the context of four years of campus life?

A college is many things. It is a collection of dormitories, libraries, social clubs, *incorrigibly* terrible cafeterias. But above all, it is a faculty. It used to be said, when this country was much younger, that a log lying on the side of the road with a student sitting on one end and a professor on the other was a university.

That essence has not changed. It is the relationship between teachers and their students that gives a campus its own special genius. "Like a contagious disease, almost," William James wrote, "spiritual life passes from man to man by contact." Above all, a student should look for—and expect to find—professors who can bring to life the subject at hand.

What else should students find at college? They should discover great works that tell us how men and women of our own and other civilizations have grappled with life's relentless questions. What should be loved? What deserves to be defended? What is noble and what is base? As Montaigne wrote, a student should have the chance to learn "what valor, *temperance,* and justice are, the difference between ambition and greed, loyalty and servitude, liberty and license; and the marks of true and solid contentment."

This means, first of all, that students should find wide exposure to all the major disciplines—history, science, literature, mathematics and foreign language. And it means that they should be introduced to the best that has been thought and written in every discipline.

College is, for many, a once-in-a-lifetime chance to discover our civilization's greatest achievements and lasting visions. There are many great books, discoveries and deeds that record those achievements in unequaled fashion. There are many more that do not. A good college will sort the great texts and important ideas from the run-of-the-mill and offer the best to its students. And that offering will be the institution's vision of a truly educated person.

All students have different notions about where they want a college degree to take them. For some, it is law school or journalism. For others, it's public service. That's fine. College *should* be a road to your ambitions. But every student should take the time to tread the ground outside his or her major and to spend some time in the company of the great travelers who have come before.

Why? Put simply, because they can help you lead a better and perhaps happier life. If we give time to studying how men and women of the past have dealt with life's enduring problems, then we will be better prepared when those same problems come our way. We may be a little less surprised to find treachery at work in the world about us, a little less startled by unselfish devotion, a little readier to believe in the capacity of the human mind.

And what does that do for a future career? As Hamlet said, "Readiness is all." In the end, the problems we face during the course of a career are the same kind that we face in the general course of life. If you want to be a corporate executive, how can you learn about not missing the right opportunities? One way is to read *Hamlet.* Do you want to learn about the dangers of overweening ambition? Read *Macbeth*. Want to know the pitfalls of playing around on the job? Read *Antony and Cleopatra*. The importance of fulfilling the responsibilities entrusted to leadership? Read *King Lear.*

Even in the modern world, it is still that peculiar mix of literature, science, history, math, philosophy and language that can help mature minds come to grips with the age-old issues, the problems that *transverse* every plane of life. Students who bring to college the willingness to seek out those issues, to enliven the spirit and broaden the mind, will be more likely to profit in any endeavor.

Reprinted by permission of the author.

 Vocabulary

As you think about this essay, these definitions may be helpful to you:
1. **sophisticated**   worldly, wise, knowing
2. **dictum**   a formal authoritative pronouncement of a principle or opinion
3. **incorrigible**   not capable of being corrected, permanently wrong, stubborn
4. **temperance**   moderation in action, thought, or feeling
5. **transverse**   set crosswise

 Discussion Questions

1. How did Bennett and his fellow students initially react to their philosophy class? How did their reactions change?
2. What does Bennett ask undergraduates to do in order to expose themselves to the same wonders of learning that he enjoyed?
3. According to Bennett, what gives each campus its own "special genius"?
4. What should students find at college in addition to good teaching?
5. What does the college experience do for a future career, according to Bennett?

 How Can These Ideas Apply to You?

1. Have you ever been required to enroll in a course you didn't want to take? What was your reaction?
2. Have you ever had a teacher who affected you as strongly as Bennett's philosophy teacher affected him? Who was it? How did he or she affect you?

3. What did William James mean by saying "spiritual life passes from man to man by contact"?
4. Do you agree that reading great literature can teach you about life's problems and how to handle them?
5. How can you discover your institution's "vision of a truly educated person"?

The Difference Between High School and College

Jack W. Meiland

Jack Meiland is a former director of the Honors Program at the University of Michigan at Ann Arbor. This essay is from his book *College Thinking: How to Get the Best Out of College.*

Most high school students believe that college work will be similar to the content of their high school courses, which involved factual information. This essay describes how the expectation of college courses is different and what new types of intellectual work are required.

Since you know what high school work is like, we can approach the nature of college work by comparing college with high school. College freshmen believe that there must be a difference between high school and college, but their ideas about what the difference is are often radically mistaken. Students often see the function of high school as the teaching of facts and basic skills. They see high school as a continuation of elementary and junior high school in this respect. In senior high school, one learns physics and chemistry, trigonometry, American and world history—all subjects in which the "facts" to be learned are harder, but in which the method is much the same as in elementary and junior high school. The method of study most commonly used is memorization, although students are also called upon to apply memorized formulas in working problems and to make deductions in mathematical proofs. There are some exceptional high school classes, and some exceptional high schools, in which this is not so. But by and large, the perceived emphasis in secondary education is on learning facts through memorization. The secondary schoolteacher holds a position of authority because he or she has mastered factual information. Tests demand recitation of facts; papers require compilation of facts.

It is only natural, then, that the typical student sees college along these same lines. Reinforced by the relation between elementary school, junior high, and high school, the students usually believe that the relation between high school and college is the same as that between junior high school and high school. They believe that the difference between high school and college is that college courses are simply more difficult and that they are more difficult because they present more difficult factual information; they examine more difficult factual information; they examine more difficult topics; they go over topics covered in high school but in a more detailed and painstaking way.

College is taken to be different from high school only in being more difficult. Unfortunately this belief is reinforced by the actual content and method of presentation of typical freshman courses and programs. For example, in the first semester, a freshman might take a course in English composition, a beginning physics course, a course in a foreign language, and perhaps a lower-level survey course in social science or history. These courses are often indistinguishable from high school courses.

New Types of Intellectual Work

At the same time, college freshmen sometimes suspect or expect that college is or should be different *in kind* (not just in difficulty) from high school—that somehow intellectual activity in college is or should be of a distinctly different and higher level. And this expectation is fulfilled when the student gets beyond the introductory survey courses. There the instructors do seem to expect something different *in kind* from the student, though without telling the student explicitly and in detail what this is.

The good college teacher presents some information, in the sense of "what is currently believed." But such a teacher also spends much time talking about *the basis* on which this information is currently believed. *A large part of college work consists of discussing and examining the basis of current beliefs.*

The difference between high school and college is not that there is intellectual activity in one and not in the other. The difference is that college work requires that students engage in a *different kind* of intellectual activity, in addition to the activity of understanding the material that is presented. The first type of intellectual activity in both high school and college is understanding the material. Even here, though, college requires a different and higher type of understanding. Once the material is understood, the college student must perform another sort of intellectual work on the material, namely critical examination and evaluation. A main difference, then, between high school and college is that *new types of intellectual work* are required at the college level.

Material is presented in college not as something to be believed on the basis of authority but as something to be believed because such belief is rationally justified and can be rationally defended. Thus, much work in college—and, I would say, the work that is characteristic of college—deals with the rational justification of belief. College teachers are concerned not merely with imparting information but also, and mainly, presenting and examining the basis on which this information is or should be believed. They do this because they want this material to be believed on the basis of reason rather than on the basis of authority. It is a basic *presupposition* of the modern mind that rationally based belief is better than belief based on authority, on faith, or on some other nonrational process. Thus, much time in college is spent investigating the *rationality* of this or that belief.

It is important to notice that once we make this shift from authority to rational evaluation, the mode of presentation of the material—and the way in which we regard the material—also changes. Material that is presented on the basis of authority is presented as factual and given an air of being absolutely and unchangeably true. Material that is presented on the basis of rational justification is presented as belief, as theory, as *hypothesis,* sometimes as *conjecture*—as material supported to a greater and lesser degree by argument and evidence. And this difference in mode of presentation makes an enormous difference in how the material is regarded. What is treated in high school as eternal and unchangeable fact that human beings have discovered in their continual and relentless progress toward total knowledge will be treated in college as belief that may perhaps be well supported at the present but that could turn out to be wrong. Another way of putting this is: what is fact in high school is often only theory—perhaps well-supported theory but nevertheless only theory—in college. And theories must be treated as such: one must examine the evidence to see how much support it gives the theory, and alternative theories must be examined to see which is better, that is, to see which theory should be believed.

Vocabulary

As you think about this essay, these definitions may be helpful to you:
1. **presupposition**   supposing beforehand
2. **rationality**   reasonableness
3. **hypothesis**   a tentative assumption
4. **conjecture**   a conclusion deduced by guesswork

Discussion Questions

1. What, according to Meiland, do high school students assume about high school teaching?
2. What does a college course expect that is different from high school?
3. What does Meiland mean by "a rational justification of belief" when referring to college course work?
4. What is the difference in material being presented by an "authority" versus material presented for "rational justification"?
5. Why is "fact" in high school treated as "belief" in college courses?

How Can These Ideas Apply to You?

1. What were your impressions of the difference between high school course work and college work when you entered college?
2. Have you found first-year courses to be similar to high school courses in the way that Meiland contends?
3. In your experience, does college-level work require you to use evidence to support the factual material you are learning?
4. How has this extended approach to college course work material influenced your way of thinking and learning?

A New Debate Is Joined over an Old Question: Is College an Investment or an End in Itself?

James Cicarelli

James Cicarelli is currently dean of the Walter E. Heller College of Business Administration at Roosevelt University in Chicago, Illinois.

In this essay, Cicarelli discusses the objectives of higher education and how to measure its impact on students. He outlines two philosophies and discusses how each is supported by different types of disciplines and institutions.

The seemingly endless debate about higher education is now focusing on the question of what the purpose of higher education is and how best to determine how well colleges and universities are achieving it. Particularly heated right now is the discussion over the pros and cons of so-called value-added *assessment.*

On one side of the debate are proponents of the relatively new view of college as a place where students go to add to their individual reservoirs of information. This philosophy of education emphasizes quantifiable knowledge that can be measured by student performance on nationally standardized tests. The idea is that by testing students before, during, and at the end of their college careers, an institution can discover its educational strengths and weaknesses through "outcomes evaluation"—measuring exactly how much has been added to each student's store of knowledge by the education he or she has received.

On the other side of the debate are those who hold a more traditional view of college as a place where students go to learn to appreciate their cultural heritage, *hone* their skills in critical thinking and communication, and otherwise transform themselves from self-centered individuals into decent and caring citizens. In this view, the emphasis in college should be more on the development of moral principles than on the accumulation of knowledge, per se. Since that sort of outcome is difficult, if not impossible, to measure, the *traditionalist* institution looks to "input" rather than "output," measuring success in terms of the variety and depth of experience to which its students have been exposed.

Despite obvious differences, the two philosophies are not mutually exclusive. Actually, both can be seen as variants of "*developmentalism*," an approach to education concerned with both the content and the *cognitive* aspects of learning. What set the two views apart are their conflicting methods of assessment, and the resulting controversy is going to dominate the discussion of evaluation for the foreseeable future.

While each side aims to improve higher education, both systems have disadvantages that would make them less effective than their proponents promise. For example, it is foolhardy to judge the success of a college education in terms of how much information the students have accumulated, because so much of it is already obsolete by the time they graduate. Students need to learn how to learn and how to teach themselves—talents that are nurtured by the ability to think clearly and read and write effectively, rather than by the mastery of information whose half-life is often measured in months.

On the other hand, it is pretentious to suppose that a college can teach values or should even try to do so. While most people can accept the broad principles embodied in the old Superman motto—"Truth, Justice, and the American Way"—it's difficult to translate them into working precepts. *Whose* truth? *What* system of justice? *Which* American way? Only in a dictatorship is one set of values taught to all. Yet simply exposing students to competing value systems, without discrimination, leads to confusion, if not anarchy.

Contributing to the controversy are the differences between professional, career-oriented education and general, liberal arts education. The former readily lends itself to the value-added approach because a profession is based on a body of knowledge that must be mastered before the student becomes a practitioner. Mastery of factual information can be demonstrated by passing a standardized test. Such a test shows how well an institution has prepared its students for entry into a profession. In other words, it measures the effectiveness of the education provided. Thus, prospective students interested in a particular career might consider such test results when deciding which college to attend. Unfortunately, that is not foolproof.

A decade ago, for example, when the boom in the oil industry led many colleges to expand their geology programs and others to begin new ones, a bachelor's in petroleum engineering was the hottest degree an undergraduate could earn. Today, most of those programs are as inactive as the West Texas oil fields where all the new geologists and engineers were supposed to find work. Educating for a job can produce graduates who are fit for that job and little else. A liberal arts education, on the other hand, can provide students with skills that transcend specific jobs and can be usefully applied in virtually any occupation.

The general-vs-professional issue is part of the larger question of whether college should be seen as an investment or as an end in itself. Advocates of the value-added philosophy tend to consider higher education an investment, an expenditure of time and resources that should yield a payoff large enough to justify the initial cost. In their view, society invests a great deal in education, in part because of the hope that the schools and colleges will produce productive citizens who will then ensure that the next generation has the wherewithal to renew the investment. Traditionalists are more apt to view higher education as something one acquires for its own sake, not because it may lead to a good job or some other material gain. If it does result in enrichment in monetary as well as intellectual terms, fine; but the purpose of a college education is to make one better, not necessarily richer.

Whatever else is involved in the debate, a big part of it, for me, has to do with romanticism versus realism. My romantic side, the one that envisions college as a mind-expanding experience, sees the value-added philosophy as an educational straitjacket that demands curriculum conformity at the expense of individualism and experimentation. Reducing the purpose of college to producing graduates who can demonstrate their proficiency on national examinations risks our turning out intellectual clones whose creativity and imagination are suppressed, if not obliterated. Only the traditional approach promises to develop free-thinking citizens who cherish liberty and, therefore, are willing to question authority rather than just accept it blindly.

My realistic side, however, characterizes this line of reasoning as so much drivel. The colleges and universities in the United States represent the entire spectrum of values, from secular liberalism to religious fundamentalism. Students are free to choose the institution that best fits their individual preferences, and national value-added tests would not restrict their choice one iota. In fact, such a system would take some of the guesswork out of choosing a college, because it would show prospective students just how well an institution has done in delivering what it promises.

At this point, it's hard to tell how, if at all, the debate will be resolved. Institutions with no national reputation and few resources will probably embrace the value-added philosophy, since they have everything to gain by doing so and little to lose. Conversely, the better-known, better-endowed institutions will tend to stick with tradition, because they have little to gain and a lot to lose. If the students from the nation's top colleges do well on national standardized tests, they will simply be performing as expected. Should they do poorly, however, even in relative terms, their performance would be taken as a sign that the college or university was doing a poor job, and its reputation would suffer accordingly.

The unknown quantity so far is which side the institutions in the middle, the ones with "average" students and reputations and resources, will take in the controversy. They constitute the majority, after all, and it is their response that will determine the outcome of the debate. Should they tilt toward the value-added side, then evaluating educational results by numbers will become an integral part of the American college system. If, however, they stay on the side of tradition, then "value-added" will, like "relevance," become an interesting footnote in the history of higher education.

Reprinted by permission of the author.

Vocabulary

As you think about this essay, these definitions may be helpful to you:
1. **assessment**   a determination of the importance, size, or value
2. **hone**   to make more acute, intense, or effective
3. **traditionalists**   people who believe an inherited or established pattern of thought
4. **developmentalism**   belief in a process of growth, differentiation, or evaluation by successive changes
5. **cognitive**   capable of being reduced to empirical factual knowledge

Discussion Questions

1. What do advocates of the value-added philosophy consider to be the worth of a college education?
2. According to Cicarelli, how do traditionalists view higher education?
3. What are the differences between a specific, career-oriented education and a general, liberal arts education?
4. How does Cicarelli distinguish between romanticism and realism? Which do you think is the better view? Why?
5. Does Cicarelli think the question of value-added assessment will be resolved? How?

How Can These Ideas Apply to You?

1. Are you inclined toward a career-oriented education, or do you prefer a more general liberal arts education? What are the advantages of each to you personally?
2. Do you think standardized tests or grades are an accurate measure of what you learn? Why? What other methods could be used?
3. What is "critical thinking"? How do you use this skill in and out of the classroom?
4. Do you think the general education courses required for most undergraduate degrees help to make you knowledgeable about areas you would not be exposed to otherwise? Why?
5. How will you measure the success of your own college experience? Intellectually? Personally? Socially?

An Uncluttered Perspective: The True, the Beautiful, and the Good

Howard Gardner

Howard Gardner is the John H. and Elizabeth A. Hobbs Professor in Cognition and Education at Harvard. The author of 18 books and several hundred articles, Gardner has argued that there are many kinds of intelligence, not just one, and therefore that there cannot be only one way to measure intelligence. This selection is from his 1999 book *The Disciplined Mind: What All Students Should Understand.* In this essay, he describes three important ideals that should inspire education.

I want everyone to focus on the content of an education—the meat and potatoes: on how that content should be presented, mastered, put to use, and passed along to others. Specifically, I believe that three very important concerns should animate education; these concerns have names and histories that extend far back into the past. There is the realm of truth—and its underside, what is false or indeterminable. There is the realm of beauty—and its absence in experiences or objects that are ugly or *kitschy.* And there is the realm of morality—what we consider to be good, and what we consider to be evil.

To make clearer what I include in these realms, let me mention three topics that I would like individuals to understand in their fullness. My example in the realm of truth is the theory of evolution, as first articulated by Charles Darwin and as elaborated upon by other scientists over the last one hundred and fifty years. This is an important area of science, with particular significance for a developmental psychologist like me. Unless one has some understanding of the key notions of species, variation, natural selection, adaptation, and the like (and how these have been discovered), unless one appreciates the perennial struggle among individuals (and populations) for survival in a particular ecological niche, one cannot understand the living world of which we are a part.

The processes of evolution are fascinating in their own right, as countless budding scientists have discovered. But such understanding has also become necessary if one is to participate meaningfully in contemporary society. Absent a grasp of evolution, we cannot think systematically about a whole range of topics that affect human beings today: the merits and perils of cloning; the advisability of genetic counseling, gene therapy, and various forms of *eugenics*; assertions that "lifelike entities" have been created computationally and that these entities evolve in a manner similar to organic matter; claims that human behavior is best explained by sociobiology or evolutionary psychology.

As my example in the realm of beauty, I select the music of Mozart: to be specific, his opera *The Marriage of Figaro.* This choice begins in the personal.

I love classical music, and in particular the works of Mozart; for me, at least, they represent the pinnacle of beauty fashioned by human beings. I believe that everyone ought to gain an understanding of rich works like *Figaro*—their intricate artistic languages, their portrayals of credible characters with deeply felt human emotions, their evocation of the sweep of an era.

Again, such understanding is its own reward; millions of people all over the globe have been enriched by listening to Mozart or immersing themselves in other artistic masterpieces from diverse cultures. Moreover, a sophisticated grasp of Mozart's achievement can be brought to bear on unfamiliar works of art and craft and perhaps also inspire beautiful new creations. And such understanding also proves relevant to the decisions that we make as citizens; which arts, artists, and other creative individuals to support; how to support them; how best to encourage new works; whether there are artistic creations that ought to be censored or regulated, and, if so, by whom; whether the arts should be taught in school, after school, or not at all.

Finally, as my example in the realm of morality, I would like individuals to understand the sequence of events known as the Holocaust: the systematic killing of the Jews and certain other groups by the Nazis and others, before and especially during the Second World War. This event has personal significance, since my family came from Germany and several of its members were victims of the Holocaust. But every human being needs to understand what it is that human beings are capable of doing, sometimes in secret, sometimes with pride. And if the Holocaust is mostly an account of unprecedented human evil, there are scattered incidents of goodness and heroism even in that grim chapter.

Like the study of science and art, accounts of historical events can be intrinsically fascinating. But they have a wider significance. I believe that people are better able to chart their life course and make life decisions when they know how others have dealt with pressures and dilemmas—historically, contemporaneously, and in works of art. And only equipped with such understanding can we participate knowledgeably in contemporary discussions (and decisions) about the culpability of various individuals and countries in the Second World War. Only with such understanding can we ponder the responsibility of human beings everywhere to counter current efforts at genocide in Rwanda and the former Yugoslavia and to bring perpetrators to justice.

The understanding of striking examples of truth, beauty, and goodness is sufficiently meaningful for human beings that it can be justified in its own right. At the same time, however, such an understanding is also necessary for productive citizenship. The ways of thinking—the disciplines—that have developed over the centuries represent our best approach to almost any topic. Without such understanding, people cannot participate fully in the world in which they—*we* live.

One might think that at least some understanding of these well-known topics is widespread. It is therefore sobering to discover that the theory of evolution is considered to be false by one out of every two Americans, and even by 20 percent of science educators. According to the noted scientist Carl Sagan, only 9 percent of Americans accept that humans have evolved slowly from more ancient beings without any divine intervention. As for the Holocaust, about one-third of all Swedish high school students believe that the Holocaust did not take place. Comparable skepticism (if not outright denial) is expressed by various American groups; 20 percent of Americans admit that they do not know what happened in the Holocaust and 70 percent wish that they were better informed about it. Robert Simon, who teaches philosophy at Hamilton College, reports that anywhere from 10 to 20 percent of his American students cannot bring themselves to say that the Nazi attempt at genocide was wrong.

It is not difficult to anticipate a response to this trio of topics: How can one call this an education for all human beings? It is time-bound (the modern era); it is place-bound (Western Europe and places influenced by it); and it is even linked to the author's personal concerns.

"Right and not right," as they say, I would indeed be pleased if all human beings became deeply immersed in the themes of evolution, Mozart, and the Holocaust. There are worse ways to enlarge one's universe. *But—note well—these choices are not privileged, and certainly not uniquely so.* Within the West, there are numerous other scientific theories of importance (Newtonian mechanics and plate tectonics, to name just two examples); other singular artistic achievements (the works of Michelangelo or Rembrandt, Shakespeare or George Eliot); other morally tinged historical events (the French and Soviet revolutions; the American struggle over slavery). And within other cultural traditions, there are abundant examples of the true (these would include folk theories about healing or traditional Chinese medicine); the beautiful (Japanese ink and brush painting; African drum music); and good and evil (the precepts of *Jainism,* the stories of Pol Pot and Mao's Cultural Revolution, the generosity of bodhisattvas).

I am not contending, then, that everyone needs to be able to explain what constitutes a species or to discern the development of melodies and the intermingling romances in a work like *Figaro,* or to analyze the reasons why so many Germans were complicitous in the Holocaust. Rather, what I claim is that "an education for all human beings" needs to explore in some depth a set of key human achievements captured in the venerable phrase "the true, the beautiful, and the good."

Another possible objection. Aren't the categories "true," "beautiful," and "good" themselves time- and culture-bound? Again, this is a valid point, but not a decisive one. The articulated concepts of "truth," "beauty," and "goodness" reflect a philosophically oriented culture; indeed, our first records of explicit discussion of these virtues are the dialogues recorded by Plato in Greece nearly 2500 years ago. Other cultures have developed similar notions, although how they parse the three domains may well differ. However, the beliefs and practices of cultures—the beliefs and practices that they value, transmit, punish, or prohibit—reveal that each culture harbors specific views of how the world is and how it should (and should not) be. And these views embody implicit senses of truth, beauty, and morality.

There is another, more important reason for my endeavor. In the end, education has to do with fashioning certain kinds of individuals—the kinds of persons I (and others) desire the young of the world to become. I crave human beings who understand the world, who gain sustenance from such understanding, and who want—ardently, perennially—to alter it for the better. Such citizens can only come into existence if students learn to understand the world as it has been portrayed by those who have studied it most carefully and lived in it most thoughtfully; if they become familiar with the range—the summits, the valleys, the straight and meandering paths—of what other humans have achieved; and if they learn always to monitor their own lives in terms of human possibilities, including ones that have not been anticipated before....

I've selected my three textbook examples because they are familiar to me, and because they will be familiar to many readers. But I must repeat: there is nothing *sacrosanct* about this trio. Another book, on another day, could focus upon relativity, revolutions, and the *ragas* of southern India. And I would devour such a book....

Reprinted by permission of Simon & Schuster from *The Disciplined Mind*, by Howard Gardner. © 1999 by Howard Gardner.

• •

Vocabulary

As you think about this essay, these definitions may be helpful to you:
1. **kitschy**   adjective form of *kitsch,* which means sentimentality or tastelessness in decoration or the arts
2. **eugenics**   the science that deals with the improvement of races and breeds through the control of hereditary factors and mating
3. **Jainism**   a Hindu religious sect that teaches reverence for wisdom and respect for animals
4. **sacrosanct**   very holy or sacred
5. **ragas**   musical works that follow a traditional form of the classical music of India

Discussion Questions

1. What is the purpose of education, according to Gardner?
2. What does Gardner mean when he says "the range—the summits, the valleys, the straight and meandering paths—of what other humans have achieved ..."? Is his metaphor from geography useful?

3. Gardner chooses Charles Darwin's theory of evolution as his example of "the True." Explain why this is a controversial choice.
4. Gardner says that his selection of examples is based in his cultural framework. Using the examples as your clues, characterize Gardner's personal cultural background.

 # How Can These Ideas Apply to You?

1. Select one example for each of Gardner's three categories (the True, the Good, and the Beautiful) but draw them from a different cultural context. How did you become familiar with that other culture?
2. Gardner's examples for "the True" in modern western culture are all drawn from science. Can you cite other examples of things that are true but are not from science? How can you know that your examples represent the truth?
3. Define your personal values by giving three important examples of what you believe is "the Good."
4. Assuming that Gardner is right about the purpose (or "end") of education, how can you best work to achieve that goal for yourself?

American Higher Education: A Brief History

William H. Halverson

William H. Halverson is associate dean emeritus of University College at The Ohio State University, Columbus, Ohio. A philosopher by training, Dr. Halverson is now widely known for his recent translations from Norwegian.

This essay presents a brief history of higher education in the United States. Although modeled initially after the great English universities, the American university has developed into a unique institution.

• • • • • • • • • • • • • • • • • • • •

The modern American university is the product of a number of historical developments occurring over a period of several centuries. The story of higher education in America begins with the establishment of a small number of colonial colleges in the seventeenth and eighteenth centuries. Harvard College, founded in 1636, was first, followed by the College of William and Mary (1693), Yale (1701), the College of New Jersey, now Princeton (1746), King's College, now Columbia (1754), the College of Philadelphia, now University of Pennsylvania (1755), the College of Rhode Island, now Brown (1765), Queen's College, now Rutgers (1766), and Dartmouth (1769). These nine institutions, all of which are still in existence, constitute a complete roster of the colleges established in colonial America.

The colonial colleges were deliberately modeled after the great English universities, Oxford and Cambridge. Harvard's first degree formula makes it very explicit: the degree is being bestowed "according to the manner of Universities in England." Degree requirements, curriculum, administrative regulations, procedures for handling matters involving student discipline—all were initially copied from the English universities. The familiar names for the four college classes—freshman, sophomore, junior (*sophister*), and senior (sophister)—come from the same source.

The colonial colleges were established in order to ensure that the colonies would be supplied with literate and humane intellectual leaders, especially clergymen. A college had to be established in the middle colonies, says an early Princeton historian, because "the bench, the bar, and seats of legislation, required such accomplishments, as are seldom the spontaneous growth of nature, unimproved by education" (Samuel Blair, *An Account of the College of New Jersey,* 1764). Yale was established in order that there might be a school "wherein youth may be instructed in the arts and sciences, who through the blessing of Almighty God may be fitted for public employment, both in church and civil state" (Franklin B. Dexter, *Documentary History of Yale University*, 1916). The *perpetuation* of humane learning in the New World and, as an integral part of this, the training of a literate clergy—these were the aims in the service of which the colonial colleges were established.

Given the same Old World models and similar aims, the colonial colleges quite naturally developed similar educational programs. These programs had the following characteristics:

1. They were intended for men only, indeed, for men who aspired to the Christian ministry or to some other position among the "learned elite."
2. All students in a given institution took exactly the same course of study.
3. The prescribed course of study consisted of those things that every "educated gentleman" was expected to know. A student was required to have mastered both Latin and Greek before being admitted to college. Once admitted he spent by far the greatest amount of his time studying the classics: Livy, Xenophon, Herodotus, Thucydides, Horace, Demosthenes, Plato and Aristotle, Cicero, Euclid, Homer and Tacitus. In addition to the classics the curriculum included such subjects as Hebrew (once required of all students at Yale), ethics, politics, mathematics, botany, and theology.

Change occurred very slowly in the curriculums of the colonial colleges. No one seriously questioned the assumption that classical studies should form the bulk of a gentleman's education. As the impact of the Enlightenment began to be felt in the New World, however, pressures began to mount to broaden the curriculum to include more mathematics and natural science, some exposure to English language and literature, and some study of modern foreign languages (especially French). Philadelphia College under Provost William Smith, and the College of William and Mary under the influence of Thomas Jefferson (who was a member of the Board of Visitors), led the way in establishing these curricular changes. In varying degrees the other colleges moved, though more slowly, in the same direction. In the main, however, the colonial colleges continued throughout the colonial period to educate their young men according to the model brought to the New World by the English settlers.

The Post-Revolutionary Era

The decades immediately following the close of the Revolutionary War, from about 1780 to 1860, saw a number of developments that were to have a permanent effect on the shape of higher education in this country. In terms of sheer size, the enterprise of higher education increased from just nine permanent colleges at the end of the colonial era to 179 by the year 1860. Nearly all the permanent institutions established during this period—152 of the 173—were private colleges founded and controlled by various religious denominations. The remaining 21 were public institutions with either state or city support and control.

Curriculums also underwent some important changes during this period. As colleges were established in the new territories opened up by the Louisiana

Purchase of 1803, it became apparent to many that a strict "classical education" was ill suited to meet the highly *utilitarian* needs of a new nation. Vast new territories needed to be brought under cultivation, cities needed to be established, railroads needed to be built, minerals lay waiting to be discovered and mined. For these purposes, what was clearly needed was not familiarity with Virgil and Homer but increasing mastery of science and technology. The age of higher education for "gentlemen only" was past: the system needed to be changed to "furnish the agriculturalist, the manufacturer, the mechanic, or the merchant with the education that will prepare him for the profession to which his life is to be devoted" (Francis Wayland, *Report to the Corporation of Brown University,* 1850).

Mounting pressures for an educational program specifically designed to serve such needs led in 1824 to the establishment of Rensselaer Polytechnic Institute "for the education of Architects, Civil, Mining, and Topographical Engineers." The older colleges, which heretofore had responded to similar pressures by adding such things as chemistry, geology, economics, law, medicine, and other profession-oriented studies to their curriculums, now began to establish separate departments or schools of engineering on their campuses. Within a period of eight years (1847 to 1855) technical schools or departments were established at Harvard, Yale, Dartmouth, Brown, and the University of Pennsylvania. Scientific and technical training had quite evidently become a permanent and important part of higher education in America.

With the broadening of curriculums and the establishment of professional courses of study, the old practice of requiring all students to take the same courses was no longer tenable. Students were still required to take certain courses that were presumed to be essential to any educated person, but beyond this each student elected those courses that he and his adviser judged best in terms of his particular goals. This system continues to be used in most American colleges and universities today.

This period also saw the beginning of the training of teachers as a specific and identifiable educational task. The "*normal school* movement" began, actually, in two small private schools established during the 1820s in Vermont and Massachusetts. The first public normal school was established at Lexington, Massachusetts, in 1839, and by 1860 similar institutions had been established in nine of the then thirty-four states. The first permanent university professorship in education was established at the State University of Iowa in 1855.

Higher education for women also made its first appearance in this country during the first half of the nineteenth century. An early product of the feminist movement, colleges for women were first established in the South—Wesleyan Female College in Georgia (1836), Judson College in Alabama (1838), and Mary Sharp College for Women in Tennessee (1852). Despite a widespread belief that women were intellectually inferior to men and, moreover, too delicate to endure prolonged intellectual effort, the practice spread to Illinois (Rockford College), to New York (Elmira College), and finally even to that citadel of masculine education, venerable old New England. Vassar, Wellesley, and

Smith were among the first to institute a curriculum based on the traditional pattern in men's colleges.

Meanwhile, a number of colleges were taking the daring step of admitting *both* men and women. Oberlin, founded in 1833, was the first coeducational college in North America, admitting women as well as men as early as 1837. The University of Utah opened its doors in 1850 to both male and female students, and thus became the first *public* institution of higher education to "go coeducational." By 1860 there were about a dozen coeducational colleges, and by the end of the century coeducation was the standard pattern in most American colleges and universities.

The period from 1780 to 1860 may be characterized, then, as one of great "horizontal" growth in American higher education. Existing curriculums were broadened, new curriculums were added, new institutions were established, the opportunity for higher education was made available to greatly increased numbers of students. Yet, as recently as 1860, the university as we know it today did not exist. Some very important ingredients had yet to be added.

The Late Nineteenth Century

Although a number of attempts were made prior to 1860 to establish "public" universities, the principles of public support and public control of institutions of higher education did not catch on easily. When Americans thought of institutions of higher learning, the models that immediately occurred to them were the privately controlled older colleges and the denominationally controlled colleges established by various religious groups as the settlers moved westward. Even when public funds were appropriated for the support of a "state university," the board of control of the institution was commonly self-perpetuating and looked upon any attempt at public control as unwarranted interference in its affairs.

The great breakthrough for public education occurred in 1862 with the passage of the Morrill Act. This act, which was the subject of much controversy for several years prior to its adoption under President Lincoln, authorized grants of land to each state "for the endowment, support, and maintenance of at least one college where the leading object shall be, without excluding other scientific and classical studies, and including military tactics, to teach such branches of learning as are related to agriculture and the mechanic arts, in such manner as the legislatures of the states may respectively prescribe, in order to promote the liberal and practical education of the industrial classes in the several pursuits and professions of life." Within nine years (despite the intervening Civil War), thirty-six states had taken formal action to take advantage of the new law. Today every state in the union has at least one land-grant school.

The impact of the land-grant concept on American higher education cannot be overestimated. The principle of public support for higher education was established once and for all. Moreover, the Act makes it clear that higher education is not only for the wealthy or for those entering the learned professions: these institutions are to "promote the liberal and practical education of the industrial classes in the several pursuits and professions of life." Henceforth colleges would teach whatever was necessary in order to prepare young men and women for the infinite variety of roles required in a dynamic and growing society.

Notwithstanding the Morrill Act, very few African-American students received the benefits of public higher education during the nineteenth century, and several institutions devoted to the education of these neglected students were established to fill the void. Morehouse College (Georgia), Howard University (Washington, D.C.), and Fisk University (Tennessee) were all founded in 1867.

A second major influence on American higher education at this time was the example of the great German universities, especially the University of Berlin. The German university in the nineteenth century was not primarily a place of instruction: it was a place of bold and original research. The proper business of a professor, according to the German model, was not to instruct the young but to push forward the frontiers of human knowledge, to discover truths that had not been known before. He would, indeed, share the results of his efforts with mature young scholars—graduate students—who might wish to study with him, but routine instruction in the simple rudiments of his subject was no part of his task.

Some few universities were established in this country for the explicit purpose of emulating the German model—Johns Hopkins in 1876, Clark University in 1889, and the University of Chicago in 1892. In the main, however, American educators responded to the German example by superimposing a graduate school upon the undergraduate structure that was already there. With the completion of this two-story structure, the modern university came into being.

Imagine, then, an institution that combines on one campus all of the developments catalogued in the preceding pages: it is a picture of the modern American university. The colonial college, suitably modified, lives on in the college of arts and sciences. The learned professions have their respective homes in the colleges of law and medicine. Engineering, agriculture, business, education—all are integral parts of virtually every large public university today. And overarching all of these, serving as a place of advanced study and research for thousands of scholars from all over the world, is the graduate school.

Three Major Tasks

Hundreds, perhaps thousands, of different activities are carried on in the various colleges and schools of a modern university. How does all of this activity "fit together" to constitute some kind of definable mission? What does society now expect its universities to accomplish? One of the major tasks of a university, obviously, is *instruction,* both undergraduate and graduate. Our society, being highly complex, requires many more highly trained people than were required when the colonial colleges were established. It is to the universities, and increasingly to the public universities, that society looks for its needed supply of doctors, lawyers, engineers, teachers, business executives, etc., without which our kind of civilization could not exist.

A second major task of a modern university is *research*. A modern university without a significant effort in research is as unthinkable as a university without students: it is implicit in the very concept of a university. Most of the major advances in human knowledge in the past hundred years have been made by researchers whose work has been carried out under the auspices of a major university. Since World War II much of this research effort has been supported by federal funds provided under research contracts between the federal government and the participating universities.

A third major task of a modern university is *public service*. This task, too, is implicit in the concept of a land-grant university. County agents, whose task it is to assist farmers to benefit from the findings of agricultural research—to promote "scientific farming"—are typically affiliated with the College of Agriculture of a land-grant university. Many universities maintain testing and research centers where local industries can, on a contract basis, refine and improve their products. University professors are often called upon to serve as expert consultants to business firms, school systems, federal and state agencies, and other organizations who have need of their particular expertise.

Virtually everything that a university does is related to one or more of these three major tasks. Together they constitute what may be called the overall "mission" of the university.

These three major tasks are interrelated in a wide variety of ways. The graduate students who assist a professor in pursuing a research project are, in the process, acquiring the up-to-date knowledge that they will need in order to serve as effective instructors of undergraduate students. The research professor who develops a new process for, say, increasing the durability of rubber becomes thereby a uniquely valuable consultant to the tire industry. The historian whose research turns up new evidence regarding the administration of Abraham Lincoln may, as a result, produce changes in the content of an undergraduate course in American history. Instruction, research, and public service may, at times, vie with one another for the university's human and material resources, but ideally they are complementary and in fact are mutually reinforcing in numerous ways.

Reprinted by permission of the author.

• • • • • • • • • • • • • • • • • • • •

Vocabulary

As you think about this essay, these definitions may be helpful to you:
1. **sophister**   one who uses a plausible but incorrect argument to deceive; in this essay, philosopher, thinker
2. **perpetuation**   causing to last indefinitely

3. **utilitarian**   useful or designed for use rather than beauty
4. **normal school**   a two-year school for training teachers

 ## Discussion Questions

1. Where did American higher education have its origins?
2. Why were the colonial colleges established?
3. What were the first curricula like?
4. What significant changes were made in the post-Revolutionary period?
5. What significant event happened in the late nineteenth century? What impact did it have on higher education even to today?
6. A second Morrill Act passed in 1890. It stipulated that no federal money would go to a state that denied admission to its land grant college on the basis of race—unless "separate but equal" facilities were available to students who would be denied for the reason of race. In your view, was this second Morrill Act, which established the so-called "1890 schools," a good or bad piece of federal legislation? Why?

 ## How Can These Ideas Apply to You?

1. How would you be different as a student in an early colonial college as compared with what you experience today?
2. What changes in the post-Revolutionary era would have affected you the most as a student of that period (e.g., as a pre-engineering student, as a teacher-in-training, as a woman, as an African American)?
3. How would your education as a community college student differ from your education as a four-year college student?

UNIT SUMMARY

In this unit you have examined many different perspectives about college as an American institution and its meaning and value to you as a student. The following questions can help you think about the viewpoints represented in these readings.

Summary Questions

1. What is a liberal education according to the authors in this unit? How will it prepare you to become a lifelong learner?
2. What are some general goals and objectives of higher education according to these readings? How do they compare with your personal reasons for being in college?
3. Many college students have traversed your campus in the past. What aspects of the history and traditions of your campus are most interesting and important to you?

Suggested Writing Assignments

1. Write an essay about your reasons for being in college. In it describe five goals you wish to accomplish during your first year.
2. How is college different from high school (e.g., teachers, assignments, classroom behavior, course content, learning expectations)? Write about your most difficult academic adjustment.
3. Interview a college teacher in whose class you have learned a great deal. Discuss learning from this teacher's perspective. How does this teacher think learning his or her subject matter can be useful in life?

Suggested Readings

Bloom, Allan. *The Closing of the American Mind.* New York: Simon & Schuster, 1987.
Gardner, Howard. *Multiple Intelligences: The Theory in Practice.* New York: Basic Books, 1993.
Hutchins, Robert M. "The Autobiography of an Uneducated Man." In Robert M. Hutchins, *Education for Freedom,* 1–18. Baton Rouge: Louisiana State University Press, 1943.
Willie, Charles. *The Ivory and Ebony Towers.* Lexington, MA: Heath, 1981.

What Can I Expect from College and How Will I Change?

What do you expect will happen to you during your college years? The college years are known for the personal and social changes that take place in individuals. New students are likely to notice, first, the academic challenges in the classroom and the social opportunities present at every turn. For many, the increased difficulty of college course work comes as a surprise, and the social freedom, which may have been predictable, is more overwhelming than expected.

Furthermore, students usually expect that college will prepare them for a career and will accomplish this in some very specific ways. Students often expect a direct-line or one-to-one relationship between what they study in college and the job that follows graduation. Direct relationships do occur in such fields as engineering and nursing, but more often, college courses teach general skills, not specific job tasks. Students who expect specific training may not see the relevance or importance of this more general instruction.

As time passes, they may become even more confused. For many

What we anticipate seldom occurs; what we least expect generally happens.

—BENJAMIN DISRAELI

first-year students, uncertainty about their future career and life is unsettling and worrisome. Their expectations for clear-cut decisions regarding their future may not be fulfilled.

According to many student developmental theorists, these unsettling feelings are common and can be considered normal. Most students need time to master certain developmental tasks that lead to a mature way of thinking and being. For example, as far as personal development is concerned, students need to cope with leaving home, perhaps for the first time. Often both parents and students find this transition difficult.

Some of the best features of college life are the opportunities to make new friends and to meet people who are different from yourself. Some students may find it easy to strike up new friendships, while others struggle with shyness and uncertainty. However, in time these relationships can become one of the most rewarding aspects of college life.

In classes, students are thrust into new experiences with demanding course work. They need to master rapidly moving and complex course content, and some will find they need help with basic learning skills. Academic freedom and the occasional need to drop a course may be new to many students. Some think they can succeed if they work harder, a strategy that doesn't always work. A student's expectations for academic success may take a few detours.

All these developmental concerns are in some sense predictable, as the essays in this section demonstrate. The essay outlining the theories of Perry and Chickering (Gordon) describes the importance of mastering the various developmental tasks. Another essay outlines how one professor (Finster) has adapted his teaching methods to challenge this development in his students. Also predictable for the 2 million or so new students each year are some shared demographic factors that suggest certain experiences will also be shared, as Habley points out. The poem by Denise Levertov provides another perspective on how we develop and on how a latent sense of identity can make you feel.

On a personal level, Zinsser describes the diverse pressures many college students experience. The essay by Newman and Newman deals with the feelings of loneliness that some students may feel, especially at the beginning of their college experience. Gee offers a light essay on life in a residence hall.

Most students expect college to be a time for increasing their knowledge. Acquiring knowledge is important, but many would agree that learning to think, reason, and solve problems is even more important because these are life skills. In his essay on learning, Highet encourages students to *enjoy* learning, which he sees as an instinctive, natural pleasure rather than an act that is forced upon us by others.

Setting goals, both short-term and long-term, is an important element in the evolution of this highly personal process. Your expectations for what you want to receive and accomplish during the college years will probably change. It will be natural for you to expand and refine your expectations. The essays in this unit may give you some appreciation for the tasks that others consider important as you progress toward graduation.

Two Million Futures . . .

Wesley R. Habley

Wesley R. Habley is director of the American College Testing (ACT) Center for the Enhancement of Educational Practices. He has served as director of academic advising at Illinois State University and the University of Wisconsin-Eau Claire. The author of numerous articles and three monographs on academic advising, Habley joined Virginia Gordon, author of the essay directly following this one, as editors of *Academic Advising: A Comprehensive Handbook,* a major book for college advisers.

In this essay, Habley raises for discussion some important factors that will influence the college students of the future. Knowing what we already know about the next ten years in America, Habley points to demographic data that will be important facts of life for college students to think about and come to terms with.

In a pattern nearly as predictable as the sun rising and setting or the tide ebbing and flowing, the fall of each year brings an influx of first-time students to colleges and universities throughout this nation. Nearly two million of them bring their dreams and expectations, their hopes and fears, their aspirations and goals with them as they enter college. Each person, shaped by a unique set of life experiences, enters college with an individual set of traits, attitudes, and opinions about college life. Equally predictable is the annual outpouring of pronouncements made by market researchers, generational analysts, and demographers who provide group descriptions of the traits, attitudes, opinions, and characteristics of this group of students.

Studies of first-year students in 2000 suggested several characteristics of the entering class: growing stress, academic disengagement, inflated high school grades, declining commitment to social activism, a decline in smoking and drinking, and a growing interest in teaching and the arts. (This information is from *The American Freshman,* an annual publication described later in this essay.) In a similar vein a recent poll carried out by Lewis Harris and Associates cited eleven major findings on the attitudes of "Generation 2001," the first graduating class of the new millennium. Most of these individuals feel that they are basically not much different from other generations. However, they are described as a generation with a greater belief in the importance of marriage and family, a greater recognition of mom and dad as significant role models, and a greater commitment to helping others as a high priority. These and several other characteristics set them apart, if ever so slightly, from the generations of their elders. Reading these studies, it is important also to realize that generational patterns are cyclical. Studies of 13 generations of American culture not only describe the beliefs, attitudes, and normative structures of a given generation but also predict these same characteristics of future generations.

Lost in the mound of aggregate data is the reality that these reports may accurately describe a group but do not necessarily describe any single individual who is a member of that group. In fact, most of these group statistics capture the prevalent attitudes or opinions of only a plurality or a slim majority of the individuals within the group. So, regardless of an individual's characteristics, opinions, and attitudes, that person is still described by aggregated data. This resulting composite captures *macro* level trends, experiences, and socioeconomic forces, yet is not applicable at the *micro* level because it does not explain the way individual college students think about, respond to, and assign value to the college experience.

Nevertheless, it can be very useful to understand the composite description, or "*template,*" that statisticians put together. The template consists of demographic descriptions, defining movements or moments, and other real-world variables such as the economy, political environment, technology, and popular culture. Some of these variables are known, while others are not. The impact of these influential variables may really be understood only in the context of the issues that will confront these individuals as college students. It is not possible to capture all the variables that will have an impact on the college student of the future, but it is possible to identify several factors that will influence student expectations for the college experience. More than one futurist has convincingly argued that demography is destiny. And indeed, demography will play an inexorable role in the life of the college student of the future. As a result, one piece of the template is based on demographic variables. Demographics, like those that follow, are predictable and obvious. Demography is certain to have an impact on the college student of the future, even if the nature of that impact is not predictable.

What predictable demographics will affect the college student of the future? The first influential demographic theme is sheer population growth. During the first half of the 21st century the U.S. population is projected to grow from 275 million to 350 million, while world population will grow from just about 6 billion to more than 9 billion people. Such growth will bring about the need for global cooperation in the management of and care for scarce resources. The competition for those resources and the competition to create new, sustainable resources will have a significant impact on world economy and political alliances. In turn, the world's response to population growth will set a context for establishing one's identity in the college environment.

The second demographic theme is that there will be no shared definition of the concept of family unit. At one time in American culture, the definition of the family unit included a father at work and a mother at home with two school-aged children. In 1998, only 11 percent of U.S. family units met this definition. Among the trends increasing in American life are blended families, single parent families, and families headed by two persons of the same sex. In addition, the number of couples choosing not to have children is on the rise.

The final demographic theme is that, as analyst Amitai Etzioni has remarked, the United States is becoming a nation of minorities. Among the indicators of this theme are population growth rates among Asian-, Hispanic-, and African-Americans. The very idea that a social or political identity can be gained from aligning with groups called Asian-Americans or African-Americans is already a statistical artifact. Since 1970 for instance, the proportion of marriages among people of different racial or ethnic origins has increased by 72 percent. This proportion is expected to rise in the future. Moreover, each group identified by race or ethnicity represents a gross categorization at best. Are Asian-Americans Chinese, Korean, or Japanese? Or are they Southeast Asian–Americans (Vietnamese, Thai, Cambodian, or Malaysian)? Etzioni suggests that American society has always had room for the pluralism of subcultures, a pluralism which allows people to play and pray in their own way. This pluralism also allows some people to uphold some of the traditions and values of their country of origin while generally adhering to the *mores* of the American mainstream.

Because demography is quantifiable and definable, it can help us describe who we are, but the real-world experiences we have during the formative years leading up to college have an even greater impact on our expectations of college. These experiences provide the context not for who we are, but rather for how we will think and how we will act. Our outlook on life, the actions we take and, for that matter, our view of the nature and purpose of higher education are all strongly influenced by the pattern of our experiences of the real world. Although many different experiential patterns or themes guide our actions, the economy, the political environment, technology, and popular culture have been chosen for brief analysis here. For instance, our economic viewpoints and actions are closely associated with just a few terms: depression, recession, unemployment, capitalism, inflation, and boom. Each of these terms, as well as any combination of them, will have a major, but currently unknown, effect on the decisions made by the college student of the future.

Just as the economy will have an impact on student decision-making, facility with technology will dictate the ways we communicate, the manner in and degree to which we will learn, as well as the nature and focus of our work. As an illustration of our rapidly changing technology, each year the staff at Beloit College in Wisconsin puts together a list of things that the newest entering college students have never experienced. Here are but a few of the technology issues included on the list for the first year class of 2000: they had never owned (maybe never seen or heard) a record player, a phone that "rang," a black and white television, an eight-track tape player, a typewriter, an Atari, or a slide rule. The list goes on, but the point is undeniable. Technological advancement will be constant and pervasive and the successful college student will be one who can adapt to and take advantage of new technology.

The political environment operates on two different stages as it contributes to the context of experience for college students of the future. The first stage is the style and integrity of political leadership in power during the formative years of future college students. A review of the style and integrity of leadership demonstrated by recent American presidents clearly illustrates the impact of political style—from charismatic and inspirational to pragmatic and cautious. And, on the matter of integrity, political behavior has ranged from inalterable and *impeccable* (or seemingly so) to shifting and self-serving.

A third experiential theme occurs in the popular culture. Yet no matter how one describes the impact of popular culture, there is a risk both of overestimating and underestimating its impact. Each generation was destined to " . . . go to hell in a handbasket" according to members of earlier generations—but none has! Yet changing modes of dress, music, film, television, the Internet, and other sources of entertainment lead to such dire predictions. Indeed it seems that every generation adopts forms of expression which extol a set of beliefs that are considered to be far from their parents' mainstream, and less than virtuous. These different ways of believing and behaving have served as a source of friction across nearly all generations.

The final category of experiences includes movements or events that have a lasting impact on individual development. These events could be global in nature and might include such things as growing terrorism, the fall of communism, and globalization of the economy. Or they may be be national movements or events such as the Challenger explosion, Waco, Columbine, hate crimes, or the Oklahoma City bombing. And finally, these movements or moments could also be highly personalized to each individual including such things as natural disasters, crime, or personal relationships.

In reality, every individual's demographic characteristics and life experiences are unique. Therefore, everyone has a different expectation of college, but a different response to college. Although expectations are both individualized and dynamic in nature, there is a constant in this discussion: the constant is that college will be a transitional shock for most students. Transitional shock occurs when there is dissonance between student expectations of college life and realities of college life. Just what are those expectations and how do they align with the realities of college life?

For more than three decades, *The American Freshman,* published by the Higher Education Research Institute at UCLA, has annually reported on the characteristics, attitudes, and opinions of a broad national population of first-year students. From these reports it is possible to capture at least some of the expectations of college students. And from a variety of reports including the normative report of ACT's *Student Opinion Survey,* it is possible to report on students' actual experiences in college. Using these two sources, the following summary illustrates the dissonance between student expectations and the realities of college experience.

- In 2000, significantly more first-time college students (up from 33 percent in 1990) report that they earned a high grade point average (A+, A, or A–) in high school, but test scores on the ACT Assessment and the National Assessment of Educational Progress have plateaued during the 1990s.
- 7 percent of first year students expect to be undecided about a major, while data sources from ACT suggest that 20 percent of all students are either undecided or not sure of the major they have chosen.

- 12 percent of first-year students think that they will change majors. Although no national study on change of major rates is available, many four-year college campuses report that 65–85 percent of students who enter with declared majors will change their major in the first two years. Campuses report that the typical number of majors in an undergraduate career is two or three.
- Only 1 percent of first-year students think that they might fail a course. In reality, a number of campus-based studies report a range from 11 percent to 26 percent of first year students who fail at least one course.
- 8 percent of first-time students think that it might take longer than four years to complete a bachelor's degree while the national five-year bachelor's degree completion rate predicts a more-than-four-year college experience for a much higher proportion of those entering each fall.

In summary, many ways in which students think about, react to, and assign value to the college experience suggest that there is no single template that can describe the college student of the future. Rather, annually 2 million college students each bring a unique set of characteristics and experiences to the college experience, and each of them seeks meaning from the college experience in a unique and personal way.

Reprinted by permission of the author.

Vocabulary

As you think about this essay, these definitions may be helpful to you:
1. **micro/macro**   (often used in combination) small-scale/large-scale, or local/global
2. **template**   a pattern or model; in this essay, one assembled statistically
3. **mores**   customs or habits
4. **impeccable**   pure, perfect, without sin or stain

Discussion Questions

1. What does it mean to say that "demography is destiny"? Is it true?
2. A familiar topic in many discussions about college is the four-year degree plan. Why do you suppose that students often do not finish their college degrees in four years?
3. Are you part of the "majority culture" of your home town or city? Describe it and how you do, or do not, fit in.

How Can These Ideas Apply to You?

1. Consider the demographic factors that Habley identifies and analyze how they might—indeed, are very likely to—apply to you. For example, how could rapid world population growth make a difference to you in your generation of college students and citizens? What can you do to stay in control in the face of these demographics?
2. What kind of family do you expect to live in 20 years from now? Is Habley right when he predicts that a highly varied notion of "family" will emerge?
3. Select two or three events from popular culture (they can be on Habley's list or of your own devising) and talk about how they have affected you. Another way to deal with this topic is to consider how your life would be different if these events had not occurred.

The Developing College Student

Virginia N. Gordon

Virginia N. Gordon, who has been a college teacher and administrator, is best known as a researcher, academic adviser, and counselor for undecided students. She received her Ph.D. in counseling from The Ohio State University and currently teaches there in the College of Education.

This essay describes two theoretical perspectives on how students change intellectually and personally during the college years. These theories are based on what students have experienced and related to researchers through personal interviews.

B y entering college you begin a very exciting and challenging period in your life. Although it may be difficult for you to imagine now, think about yourself on the day you graduate with a college degree. In addition to being a college graduate, what kind of person will you be? How do you expect to change during your college years?

After careful research, many theorists have described how students change and develop throughout the college experience. Social scientists who have studied college students have discovered some patterns and common themes in the way they change. One such theorist, Professor William Perry, of Harvard University, has studied how college students change intellectually and ethically. He developed a scheme to describe the development of the thinking and reasoning processes that takes place naturally as students mature and grow intellectually. Each phase of this development may be likened to a set of filters through which students see the world around them.

Dualistic students see the world in polar terms; that is, they believe that all questions have a right answer and, therefore, that all answers are either right or wrong. Such students are happiest when they find simplistic answers to their questions about the world, and they want to view their teachers and advisers as experts who can give them the right answer. They believe that hard work and obedience pay off. They depend on others to make important decisions for them. Many freshmen begin their college experience seeing through this dualistic lens.

As students develop, however, Perry says they become capable of more complex reasoning and dissatisfied with simplistic answers. They are moving into a "*multiplistic*" view of the world. They begin to see and understand cause and effect relationships. Diversity becomes legitimate because they realize that no one has all the answers. They believe everyone has the right to his or her opinion. They still, however, depend on others to make decisions for them. Some freshmen and sophomores view their experiences through this multiplistic lens.

Perry identifies the next phase, "relativism," as the time when students begin to synthesize diverse and complex elements of reasoning. They are able to view uncertainty as legitimate. They see *themselves* as the principal agent in decision making and acknowledge that they must not only make their own decisions, but also take responsibility for those decisions, regardless of how well or badly those decisions may turn out. Many juniors and seniors fall into this category of "relativistic" thinkers. Because the emphasis in Perry's system is always on how college students tend to think and reason, his theory is called a theory of *cognitive* development.

For Perry, the most advanced phase of cognitive development is one in which students make a commitment to a personal identity and its content and style. Each develops a sense of being "in" one's self, along with an awareness that growth is always transpiring, that change is inevitable and healthy. Students also make a commitment to a defined career area and are able to develop a lifestyle that is appropriate for them. Many students continue in this state of personal growth and development after college.

Through his theory of cognitive development, Perry helps us understand how students view, react to, and assimilate knowledge as they progress through college. It is important to recognize that while college experiences encourage and foster this development, non-college students also mature and develop in much the same way. (It is also important to remember that any theoretical model, no matter how carefully established, is just that: a model. Judgments about how individuals may be measured against a model require great care. And, as you see later, other models are also well established.)

Perry theorizes that growth occurs in surges, with pauses between the surges when some students might need to detach themselves for a while, while others even retreat to the comfort of their past ways of thinking. Ask five seniors to look back on how they have changed intellectually. While they will be able to reflect on their intellectual development in unique and personal terms, the patterns of growth that Perry describes will usually be evident. However, it sometimes takes courage to confront the risks each forward movement requires. Every student has the freedom to choose what kind of person he or she will become, but the forces of growth, according to Perry, will not be denied.

Developmental Tasks

Another theorist, Arthur Chickering, suggests that college students develop in an orderly way on many dimensions: intellectually, physically, psychologically and socially. He describes several developmental tasks, or "*vectors,*" through which students move during their college years. A vector, according to Chickering, is a developmental task that (1) has specific content, (2) shows up at certain times in our lives, and (3) takes two to seven years to resolve. The process is ongoing throughout our lives, and even though we may resolve a task once, it may resurface later. These tasks build on each other; how we resolve one may affect the ones that follow. While these tasks develop in order, they may also be concurrent, so we may be dealing with several at one time. The seven developmental tasks that Chickering has proposed are described next.

1. Achieving Competence

The first task is achieving competence. College students need to achieve competence in several areas: intellectually, physically, and interpersonally. Chickering likens this to a three-tined pitchfork, since all three happen simultaneously.

Intellectual competence involves the skill of using one's mind in "comprehending, analyzing and synthesizing." It means learning how to learn and acquiring knowledge. Most students enroll in college in order to develop intellectual competence. They begin to develop good study habits and the skills of critical thinking and reasoning. They will be able to appreciate and integrate many points of view in their thinking. Ideally, they will enjoy learning for its own sake and feel the excitement of entering new realms of knowledge. Physical competence involves manual skills as well. The recreational value of, and prestige associated with, athletic skills or the creative value of arts and crafts are important to many students. More and more we are concerned that lifelong fitness is important. Recreational skills and interests that one develops in college continue throughout life. Colleges provide many physical facilities for students who seek to develop competency in this area.

Probably the greatest concern of many students is how to develop interpersonal and social competence. They feel a need for communication skills, such as listening and responding appropriately, so they can relate to others individually or in groups. Learning the social graces and how to interact with peers is an important task that most students accomplish early in their college years. Much of this learning happens as a result of observation, feedback from other students, and experience.

When these three competencies are achieved, students feel a *sense* of competence; they sense that they can cope with whatever comes. They are confident of their ability to achieve successfully whatever they set out to do. They respond to new challenges by integrating old learning with new. The task of developing competence is especially important during the freshman year.

2. Managing Emotions

Two major emotional impulses that need to be managed during college are sex and aggression. Maturity implies that legitimate ways have been found to express anger and hate. Sexual impulses are more insistent than ever. Students feel pressured to find answers to questions concerning interpersonal relationships. They move from being controlled by the external rules of their heritage to control by internal norms of self. (Students from rural areas may have different sets of rules, for example, than inner-city students.) Many students are still controlled by the external norms of their peers. Exaggerated displays of emotion are not uncommon: in the past, for example, college students initiated panty raids or held contests for swallowing the greatest number of goldfish.

People often feel boredom, tension and anxiety as normal emotions while their impulsive feelings need to be controlled. Becoming aware of positive emotions such as sympathy, yearning, wonder and awe is also important. Eventually, students learn to be controlled by their own internal set of norms.

Achieving competence in the management of emotions means moving from an awareness of the legitimacy of emotions, to acting on them, to controlling them internally.

3. Moving through Autonomy toward Interdependence

Another important task for new college students during the first months of college is to achieve independence. A student may be hesitant to try certain new experiences or to approach new people. Such a student is trying to become independent but, as Chickering says, is like a "hog on ice," a little shaky at first. For probably the first time in their experience, many students may be living with no restraints or outside pressures, with no one to tell them when to study or to be home by 11 o'clock. As they act on their own, they may flounder at first. Beginning students may wonder, for example, why they have so much free time. They attend classes for only three or four hours a day and then may squander the rest of the day—until they realize the importance of quality study time.

The student who achieves *emotional* independence has learned to be free of the continual need for reassurance, affection or approval. Such a student has learned to deal with authority figures and feels comfortable with professors or other very important people on campus. There is less reliance on parents and more on friends and nonparental adults. Achieving *instrumental* independence means students can do things for themselves that parents used to do, such as washing the laundry or managing money. They are able to solve problems and use resources on their own.

When the student finally comes to recognize and accept *inter*dependence, the boundaries of personal choice become clearer and the ranges within which one can give and receive become more settled. Autonomous students feel less need for support from their parents and begin to understand that parents need them as much as they need their parents. They begin to see their parents for what they are: middle-aged people with weaknesses just like themselves. Becoming autonomous is a very important task for freshmen to accomplish.

4. Developing Mature Interpersonal Relationships

Developing mature relationships means that students become less anxious and less defensive, more friendly, spontaneous and respectful. They are more willing to trust and are more independent. They develop the capacity for mature intimacy. They can participate in healthy relationships that incorporate honesty and responsiveness. They finally realize that perfect parents don't exist and that Prince or Princess Charming is not coming to sweep them off their feet. They also have an increased tolerance for people culturally different from themselves. They have acquired increased empathy and altruism and enjoy diversity. They are able to develop mature relationships with many types of people.

5. Establishing Identity

The fifth vector, according to Chickering, is establishing identity. This task is really the sum of the first four vectors: developing competence, managing emotions, developing autonomy through interdependence, and developing mature interpersonal relationships. Success at achieving identity will often hinge on how these former tasks have been accomplished. Studies suggest that students generally achieve a coherent, mature sense of identity during their sophomore or junior years.

In addition to these inner changes, students need to clarify their conceptions of physical needs, personal appearance, and sex-appropriate roles and behavior. They identify a personal life-style that is theirs. Once such a sense of identity is achieved, other major vectors may be approached. Establishing an identity is the hinge on which future development depends.

6. Developing Purpose

Developing purpose is the vector related to career choice. The questions to be faced for this vector are not only "Who Am I?" but also "Where Am I Going?" Interests tend to stabilize; vocational exploration becomes a serious task. A general orientation toward a career area is achieved first, and then more specific career decisions are made. Students begin to formulate plans and integrate vocational and lifestyle considerations into those plans. An initial commitment to a career goal is made with the move into adulthood.

7. Developing Integrity

Students also need to clarify a personally valid set of beliefs that have some internal consistency. This happens in three stages, according to Chickering. Their values are first (1) humanized, then (2) personalized, and then (3) their beliefs and actions begin to suit each other. During childhood, students assimilate their parents' values. In college, students begin to examine these inherited values to see if they fit them personally. Some values may be rejected while others may be retained. The student's task is to personalize these values by achieving behavior consistent with them and being willing to stand up for what he or she strongly believes. Such a degree of commitment leads to congruence between one's beliefs and values and one's actions. Standards for assessing personal actions are set and are used as guides for all behavior.

Working through these seven developmental tasks is crucial to the college student's successful passage into mature adulthood. How will you be different on graduation day? I hope that you will have no regrets about missed opportunities to become involved in your own development. The college environment offers an almost unbelievable assortment of opportunities in and outside the classroom. There are many resources, including people, who stand ready to challenge and support you. As you move into the world you will be willing to assert the convictions and values you carefully (and sometimes traumatically) learned during your college years. Knowing that everyone moves through these passages of development and that change is inevitable can help you see the more difficult times as periods of growth. In this way you will be able to react positively and productively.

Reprinted by permission of the author.

Vocabulary

As you think about this essay, these definitions may be helpful to you:
1. **dualistic**   consisting of two irreducible elements or modes; a way of thinking that sees issues as black or white, rather than as shades of gray
2. **multiplistic**   numerous or various
3. **cognitive**   involving the act of knowing, including both awareness and judgment
4. **vector**   a course or direction
5. **instrumental**   serving as a means, agent, or tool; in this essay, instrumental independence is the ability to live and work on your own

Discussion Questions

1. What aspect of student development does Perry's scheme address? What is its primary thesis?
2. How does a dualistic student view the world?
3. How does Perry describe commitment, which is the most advanced phase of cognitive development?
4. What are the seven developmental tasks of college students as proposed by Chickering?
5. What, says Chickering, is required to develop an identity? How are the last two tasks of developing purpose and integrity related to identity?

How Can These Ideas Apply to You?

1. Where in the phases of cognitive development described by Perry do you think you are? Explain your response.
2. Have you ever consciously experienced a period of intellectual growth? How would you describe it?
3. Which of Chickering's developmental tasks do you think you have already accomplished? What indications point to their resolution?
4. Which of Chickering's developmental tasks have been or will be the most difficult for you to resolve? The easiest?
5. Overall, what do you think of these two theoretical perspectives on how college students develop?

The Thread

Denise Levertov

Denise Levertov (1923–1997) was born in Ilford, England, but moved to the United States in her twenties. Her poems are often both lyrical and mystical, two qualities present in "The Thread," a poem about feelings of personal identity. Author of many volumes of poetry, she was also an editor for two national journals and taught at many major American universities.

Something is very gently,
invisibly, silently,
pulling at me—a thread
or net of threads
finer than cobweb and as
elastic. I haven't tried
the strength of it. No barbed hook
pierced and tore me. Was it
not long ago this thread
began to draw me? Or
way back? Was I
born with its knot about my
neck, a bridle? Not fear
but a stirring
of wonder makes me
catch my breath when I feel
the tug of it when I thought
it had loosened itself and gone.

 Discussion Questions

1. What is the "something" that Levertov describes? How do you know?
2. When Levertov says, "No barbed hook pierced and tore me," she seems to be comparing herself to a fish. Is she? If so, how does this influence your understanding of what's going on in this poem? If not, then why does she introduce barbed hooks that pierce and tear?

3. Was she born with this "something" around her neck, like a knot or a bridle?
4. If Levertov has been living with this "something" all her life, why does it surprise her from time to time? How can that happen?
5. Is the "something" of the poem good or bad—or are those relevant words to describe it?

 ## How Can These Ideas Apply to You?

1. Suppose for the sake of discussion that this is a poem about identity, and that it tells how sometimes our own identity seems to get lost in our lives, only to reappear from time to time. Have you had the experience that Levertov describes by saying " ... I thought / it had loosened itself and gone"? If so, were you pleased or disappointed when "it" resurfaced?
2. Is it important to you to understand yourself? Why, or why not?
3. How can college contribute to your self-knowledge? Do you think improved self-knowledge is a liberating force, or is it too much concentration on—even enslavement to—your own ego?

Freshmen Can Be Taught to Think Creatively, Not Just Amass Information

David C. Finster

Dr. David C. Finster is professor of chemistry and chair of the chemistry department at Wittenberg University of Springfield, Ohio. He has been a recipient of the Wittenberg Distinguished Teaching Award.

Finster describes how he applies Perry's theory of cognitive development to his teaching methods and how he uses student-based teaching in his classes. He challenges his students to think about *how* they solve a chemistry problem in addition to finding the solution.

Not long after I embarked on my teaching career, I realized that to be an effective teacher one must first know something about learning. To try to convey knowledge with no understanding of the process of receiving it is to forget the principles of communication. My questions about learning led me to the work of the educational psychologist Jean Piaget on *cognition* in children. His insights, which beautifully explain how children learn to think about problems and to make sense of the world around them, were critical for me. Indeed, understanding how to foster a child's natural growth from simplistic to more complex and abstract thinking processes seems to me vital for any teacher.

But what about college freshmen? Are they just "big children"? In the sense that they are still wrestling with the turmoils of adolescence, now compounded by the independence and responsibility of college life, perhaps so. But in the sense that they are making the transition to what Piaget calls formal *operational* thought, they are not.

A clearer view of cognition in college students came to me from the work of William Perry. He studied the college experience through lengthy interviews with students over several years and then formulated a "developmental scheme" based on his findings. His charting of the intellectual and ethical growth of college students reveals much about the processes of learning and teaching.

Perry's scheme describes progressive stages of development in young people of the ability to comprehend the difference between information and knowledge, to understand the roles of teacher and student, and to make considered decisions in resolving life's simple and complex dilemmas. At the first stage, they are "dualists," with a right-or-wrong view of the world. They see knowledge as a collection of facts to be memorized and authority figures as having all the answers. At the middle stage, they develop a more complex worldview, recognizing that there can be a variety of opinions and viewpoints on an issue. Later they become capable of evaluating those different perspectives through reasoning and judgment, and, finally, they are able to make decisions and commitments based on their own value system. This latter stage is crucial in the formulation of individual identity.

Perry notes nine distinct developmental "positions" along the way to maturity, which must be gone through sequentially—that is, one cannot advance from the second to the fifth position without going through the third and fourth. Most students come to college in "late *dualism*," or at the third position, believing that the purpose of education is to accumulate information and that people in authority have the right answers. Their ability at that stage to see multiple perspectives on an issue is very limited. The way to promote their progress along Perry's scheme is to challenge them to think of the stage just beyond their current level while providing the necessary support to help them do so.

A good teacher seeks not only to build students' knowledge of the content of a discipline but also to teach them to think critically as they learn. The second aim may explain the difficulty some students have in learning at the college level. Critical thinking—that is, the ability to evaluate different perspectives and challenge assumptions—comes at a stage in the Perry model that is beyond students in the "dualist" position. Teachers naturally prefer teaching their disciplines at that level, however, and many expect their students to welcome this broadening aspect of their education. Dualists, on the other hand, see education differently.

A problem arises when the gap between where students are in their intellectual development and where their teachers teach is too large. Most teachers are aware of the gap, but find that time-honored teaching methods do not readily bridge it. Some choose to ignore it, because they are loath to "water down" their courses. Others eliminate it by reducing their goals to a more elementary level and teaching information rather than thinking skills.

The latter tactic is encouraged in our educational system, because content is readily measured by testing, and so "mastery" of a subject can be easily demonstrated. Unfortunately, teachers who resort to it *entrench* their students in the early stages of development by reinforcing a simplistic view of education.

An alternative solution to the problem would be to adopt a developmental instructional method. Using that approach, a teacher begins by recognizing where students are in their ability to understand the purpose of education, to see a difference between information and knowledge, and to think for themselves in the classroom. The aim is then to foster their intellectual growth from that point on.

A favorite saying of mine is that the purpose of college is to calm the disturbed and disturb the calm. Part of good teaching is challenging the way students think, while at the same time providing them with mental and emotional tools to resolve the dilemmas they face. In this manner, we help them grow *incrementally* and become mature adults.

Developmental-instruction theory holds that success in fostering intellectual growth depends in large part on the degree of personal interaction in the educational environment. Small classes are therefore important, because in addition to avoiding the impersonal atmosphere of large lectures, they allow a two-way exchange between teacher and student. Such exchanges play a vital part in active participatory learning and in the development of critical-thinking skills.

Another tenet of development theory is that the first year of college is crucial in tapping students' potential to grow intellectually. So, while large sections of introductory courses are efficient in terms of allocating teaching resources, the freshman year is the worst time for "mass education" because it reinforces the early stage idea that the purpose of education is to amass information.

As a chemistry professor, I have adopted developmental theory in teaching science courses. I begin by challenging the notion that science is Truth—a classic dualistic belief woven into our culture from the time of Galileo and Newton. There are multiple perspectives possible in many aspects of science, and, while I point out that in some cases only one answer to a scientific question is the right one, I present alternative perspectives as often as I can in class. Discussing applications of science that both create and solve special dilemmas provides ample opportunity for examining different perspectives.

In teaching my chemistry classes, I focus on process as much as on content. *How* one solves a problem in chemistry is as important as the solution, particularly when one is learning. I therefore avoid multiple-choice tests in favor of examinations that force my students both to solve the problem and to explain how they approached it. I try to lecture in an interactive way also, by engaging students in the process of thinking through an argument rather than just presenting them with the facts and theories. They begin to become educated scientists by discussing historical and current scientific issues in class, in assignments, and on tests.

Writing is a well-recognized method of exposing students' thought processes to themselves, and I assign my students term papers that require them to investigate a contemporary, controversial issue in science and then present their conclusions clearly. In fact, I "think developmentally," even when I am prescribing the format for writing up their lab reports.

The changes in the way I approach my classes that have resulted from my study of developmental theory may seem insignificant individually, but in combination they have added, for me, a new and exciting dimension to my teaching. As I listen to students talk about learning and life, I hear Perry's positions and stages review themselves. His model has given me a framework for understanding my students' assumptions about education—particularly as they conflict with mine. It helps me guide their progress with a sense of direction. Student-based teaching has worked for me, and I am convinced that the Perry model can be applied profitably to any discipline.

Vocabulary

As you think about this essay, these definitions may be helpful to you:
1. **cognition**   the process of knowing, including awareness and judgment
2. **operational**   ready to undertake a destined function
3. **dualism**   a theory that considers reality to consist of two irreducible elements or modes
4. **entrench**   to establish solidly
5. **incrementally**   changing by small amounts or degrees

Discussion Questions

1. How has the work of Piaget, a French psychologist and philosopher, influenced Finster's understanding of cognition, or how individuals learn in the broadest sense?
2. Describe the "dualists'" way of thinking according to Perry.
3. How can students be encouraged to progress beyond their current level of thinking, according to Perry?
4. How does Finster describe a "good teacher"?
5. What specific steps does Finster take to apply Perry's ideas in his teaching chemistry?

How Can These Ideas Apply to You?

1. Are you a "late dualistic" thinker according to Finster's definition? Explain.
2. Do you agree with Finster's description of a "good teacher"?
3. Have you ever experienced a teacher who is teaching "above your head"? What did you do?
4. Why does Finster think the first year is the worst time for "mass education"?
5. Do you think Finster's methods of teaching are effective? Why? Would you enjoy chemistry if taught by Finster's methods?

College Pressures

William Zinsser

William Zinsser was a professor and dean at Yale University. As a university administrator, Dean Zinsser has witnessed firsthand what first-year students experience. In this
extract, he describes the pressures students feel from trying to living up to the
expectations of their parents.

• • • • • • • • • • • • • • • • •

I see four kinds of pressure working on college students today: economic
pressure, parental pressure, peer pressure, and self-induced pressure. It is easy
to look around for villains—to blame the colleges for charging too much
money, the professors for assigning too much work, the parents for pushing their
children too far, the students for driving themselves too hard. But there are no
villains, only victims.

Along with economic pressure goes parental pressure. Inevitably, the two
are deeply intertwined.

I see many students taking pre-medical courses with joyless *tenacity*. They
go off to their labs as if they were going to the dentist. It saddens me because I
know them in other corners of their life as cheerful people.

"Do you want to go to medical school?" I ask them.

"I guess so," they say, without conviction, or, "Not really."

"Then why are you going?"

"Well, my parents want me to be a doctor. They're paying all this money
and . . ."

Poor students, poor parents. They are caught in one of the oldest webs of
love and duty and guilt. The parents mean well; they are trying to steer their
sons and daughters toward a secure future. But the sons and daughters want to
major in history or classics or philosophy—subjects with no "practical" value.
Where's the payoff of the humanities? It's not easy to persuade such loving parents that the humanities do indeed pay off. The intellectual faculties developed
by studying subjects like history and classics—an ability to *synthesize* and relate, to weigh cause and effect, to see events in perspective—are just the faculties that make creative leaders in business or almost any general field. Still,
many fathers would rather put their money on courses that point toward a specific profession—courses that are pre-law, pre-medical, pre-business, or, as I have
sometimes heard it put, "pre-rich."

But the pressure on students is severe. They are truly torn. One part of
them feels obligated to fulfill their parents' expectations; after all, their parents
are older and presumably wiser. Another part tells them that the expectations
that are right for their parents are not right for them.

I know a student who wants to be an artist. She is very obviously an artist and will be a good one—she has already had several modest local exhibits. Meanwhile she is growing as a well-rounded person and taking humanistic subjects that will enrich the inner resources out of which her art will grow. But her father is strongly opposed. He thinks that an artist is a "dumb" thing to be. The student vacillates and tries to please everybody. She keeps up with her art somewhat *furtively* and takes some of the "dumb" courses her father wants her to take—at least they are dumb courses for her. She is a free spirit on a campus of tense students—no small achievement in itself—and she deserves to follow her muse.

Peer pressure and self-induced pressure are also intertwined, and they begin almost at the beginning of the freshman year.

"I had a freshman student I'll call Linda," one dean told me, "who came in and said she was under terrible pressure because her roommate, Barbara, was much brighter and studied all the time. I couldn't tell her that Barbara had come in two hours earlier to say the same thing about Linda."

The story is almost funny—except that it's not. It's *symptomatic* of all the pressures put together. When every student thinks every other student is working harder and doing better, the only solution is to study harder still. I see students going off to the library every night after dinner and coming back when it closes at midnight. I wish they would sometimes forget about their peers and go to a movie. I hear the clacking of typewriters in the hours before dawn. I see the tension in their eyes when exams are approaching and papers are due: *"Will I get everything done?"*

Probably they won't. They will get sick. They will get "blocked." They will sleep. They will oversleep. They will bug out.

Part of the problem is that they do more than they are expected to do. A professor will assign five-page papers. Several students will start writing ten-page papers to impress him. Then more students will write ten-page papers, and a few will raise the ante to fifteen. Pity the poor student who is still just doing the assignment.

"Once you have twenty or thirty percent of the student population deliberately overexerting," one dean points out, "it's bad for everybody. When a teacher gets more and more effort from his class, the student who is doing normal work can be perceived as not doing well. The tactic works, psychologically."

Why can't the professor just cut back and not accept longer papers? He can, and he probably will. But by then the term will be half over and the damage done. Grade fever is highly contagious and not easily reversed. Besides, the professor's main concern is with his course. He knows his students only in relation to the course and doesn't know that they are also overexerting in the other courses. Nor is it really his business. He didn't sign up for dealing with the student as a whole person and with all the emotional baggage the student brought along from home. That's what deans, masters, chaplains, and psychiatrists are for.

To some extent this is nothing new: a certain number of professors have always been self-contained islands of scholarship and shyness, more comfortable with books than with people. But the new *pauperism* has widened the gap still further, for professors who actually like to spend time with students don't have as much time to spend. They also are overexerting. If they are young, they are busy trying to publish in order not to perish, hanging by their fingernails onto a shrinking profession. If they are old and tenured, they are buried under the duties of administering departments—as departmental chairmen or members of committees—that have been thinned out by the budgetary axe.

Ultimately, it will be the students' own business to break the circles in which they are trapped. They are too young to be prisoners of their parents' dreams and their classmates' fears. They must be jolted into believing in themselves as unique men and women who have the power to shape their own future.

This is an excerpt from "College Pressures," written while William Zinsser was teaching at Yale University. Reprinted by permission of the author © 1979 by William K. Zinsser.

• •

 # Vocabulary

As you think about this essay, these definitions may be helpful to you:
1. **tenacity**   persistence in maintaining or adhering to something valued
2. **synthesize**   to combine parts or elements to make a whole
3. **furtively**   slyly, as the look of someone with something to hide
4. **symptomatic**   characteristic
5. **pauperism**   the state of being reduced to poverty

 # Discussion Questions

1. The author says there are four kinds of pressures working on college students today. What are they? Can you think of others?
2. What kinds of pressures does the author indicate come from parents? What is the motivation for these pressures?
3. What other kinds of pressures do students feel? Give an example from the reading.
4. How do students react to these pressures?
5. How do these pressures affect the faculty and other professionals on campus?

How Can These Ideas Apply to You?

1. Have you ever felt any of the four pressures the author indicates in the opening paragraph? Which ones and why?
2. Which of the four pressures have been most difficult for you? Why?
3. How do you personally deal with the stress that accompanies pressure?
4. Do you agree with the author that faculty members typically have not "signed up for dealing with the whole person"? Do you think they should? Why?
5. What can you do to gain the "power to shape your own future"?

Dorm Do's and Don'ts

E. Gordon Gee

E. Gordon Gee, now chancellor of Vanderbilt University, has been president of five colleges. When he was at Ohio State, this essay was sent to Ohio high school newspapers. Many high school students make the transition to college life living in a residence hall. Here are tips for what to expect from dorm life and how to take advantage of the experience.

From time to time, I spend a night in one of Ohio State's residence halls. I view it as a reality check. It gives me a chance to catch up on the latest trends in slang, music, and snack food. Plus, I learn a lot from reading the T-shirts—sometimes more than I would like!

With each overnight, I get a little wiser. Recently, when the inevitable prankster set off the fire alarm at 2 A.M., I emerged fully dressed in suit and bow tie. They are not going to catch me in my pajamas again! On another occasion, I learned just how much pizza college students can consume. My offer to treat was taken up by so many that I had to write a check for $275 to send the pizza delivery guy on his way.

Needless to say, when the president of the university sleeps over, students clean up their act. But I am aware that there is potential for anything to happen when large numbers of students share the same living space.

From my talks with hundreds of Ohio State students, I have found that a little self-reflection and some prior planning can smooth the way for surviving and even enjoying residence hall life. And I would like to take this opportunity to pass their tips on to you.

Finding the right match in a roommate depends a lot on individual lifestyle. If the school you choose sends out a questionnaire asking for your likes, dislikes, and housing preferences, answer it yourself. Don't have your parents fill it out—they might not know you as well as they think. And be honest.

Do you like heavy metal or country/western? The music on or off when you study? Maybe you are the type that stays up all night and sleeps during the day (warning—not a good idea when you are taking classes!). Are you a neat freak or a slob? Say so! It will spare you and your future roommate grief later.

Before leaving for college, you might need to pick up a few new skills, like how to separate red sweatshirts from white socks in the laundry. Or the dangers of bleach, unless you like the Grateful Dead look. Or how to balance your checkbook—and your diet. As many students learn, the human does not thrive for long on caffeine and cheese curls.

And, finally, the cardinal rule of rooming together. Never, EVER eat your roommates' food without first asking permission and offering to replace it. Otherwise, you might find your mattress in the hall.

Undoubtedly, it will take time to adjust. But I can assure you it will be worth the effort. Keep an open mind. Your mother may have said, "To make a friend, be a friend." It's true. Give it a chance.

Living in a residence hall is a wonderful opportunity to increase your understanding of the world, of the way human beings relate to each other. You will change and grow. You will learn that there are as many different ways of looking at the world as there are people in the world. And you will make friendships that last a lifetime.

If you do decide to go away to college, it will be for many of you the first taste of freedom—your first venture out from under the parental thumb. You are on your own—free to grow and equally free to make the occasional mistake. The important thing is to learn from your mistakes and move on.

You will find that a good time is a big part of the college experience. But, remember that in the long run, you and your friends are there to get an education. Don't waste that chance.

And turn down that music.

Reprinted by permission of the author.

• •

 ## Discussion Questions

1. What does the author suggest you can learn about life from dorm living?
2. If you are experiencing dorm life, is your experience similar to that described by the author?
3. What other experiences or lessons have you learned from living in a residence hall?

Loneliness

Barbara M. Newman and Philip R. Newman

Barbara and Philip Newman are the authors of many books on human development. They are especially well known for *Development through Life: A Psychosocial Approach,* now in its seventh edition.

Some students may experience feelings of loneliness as they enter a new and foreign college environment. The authors describe loneliness as a common college experience and suggest that friendships can play a key role in overcoming it.

• • • • • • • • • • • • • • • • • •

College brings new opportunities for friendship, but it also brings new experiences of isolation and loneliness. Many college students leave the comfort and familiarity of their support system at home for a new environment. Others break ties with old friends who have gone to work or entered the military right after high school. The early weeks and months of college are likely to bring deep feelings of isolation and loneliness. These feelings are intensified because students usually approach the transition to college with such positive anticipation. They often do not even consider that this change will bring any sense of *uprootedness* or loss.

Loneliness is a common experience of college life. An estimated 25 percent of the college population feel extremely lonely at some time during any given month. These feelings are likely to be most noticeable during the freshman year because of the sharp contrast between the structure of high school life and the independence expected of students in college. However, loneliness can be a theme throughout the college years. The process of becoming an individual brings with it a new appreciation for one's separateness from others. As young people discover their own uniqueness, from time to time they are bound to feel that no one else really understands them.

Your parents may also experience periods of loneliness. They miss the physical presence of a person they love. They miss the daily interactions. Now and again, they may yearn for things to be more like they were and wish to be less separate.

Loneliness can be classified into three categories: *transient,* situational, and chronic.[1] *Transient loneliness* lasts a short time and passes. College students may feel this kind of loneliness when their friends are out on dates and they are alone in the dorm. This type of loneliness may occur when a student is the only one to take a certain position in a discussion; the only black student in a class; or the only one working out in a large, empty gym.

---

[1] These categories are adapted from J. Meer, "Loneliness," *Psychology Today,* July 1985, pp. 28–33.

Situational loneliness accompanies a sudden loss or a move to a new city. Students commonly experience this kind of loneliness when they first come to college, especially if they are away from home. Most of us are *disoriented* when we move to a new town. Going to college is no different. Despite the many new and wonderful facets of college life, most young people experience situational loneliness due to the loss of the supportive, familiar environment of their homes and communities.

Your parents may undergo situational loneliness because of the loss of your presence. Even though they have planned and saved for this opportunity, they may experience intense loneliness following your departure. Rather than trying to create a myth that no one is feeling lonely, parents and college students can help each other through this time by admitting their loneliness and doing their best to reduce it. Frequent telephone calls, letters, and visits home in the first few months can ease the feelings of loss.

Chronic loneliness lasts a long time and cannot be linked to a specific event or situation. Chronically lonely people may have an average number of social contacts, but these contacts are not meaningful in helping the person achieve the desired level of intimacy. Chronically lonely people often seem reluctant to make contact with others. There appears to be a strong relationship between social skills and chronic loneliness. People who have higher levels of social skill, including friendliness, communication skills, appropriate *nonverbal* behavior, and appropriate response to others, have more adequate social support and experience lower levels of loneliness.

You may not recognize that you suffer from chronic loneliness until you are away at college. While children are living at home, parents are usually able to provide the amount of social support their children need. At college, children may find it extremely difficult to replace the level of trust and closeness that were provided by family members and high school friends.

Inadequate friendship relationships may actually interfere with your academic performance as well as your physical and mental health. Substantial research evidence supports the relationship between inadequate social support and *vulnerability* to illness. People who are part of a strong social support system are more likely to resist disease and to recover quickly from illnesses when they occur. Their general outlook on life is more optimistic.

A college student's circle of friends plays a key role in keeping the young person integrated into the social environment. Friends look in on you when you are sick; they make sure you have an assignment if you miss class; they invite you to join them if they are going to a party, a special lecture, or a campus concert. Friends worry about you and remind you to take care of yourself. Friends monitor your moods and prevent you from becoming too preoccupied or too discouraged. Friends value you and support your emerging identity. They understand the importance of the questions you are raising, and they encourage you to say what's on your mind. Building and maintaining satisfying friendships are key ingredients to feeling at home and succeeding in college.

Vocabulary

As you think about this essay, these definitions may be helpful to you:
1. **uprootedness**   in psychology, a sense of being displaced
2. **transient**   passing through with only a brief stay or sojourn
3. **disoriented**   having lost a sense of time, place, or identity
4. **nonverbal**   involving minimal or no use of language
5. **vulnerability**   openness to attack or damage

 # Discussion Questions

1. What factors may trigger loneliness in a college student?
2. What are the three categories of loneliness described by the authors?
3. How does transient loneliness differ from chronic loneliness?
4. Why are students with little or no social support more vulnerable to illness?
5. How do friendships help students feel less lonely?

 # How Can These Ideas Apply to You?

1. Did you experience situational loneliness when you started college? How did it feel?
2. At what other times have you experienced loneliness? What did you do to overcome it?
3. Do you know students who are lonely? Are they able to overcome it? If not, what can they do?
4. Why are building and maintaining friendships so helpful in overcoming loneliness?
5. How can you as a friend help another student through lonely times?

UNIT SUMMARY

The readings in this unit discussed many aspects of college life and its effect on students. Although adjusting to college may take some time, the challenge and excitement of being a student makes this experience unique and memorable.

Summary Questions

1. How do the expectations about college expressed by the readings in this unit differ from your own? How are they similar?
2. How can the college experience help you in your intellectual, personal, and career development?
3. If you were not attending college, how would your life be different? Evaluate the differences.

Suggested Writing Assignments

1. Write a brief essay on how you have changed since your first day in college. How do you expect to change by the time you earn a degree?
2. Describe one experience that you have had with taking control of your situation in life. How did you manage the change?
3. Describe one of your own college experiences that was also described by an author in this unit. Some examples are loneliness, pressure, dorm living, and classroom experience. Compare your experience with that author's account.

Suggested Readings

Chickering, Arthur W., and Linda Reisser. *Education and Identity,* 2nd ed. San Francisco: Jossey-Bass, 1993.

Gilligan, Carol. *In a Different Voice.* Cambridge, MA: Harvard University Press, 1982.

Siebert, Al, and Bernadine Gilpin. *The Adult Student's Guide to Survival and Success: Time for College.* Portland, OR: Practical Psychology Press, 1992.

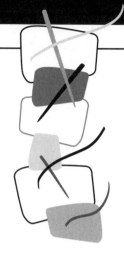

How Can I Succeed Academically?

Academic success can be defined from many perspectives. Some measure it by grade-point average (known commonly as GPA) or by "accume," which is short for cumulative point-hour ratio. A student with a 3.5 GPA, for example, is usually considered more successful academically than a student with a 1.9. Academic success is also defined by one's accumulation of knowledge. Students who, when tested, can successfully throw back to their instructors the facts and concepts they have memorized may be considered academically successful. Still others define success by the salary and prestige of the job they are able to acquire at the end of their senior year. Some students may consider what they have genuinely learned to be the true measure of their academic success. Learning how to learn is a skill that can be used for a lifetime. Successful students will always be intensely involved in their own learning.

Regardless of how a student measures academic success, certain activities in which students engage are essential to the learning process. Among them, reading and writing are

'Tis education forms the common mind. Just as the twig is bent, the tree's inclined.

—ALEXANDER POPE

59

two of the most critical. Some first-year students find themselves ill prepared in these basic skills. Most new students who understand the value of these activities work hard to improve their reading and writing skills throughout their college years.

Some other skills closely associated with academic success are:

Communication Skills. These include being able to communicate ideas and concepts effectively in a prepared presentation or in the conversational give-and-take of a committee meeting. Such skills are important in the classroom and marketable in the workplace.

Writing Skills. Students who can express themselves well in writing have a highly marketable skill. The ability to write clear and persuasive reports, proposals, and similar important documents is essential in every work environment.

Organizational Skills. Students need to set goals and priorities and to organize their time and energy accordingly. Self-discipline plays a key role in how students balance their academic life with other personal and social demands.

Analytical Skills. Learning to think critically and logically is important to academic success. Identifying problems and solving them creatively are central to accomplishing many academic tasks.

Research Skills. Students require basic research skills to fulfill many academic assignments. Defining a problem, formulating pertinent questions, using appropriate resources to study the problem, and employing a variety of research methods to solve the problem are all part of the research process that students use constantly.

The authors in this unit would certainly agree on the importance of the five categories of skill listed above. Indeed, Uchida adds several more with a list generated from input given by 55 distinguished professionals. O'Hanlon adds skill at library and Internet research, Gold suggests punctuality, and Brown requires regularity in attendance to class. Burtchaell and Raspberry offer perspectives on selecting a college major that may surprise some readers—especially those who have been conditioned to believe that selecting a college major is roughly equivalent to making a lifelong commitment to a single job. Minnick provides some ways for thinking about elective courses, which are all the classes you take that are not stipulated as some requirement. All these readings can have a bearing on your thoughtful approach to course selection.

What Students Must Know to Succeed in the 21st Century

Donna Uchida

Donna Uchida is a communications officer for Levi Strauss in San Francisco. The Council of 55 to which she refers in this essay is a group of advisers from varied fields—education, business, government, psychology, sociology, demography, and others. These experts participated in a study that asked, "What do students need to know in order to succeed in the 21st century?" This reading summarizes their conclusions and relates them to the academic content that students need to master for success in the foreseeable future.

• • • • • • • • • • • • • • • • •

What will students need to know to be well-educated for the 21st century? According to the Council of 55, here are some essential elements necessary to the content of education:

1. Use of math, logic, and reasoning skills; functional and operational literacy; and an understanding of statistics. Jan Mokros, writing in *Math Textbooks: Where Is Math?*, notes that the term "mathematics" comes from "a family of Greek words denoting to learn or search for meaning." Mokros objects to many math textbooks because "students who use them never have a chance to gather, describe, summarize, and interpret real data for themselves."

"Math must also be viewed as a language and as a way of communicating or making sense of the world," according to Stephanie Pace Marshall, executive director of the Illinois Mathematics and Science Academy. "Math is a language of relationships, patterns, and connection," she adds. "This is the mathematics we must teach."

The National Council of Teachers of Mathematics has led a pioneering effort to establish standards for the teaching of math. As with any standards, they should guide schools in developing and judging the content, teaching, and evaluation of math curriculum. An understanding of math concepts, computation, and problem solving is essential to a truly literate person.

Math is one way to generate thinking and reasoning skills among students. Performance-based assessments that ask students to reveal how they arrived at answers to math problems can also give students practice in reaching logical conclusions.

As part of the Math Counts program, *USA Today* published a poster showing a front page of the newspaper and highlighting how some knowledge of statistics was necessary to understand nearly every article. Students will need to know not only how to interpret statistics, but also how to determine their authenticity. They also will need to be able to use legitimate statistics to build a case for their ideas. In addition, well-educated students must be able to sort out and evaluate mounds of evidence bombarding them from an expanding number of sources, ranging from textbooks to the Internet....

Teaching thinking and reasoning skills goes far beyond math. It is a part of every discipline, from writing to studying the causes and the effects of historic events. "Reasoning is not a separate category of learning. It is integral to any lesson, any exercise, and any educational experience," says Mary Bicouvaris, the 1989 National Teacher of the Year, who currently is associate professor of education at Christopher Newport University in Newport News, Virginia.

2. Critical interpersonal skills, including speaking, listening, and the ability to be part of a team. "Interpersonal skills include more than speaking and listening. Students need the ability to work collaboratively with different people," says Anne Campbell. Campbell is a former Nebraska Commissioner of Education and served as a member of the National Commission on Excellence in Education, which developed the 1983 report, "A Nation at Risk."

The ability to work with and communicate effectively with others was an overarching issue in this study. In fact, it placed as an essential part of knowledge, skills, and behaviors.

The Council of 55 made several points about the importance of this critical body of knowledge and cluster of skills. "Respect for other opinions and perspectives is increasingly vital in a more demographically diverse society," says Michael Usdan, president of the Institute for Educational Leadership. "More emphasis needs to be placed on achieving these skills through the teaching of core subject areas," adds Chris Pipho, director of state/clearinghouse services for the Education Commission of the States.

The bottom line for some Council members was that interpersonal and communications skills are at the front line of "getting you hired or fired." Others emphasized that the classroom should be a laboratory for collaborative decision making and team building, urging principals and teachers to model the behavior by collaborating. One panelist remarked, "Students will not buy into the 'do as I say, not as I do' *syndrome.*"

3. Effective information accessing and processing skills using technology. The spotlight of the nation and much of the world is focused on more effectively accessing the *plethora* of information that is virtually at our fingertips. Concern continues to grow about an expanding gulf that may divide the information rich and the information poor. Education cannot stop with simply helping students learn to access information. Students also will need to understand how to process and use the volumes of often conflicting information that will reach them each and every day. "Everyone says you must be able to read," says Marvin Cetron, president of Forecasting International and a chief advisor for this study. "It's more important for us to understand that we now have videodiscs; we have tools we can use interactively. Now, with technology, you can learn by seeing and doing."

Some students will be expected to create new technologies. Others will be expected to explain technology in plain language. Thus, both technical and communication skills will continue to be valued simultaneously.

"We need more effective training for teachers to emphasize information accessing and processing, plus we need to ensure that all students have access to technology," says Mary Hatwood Futrell, dean of the George Washington University Graduate School of Education and Human Development, and a former president of the National Education Association.

Of course, both the technological tools and the knowledge and skills needed to use them are essential to education for the 21st century. "Education at all levels will require large increases in funding to provide the equipment and training for teachers to meet the demand for technology in the curriculum," according to Jack Dulaney, superintendent of the Monongalis County Schools in West Virginia. "This may require asking more businesses to become involved." Adds Marshall, "We must go beyond information accessing to include information creation and knowledge development."

4. Writing skills to enable students to communicate effectively. Writing is one of the essential elements of literacy. It is a key to effective communication, and the very act of writing demands thinking and reasoning. Writing helps individuals develop initiative as they sort through ideas, organize thoughts, and draw parallels. It develops courage, since sharing ideas leaves them open to the scrutiny of others. Writing also has been shown to contribute to even better reading skills.

Writes Kathryn Au, an education psychologist with the Kamehameha School in Honolulu, Hawaii, "If we want students to become good readers and writers, we need to involve them in the full processes of reading and writing. We should have them read literature and write for a variety of purposes, just as we want them to do in real life."

The National Council of Teachers of English has done extensive research on effectively teaching students to write. While debate continues over the importance of mechanics vs. free and creative writing, the fact remains that both are important. Ultimately, students need to be able to write to inform, to persuade, to express, and perhaps even to entertain....

We should keep in mind that language itself evolves, and so do writing styles. Members of the Council of 55 suggested continuing in-depth training for teachers, coupled with providing students with sound materials and practical experiences in writing. They also emphasized the need for students to be able to write creatively and scientifically and to be able to use tools such as hardware and software to assist them in writing, editing, and rewriting (often considered among the most important steps in the writing process)....

5. Knowledge of American history and government to function in a democratic society and an understanding of issues surrounding patriotism. "Becoming involved in our representative democracy is critical for our nation's future," said Thomas Shannon, executive director of the National School Boards Association. "When students get involved, theory touches reality," he added.

Indeed the best way to learn about civics is to become a part of it. Of course, a knowledge of history and government is key to avoiding pitfalls of the past. . . .

During 1995, the Center for Civic Education, working with a number of other groups, released standards focusing on five significant questions:

1. What are civic life, politics, and government?
2. What are the foundations of the American political system?
3. How does the government established by the Constitution embody the purposes, values, and principles of American democracy?
4. What is the relationship of the United States to other nations and to world affairs?
5. What are the roles of the citizen in American democracy?

These questions, plus a framework found in a report on those standards, "We the People . . . the Citizens and the Constitution," are essential touchstones for developing effective programs to teach students about their government and to guide them in the teaching of history. Of course, state and local history as well as family and recent history are important in connecting with the continuum of social, political, and economic development.

In "Education for Democracy," a joint project of the American Federation of Teachers, the Educational Excellence Network, and Freedom House, three convictions were presented for "schools to purposely impart the ideals of a free society." They are: "First, that democracy is the worthiest form of human government conceived. Second, that we cannot take its survival or its spread—or its perfection in practice—for granted. Third, that democracy's survival depends upon our transmitting to each new generation the political vision of liberty and equality that unites us as Americans."

The National Council for the Social Studies and other subject area organizations have intensified their focus on preparing students to function in a free and democratic society. The issue of patriotism raised several comments among members of the Council of 55. "It is important that students have knowledge about the democratic process and not just blind patriotism," emphasized former superintendent K. Jesse Kobayashi.

Panel members also appealed for integration in the teaching of history, government, geography, and other social sciences to show how they all are related and interconnected.

6. Scientific knowledge base, including applied science. "One cannot just learn *about* science," says Marshall. "Science is the active engagement with the physical world. It is risk, experimentation, failure, and discovery. It must be *experienced*."

Scientific discovery and the practical and commercial applications of discoveries have brought profound changes to the nation and the world. Most would agree that leadership in science is directly connected to our nation's capacity to maintain a sound economy and may even determine whether the nation or the planet will survive. Therefore, science education, from knowledge about scientific principles, to applied science, to an understanding that over time, evidence may suggest new theories, is essential. . . .

"All of our children and young adults, not just those preparing to be professional scientists, must have an understanding of scientific ways of thinking and science knowledge in order to function in an information age," writes Mary Lewis Sivertsen in *Transforming Ideas for Teaching and Learning Science,* published by the U.S. Department of Education. "Equally important is the ability for all citizens to make good decisions using a basic understanding of the science and technology behind the various social issues affecting their lives."

As superintendent of the Princeton, New Jersey, Public Schools, Paul Houston, currently executive director of the American Association of School Administrators, worked with a community planning group that discussed whether technology drives values or vice versa. Their answer was that technology does drive values. For example, our abilities to extend life through technology and medicine are increasing, which leads to questions about how we define "life," the morality of *euthanasia,* and more. Therefore, as science and technology are applied in real-world situations, ethics and values must be developed to guide their use. . . .

In her report, Sivertsen notes that science has remained a relatively low priority in elementary schools, yet the elementary grades are a critical time for capturing children's interest. "If students are not encouraged to follow their curiosity about the natural world in the primary grades, waiting to teach science on a regular basis in grade four may be too late. Data show that many children tend to lose interest in science at about the fourth grade," she says.

Percy Bates, director of Programs for Educational Opportunity at the University of Michigan School of Education, says that "for too long the field of science has seemed to be reserved only for the bright, the smart, the elite in our schools." In an Equity Coalition article, "Science Education and Equity," Bates cites evidence from the National Center for Educational Statistics, dated June 1992, showing that "Boys and girls are virtually even in math and science achievement in the third and seventh grades. However, by the eleventh grade boys achieve at a much higher level than girls." He encourages the "removal of all barriers in the field of science. Evidence shows that not only gender, but race, ethnicity, and socioeconomic class (SES) are acting as gatekeepers to becoming a scientist." . . .

7. An understanding of history of the world and world affairs. As much as some people would like to think of their nation as an island detached from the rest of the world, it is simply no longer possible to maintain that separation. Political, technological, sociological, economic, and environmental issues jump both natural and political borders. They affect us all. Therefore, students need to understand world history and world affairs.

An understanding of world history and world affairs could help today's students avoid future Holocausts or explore how various nations might become allies in conquering disease or reaching into inner, outer, and cyberspace.

Tom Maes, superintendent of the Adams County School District #1 in suburban Denver, Colorado, believes, "Like languages, the lack of world history has serious implications for world markets." Adds NSBA's Shannon: "Patriotism, founded on pride in our national, political culture, traditions, and institutions is clearly important. But this does not mean that knowledge, respect and appreciation of other cultures and nationalities should be *sloughed*. We are in a mutually interdependent world and must get along—but not at the price of surrendering our own values." Students need to be grounded in the cultures of other peoples, if only to understand them and to maintain peace in an interdependent world.

8. Multicultural understanding, including insights into diversity and the need for an international perspective. The world has become more interrelated as satellites, cyberspace, and jet travel bring people and nations closer together. Communication transcends political boundaries. Our nation, too, has become more cosmopolitan as new waves of immigrants come to America. In fact, except for Native Americans, the United States is a land of immigrants. All are seeking common as well as divergent purposes in a free and democratic society. Now, more than ever, an understanding of diversity is key. In the future it will only become more important.

The ability to work in collaboration with different people is critical, says Richard Warner, principal of Fargo South High School in North Dakota. "Different people means not only color, but gender, nationality, religion, and political persuasion," he adds. "The basic need is for understanding our dependency on each other," says California superintendent K. Jesse Kobayashi.

Other members of the panel also called for not only the teaching of multicultural understanding but also the modeling of it in every school and community.

Properly managed, diversity can enrich. Not properly managed, it can divide. The key is education.

9. Knowledge of foreign languages. "How can we provide a sound education and compete in world markets without learning foreign languages?" asks Maes. For that matter, how can we make ourselves understood if we aren't able to communicate in languages of the world marketplace? How can we be sure we aren't being taken advantage of because we don't understand the conversations taking place around us? How can we fully enjoy the history and culture of other nations or of the immigrants who come to this country without an understanding of other languages? These are questions demanding our attention as we approach the 21st century.

The stories are legion. Businesspeople from other countries come to the United States and speak our language. Americans go to other countries and need interpreters. As businesses become increasingly multinational and as nations pool resources to collaborate on global issues, such as the environment, the lack of ability to communicate in other languages becomes an even more costly barrier.

10. Knowledge of world geography. Similarly, a lack of knowledge about geography will be a barrier to understanding our shrinking universe.

Anthony R. DeSouza, in "Time for Geography: The New National Standards," writes: "By the year 2000, planet Earth will be more crowded, the physical environment more threatened, natural resources more depleted, the global economy more competitive, world events more interconnected, human life more complex, and the need for people to have a solid grasp of geography even more essential."

He adds, "By learning geography thoroughly, students come to understand the connections and relationships among themselves and people, places, cultures, and economies across the world."

An Integrated Curriculum

While the Council of 55 identified fairly specific disciplines or bodies of knowledge that will be required for students to thrive in the 21st century, members of the council also made clear that the curriculum should be integrated across disciplines. "Perhaps history, government, geography, and other social sciences need to be integrated," Dulaney suggests. "This will show students the connections and interrelationships."

"It seems that with the emphasis on an integrated curriculum across disciplines as well as the need for students to learn to work collaboratively, this will lead to a new curriculum of the 21st century," says J.C. Sparkman, former executive vice president of Tele-Communications, Inc. (TCI) of Denver. . . .

Reprinted by permission of the American Association of School Administrators.

• •

 # Vocabulary

As you think about this essay, these definitions may be helpful to you:
1. **syndrome**   a medical term referring to a number of symptoms that, when they occur together, characterize a specific disease
2. **plethora**   excessive in number; overabundant
3. **euthanasia**   the act or method of causing a painless death, often to protect against suffering
4. **slough** [pronounced sluff]   as a verb, to shed or get rid of

 # Discussion Questions

1. What is the purpose behind Uchida's frequent quotations from members of the Council of 55?
2. Are there any kinds of knowledge that surprised you by being included on this list? Are there any important omissions that you can think of?

3. How would you rank these ten kinds of knowledge from most important to least important? If you need to put some of them together into categories, feel free to do so, but explain why you think they fit together.
4. Uchida lists the ability to get along with others (Item 2) as an "academic content" area. Is it? Why or why not?

 # How Can These Ideas Apply to You?

1. One way to understand the ten categories in this reading is to think of them as goals for your own education. Select the one or two that will be the hardest for you to attain, and explain what about you or about the goals you select make them especially difficult.
2. The Council of 55 identified kinds of knowledge other than academic content that, in their view, students in the 21st century need to learn. Can you suggest what some of them might be?
3. Select one of these areas and explain what you can do to master the knowledge in it that you need for success in the 21st century.

Major Decisions

James Tunstead Burtchaell

Father James Burtchaell, professor emeritus of Theology at the University of Notre Dame, served as provost for many years. While holding that title, which in a university is normally the position of chief academic officer and ranks just below the president, Burtchaell lived in student residence halls and saw firsthand the student concerns that he discusses in this reading. Although many colleges strive to get students to decide on a major early, often before being admitted, Notre Dame in Burtchaell's time told students that, as first-year students, they could specify an intent but not declare a major. This essay explains why.

More than two out of every three undergraduates at this university change majors between the time they are accepted and the time they graduate. A good number change two or three times. Any decision that has so many students second-guessing must be tricky, and it is.

The difficulty comes from several directions. First, there are so many options that you had no opportunity to sample in high school. Everyone has some experience studying literature, mathematics, French and physics, but no high school in the country offers electrical engineering. Nor can you get a running start in microbiology or finance or metallurgy or philosophy. More than half of the disciplines we offer are new to you. So how can you have a responsibly cultivated preference early enough to select one as your principal interest here?

Another difficulty is pressure. Some students get pretty clear advice from their parents about what a sensible major would be. Most of that advice tends to have something to do with earning a living after college. And much of it is bad advice.

In the old days there were parents who threatened to cut off tuition money unless their child studied the subject they thought was right. That rarely happens today, but there is another kind of pressure that may be worse. There are few students at Notre Dame whose parents didn't make sacrifices for them to be here. And most students are backed by parents who didn't have, or weren't free to accept, the kind of education they worked hard to provide their children. The result: Most people on this campus walk around with an abiding and compelling sense of gratitude to their parents.

For every student here whose parents have told him what to study, there are a hundred whose parents never breathed a word of instruction on the matter. But most of those hundred, in the privacy of their hearts, want to make a choice that will satisfy their parents. They are drawn to major in subjects their parents can see as oriented toward a useful future. One somehow feels it would be ungrateful to receive a first-rate university education and not put it to maximum use from the start. That is a more *insidious* and damaging form of pressure precisely because there is nothing the parents can do to change it. They had nothing to do with imposing it.

In addition, high school counselors often talk to seniors in a way that is excessively career oriented. They make the student aware, even before she sets foot on a college campus, that she is going to higher studies with an eye toward an eventual profession or job. The message is that it is wasteful to spend four years without any clear idea of where all that expensive study is leading.

Students also have a tendency, especially in their early years at college, to feel crowded by competition. Most freshmen look up and down the corridor the first week they're here and feel intimidated. Everyone they encounter seems to have been a valedictorian, student council president, all-state breast-stroke champion, published poet.

I exaggerate, of course, but most people here *are* used to being at the head of the line. That is how you got here. Now you are at a place with a lot of others who were at the head of *their* lines, and there just isn't room for all of you at the top of this class. So you tend to figure that your choice of study here will have to be canny and careful if it's going to make you competitive with such bright and aggressive classmates.

After a few years you discover everyone else is as normal as you, but by then you've begun to worry that since Notre Dame accepted you it must be a second-rate institution. There are all those other more talented people out there at better places who, when they emerge, are going to have a running start on you. So your choice of what to study is fretful because you have these other, more quick-witted people to compete with.

Those are three difficulties that most of you have to cope with: the subjects are so unknown, the choice is so pressured, and the competition is so strong. Unfortunately these difficulties cause students to stumble into a few classical misunderstandings, which in turn lead them to wrong decisions about their major.

The first misunderstanding is to confuse education with training. An institution that offers you training is trying to provide you with the information and skills you need for a specific career. A law school must acquaint you with how to interview clients, how to plead before a court, and how to draw up proper legal documents. A welding academy will teach you the materials and methods of the trade. Advanced training in computing will prepare you not simply to keypunch or to program, but to create software, to understand the mysteries of central processing, and then to grasp the theoretical underpinnings of applied mathematics.

All of that is training: specific knowledge needed for specific professional or skilled work. It is not education.

Education is the opportunity, through studying a variety of subjects, to gain the information and the dexterity to use your wits and your expression. Education prepares you to *be* someone more than to *do* something. Education is what prepares you to hear more when you listen, to reach deeper when you think, to say more when you speak.

Education is quite different from training, which prepares you in advance to do the tasks that are well known in a given job. Education prepares you in advance to see beneath and beyond what is well known. The principal value that an educated person brings to her career is intelligence. What one wants of an educated person, beyond his skills, is the ability to see into problems that cannot be foreseen. A welder must know in advance all the techniques he has to use, but a banker or a physician or a teacher or a member of the city council is expected to move beyond previous experience and apply his wits to the heart of new problems.

A good university such as this one will give you quite a few skills and a broad grounding of information. But we do not exist to teach skills to undergraduates; we do that in our graduate and professional programs. The result of a college education should be a person whose mind is enlivened and whose imagination is limber. England's Robert Benchley put it in his own peculiar and wise way:

"Gentlemen: You are now about to embark upon a course of studies which will occupy you for several years. Together they form a noble adventure. But I would like to remind you of an important point. Some of you, when you go down from the University, will go into the Church, or to the Bar, or to the House of Commons, or to the Home Civil Service, to the Indian or Colonial Services, or into various professions. Some may go into the Army, some into industry and commerce, some may become country gentlemen. A few—I hope very few— will become teachers or *dons*.

"Let me make this clear to you. Except for the last category, nothing that you will learn in the course of your studies will be of the slightest possible use to you in after life, save only this: That if you work hard and intelligently you should be able to detect when a man is talking rot, and that in my view is the main, if not the sole, purpose of education."

People fortunate and qualified enough to receive a university education will make their living by their wits. You will be served less by what you *have* learned than by what you *can* learn.

The good thing about education is that it matters hardly at all what subjects you choose to study. You can be educated in any discipline, because there is no direct connection between an educational subject and a specific career. So never ask what you can *do* with your major.

This touches on the second classical misunderstanding that has led so many students astray. The choice of a major is not the choice of a career. Undergraduates are not making lifetime decisions. When they imagine they are, it can be paralyzing.

As you know, Notre Dame has delaying tactics to slow you down in the selection of a major. Before coming here most of you speculated about your eventual career, and then about what course of study you would select. You arrived here ready to declare a major, but the Freshman Year of Studies would not allow that. The most you were permitted was to designate an "intent." We wanted you to get the maximum exposure and experience here, and a year or two more of self-knowledge, so that your intellectual curiosity and interests could ripen and the decision would be more sound, more considered.

Let me say a bit about that. Some talents show themselves early in life. If you are an excellent athlete, you already have the coordination and stamina and pleasure from sports in your early teens. Nobody suddenly develops into a star athlete in her 30s. The same is true for mathematical ability. If you are good at quantitative understanding, you are already good at it in junior high school; in fact, you tend toward high achievement in math and other related subjects. You know science is your strong suit, and you come to college aware that you will study science and excel in it. Then things go wrong. Physics will begin to bore some of you. You will conceal from your parents that you signed up for a few extra theology courses, and you'll write poetry by flashlight under the covers at night. You may plug on and earn good grades, but with less and less appetite. It is *disconcerting* to develop a new range of interests when your track record of achievement and satisfaction is so definitely in another direction. But that is what happens when a new range of talent begins to mature and to rival other talents that had declared themselves earlier. No one tells you in advance that philosophical thinking matures later than mathematical thinking. The choice of a major needs to be slowed down to allow you to get confirmation of your emergent strong interests and abilities.

But even then, near the close of your sophomore year, you are only choosing a major, not a career. Still more developments and experiences will come. Fixing on a lifetime career when you are a sophomore in college is like getting engaged at 14.

What you study here may have little necessary connection with what you will do later. We give baccalaureate degrees in about 40 disciplines and in many combinations of subjects. But people graduate in philosophy and end up lawyers. They study mechanical engineering and end up as business executives. They get degrees in English and go to medical school, do art history and run the family business, choose chemistry and go into politics. They major in sociology and become priests. They finish in accountancy with their CPAs and choose to be homemakers and mothers.

Even if they emerge from a program most students would consider a direct pipeline to a specific profession—architecture, for example—they are really much more free than you would suppose. Do you know how many people with degrees in architecture practice architecture? About half. So consider yourself enhanced, rather than caught, by what you choose to study. You are not making a lifetime decision, you are making a decision for the next two or three years . . . or until you change that decision.

This is not to say that there should be no natural growth from study to career. It does imply, however, that educated people have such enormous advantage and versatility that they retain a basic freedom to do whatever they please in life. To have graduated in any discipline that Notre Dame offers in no way forecloses career possibilities. It has become increasingly the case that you will enter a career that requires or provides specific training. About 60 to 70 percent of you will go on to graduate or professional schools; others to corporate training programs. Do not suffer a failure of nerve by imagining that you are more attractive to employers if you have more advanced professional training. For then you will forfeit the unrepeatable and more valuable opportunity to get an education first.

You have talents that will be enormously attractive to employers, talents so superior that you are free to make your living by your wits, your versatility of understanding, your imagination. Don't double-think the future.

The temptation is to figure out your career and then choose the studies that lead up to it. That is exactly the wrong way round. You are not ready to choose a career, except in the most tentative and speculative way. You are barely ready to choose a major. Select what you want to study with the belief that it will lead you to the point of deciding—well, not quite your career, but what you will do after graduation. What educates you best is not what you figure will lead somewhere, but what you now believe will give you most enjoyment. Pick your major on the pleasure principle, for what you most enjoy studying will draw your mind in the liveliest way to being educated.

If you want to study medieval history, don't fret about what you can do with it. You are not at a trade school. If you want to study marketing, do it because you find marketing the most fascinating subject we offer. If you came to Notre Dame determined to become a physician but in your freshman year you couldn't stand math and you failed chemistry and you threw up over your laboratory frog, there's a message there. It's not that you are incapable of becoming a doctor, but that the kind of disciplines that govern a doctor's work do not really appeal to your appetite. If in the meantime drama has caught your eye, then make that your choice and let the future handle itself. Or, more accurately, let it help you to become more qualified to determine the future. If throughout the course of four years you progressively follow your intellectual nose into what fascinates you most, when you emerge you will be in a much wiser position to choose the threshold of the proper career than you were at the start.

In the meantime don't feel pushed to make the decision prematurely. Our curriculum is versatile enough that the decision can be reviewed and postponed and changed. I am not arguing for indecision or instability. I am merely pleading for a sense of freedom, a certain responsible recklessness about study, that too many students feel guilty about having.

Let me put it this way. Imagine you are told now that on graduation day you will die. It will be painless and gentle; you will slowly and beautifully fade, right here on the main quad, with family and roommates gathered round, the Glee Club singing under the trees, and *Father Hesburgh* giving you a potent final blessing. Knowing of your death now—realizing that whatever your major is, it can never lead you into a career but will be only for your pleasure and fascination—would it make any difference what you choose to study in the interim? If it would, then you ought to change. Ironically, what you then choose will lead you, by steady and proper pacing, into the most reliable future.

It is essential to realize that any major can lead to any career, and that the best major is the one you choose with no lookout out of the corner of your eye to where it will lead.

Once that is cleared up, the difficulties are less difficult. Yes, most of the majors possible here are subjects you cannot have studied before. So use the first and especially the second year to explore. Use the freedom the curriculum provides. Far too many men and women graduate from here and come to this regret: If they had it to do over again, or had had the nerve earlier, they would study another subject.

As for the pressure from parents whose approval you seek, remember: If you are mature enough to undertake university studies, you have to be mature enough to choose those studies. You might choose unwisely, but it should be your choice.

Parents who virtually demand what their children will study at college are misguided and, fortunately, rare. I think parents ought to have the freedom to suggest or lobby for a choice of major, but you take away your parents' freedom if you transform their cue into a command. Parents ought to be able to promote an idea without children complaining they are being forced or browbeaten. If your parents do suggest a course of study, give it serious thought, but don't pretend you owe it to them to follow their recommendation.

And don't get up a guilt if you choose another major, because you may in fact be trying to make *them* feel guilty for something they never did.

And if you feel tempted to make a curriculum choice to gain your parents' respect: don't. If you have anything to be grateful for, it is that your parents have wanted you to get the best education within your reach and theirs, precisely so that you could and would make these kinds of decisions responsibly for your own satisfaction. If they didn't want you to develop independent judgment they would have kept you home.

How can you choose your major to sidestep most of the rush-hour traffic of competition? By ignoring competition. Only about 40 percent of your fellow Americans manage to enroll in college, and only about half of those graduate. Virtually all of you at this University will complete your degree requirements. That puts you among the top fifth of all people your age. And among that 20 percent, only the most highly qualified are competitive for admission to a university like Notre Dame, which means you have educational opportunities that rank you among the top one or two percent in the country.

It makes one feel uneasy to hear such talk of exclusiveness, but these are simple facts. So when you get uneasy because everyone in the corridor seems pretty swift of mind, calm down. You are moving among classmates who have the same advantaged education you have, who have been *sieved* through highly selective admission processes. After a while they may begin to look ordinary enough, but they aren't. And you aren't. The older one gets and the more experience one accumulates, the more clear it becomes that the number of really quick-minded people is small. You wonder how the world gets by with so few. Rather than imagining yourself as part of a large, capable crowd trying to crush through a narrow doorway of opportunity, it is more realistic to understand you are advantaged to an embarrassing degree, and there aren't nearly enough of you to go around.

To select a major program of study wisely you need not figure out what other people want of you. You need to figure out what you want. And that's not easy. It requires much self-knowledge.

But that is both what education gives and what education requires. William Johnson Cory, a Cambridge man, expressed impatience when critics complained that English schools were offering an education that was not useful enough. Education was not supposed to be useful, he retorted.

"You are not engaged so much in acquiring knowledge as in making mental efforts under criticism," he continued. "A certain amount of knowledge you can indeed with average faculties acquire so as to retain; nor need you regret the hours that you spent on much that is forgotten, for the shadow of lost knowledge at least protects you from many illusions.

"But you go to a great school, not for knowledge so much as for arts and habits; for the habit of attention, for the art of expression, for the art of assuming at a moment's notice a new intellectual posture, for the art of entering quickly into another person's thoughts, for the habit of submitting to censure and refutation, for the art of indicating assent or dissent in graduated terms, for the habit of regarding minute points of accuracy, for the habit of working out what is possible in a given time, for taste, for discrimination, for mental courage and mental soberness.

"Above all, you go to a great school for self-knowledge."

There are crucial freedoms that others can neither keep from us nor give to us. We must take possession of them ourselves. The sense of freedom that leads one to follow his or her own sensible instincts into a major course of study, confident that if one does that, then—and only then—will one be ready to make other even more crucial decisions: that is the sense of freedom I urge upon you before it is too late, and even before it is too early. Go ahead.

And after you have made your choice, remember that your major is only a minor portion of your higher education. You are invited—prodded—to surround and enliven your mind with elective courses. Relish them. The instructors in your discipline believe that you can never study enough of it, and some of us would advise you to take every elective our discipline has to offer. That is because we hanker to have our students love what we love, and this tempts us to tempt you to forgo your education and begin training in our field. Instead, browse in the clover.

When I was an undergraduate in philosophy, we were directed to read only primary sources; only the great thinkers, not the secondary folks who wrote textbooks about them. Excellent. But in retrospect, the good times were the hundreds of hours when I got lost in the stacks of the library and read my fascinated way through an education that no one had planned, but was lavishly provided.

Your duty is to enjoy. Nothing you might do could be more useful.

Reprinted by permission of the author.

• •

 # Vocabulary

As you think about this essay, these definitions—and one identification—may be helpful to you:
1. **insidious**   harmful but enticing or having a gradual but cumulative effect
2. **dons**   the British educational system's equivalent for college teachers
3. **disconcerting**   unsettling or emotionally disturbing
4. **Father Hesburgh**   for more than twenty years, the legendary president of the University of Notre Dame
5. **sieved**   filtered

 # Discussion Questions

1. What are the three difficulties that cause undergraduates to make wrong initial decisions about a major?
2. For Burtchaell, what distinguishes training from education? Give some examples of your own for training.
3. According to Burtchaell, what should a "good university" provide its students?
4. Based on your experience and that of your friends, is Burtchaell correct in saying that new students have insufficient information to select a major?
5. Burtchaell's final two sentences may have surprised you. Did you expect a serious teacher to draw this conclusion? How does he justify it?

 # How Can These Ideas Apply to You?

1. Are there any exceptions to Burtchaell's argument that students should defer their decisions on a major for at least the first year? Are you one of those exceptions?

2. If you were not allowed to declare a major but could list three or four areas of study as your likeliest intentions, what would they be? How can you best use your first year to decide among them?
3. Do you agree that choosing a major is not necessarily choosing a career? Why or why not?
4. Burtchaell analyzes several kinds of pressure that first-year students often feel. Does his description apply to you? If not, why not?
5. Is Burtchaell convincing when he urges you to choose a major on the "pleasure principle"?

College Major Doesn't Mean All That Much

William Raspberry

William Raspberry is a widely syndicated columnist who works with the *Washington Post* Writers Group. In this brief essay, which was first published as one of his regular columns, he stepped away from his usual commentary on the Washington scene and grew more personal as he counseled his daughter about approaching the question of what college major to select.

Soon to every *fledgling* student
Comes the moment to decide.
But since Angela's a freshman,
My advice is: let it ride.

With apologies to James Russell Lowell, that is pretty much my counsel to my daughter, who is about to begin her first year in college. Soon enough, she'll have to face the sophomore necessity of choosing a major—whether or not she's decided on a career. In the meantime, I tell her, don't worry about it.

A part of the reason for my advice is the memory of my own struggle to decide on a major. I eventually had four of them, none of which related to what was to become my career. But the more important reason is my conclusion, regularly reinforced, that majors just don't matter that much. The latest reinforcement is from John Willson, a history professor at Michigan's Hillsdale College, who having heard once too often the question, "But what do I do with a history major?" has decided to do what he can to put his students at ease.

"Every sophomore has a majoring frenzy," he wrote in a campus publication. "It is typical for sophomores to say, 'I want to be an anchorman. Therefore, I will major in journalism. Where do I sign up?' They act like they have had a blow to the *solar plexus* when I say, (a) Hillsdale has no major in journalism, and (b) if we did, it would no more make you an anchorman than a major in English makes you an Englishman."

But rather than simply repeating what professionals already know, or urging colleges to dispense with the requirement for declaring a major, Willson has reduced his advice to a set of rules and principles.

The first, which college students often find incredible, is that aside from such vocational courses as engineering or computer science, any relationship between majors and careers is largely incidental. Physics majors are hardly more likely to become physicists than business majors to become *entrepreneurs*.

The rule that derives from this principle: If you wanted your major to be practical, you should have gone to the General Motors Institute.

The second principle is that students (and colleges) should delay the necessity of choosing for as long as practicable. "Most students (and even more parents) have rather vague notions of what the subject of any given subject is. . . . Talk with your parents, but don't let parents, teachers, media experts, television evangelists or fraternity brothers pressure you into a majoring frenzy before you know what the major is all about." In short: All things being equal, it is best to know what you are talking about, which may even prevent majoring frenzies.

The third is a quote from the Rev. James T. Burtchaell (writing in *Notre Dame* magazine): "Pick your major on the pleasure principle, for what you most enjoy studying will draw your mind in the liveliest way to being educated." It's good advice, and not only for students at small liberal-arts colleges. A few years ago, the University of Virginia published a booklet, "Life after Liberal Arts," based on a survey of 2,000 alumni of its college of arts and sciences. The finding: 91 percent of the respondents not only believe that liberal arts prepared them for fulfilling careers but would also not hesitate to recommend liberal-arts majors to students considering those same careers. The "winning combination" derived from the Virginia survey: a liberal-arts foundation, *complemented* with career-related experience and personal initiative.

Colleges aren't assembly lines that, after four years, automatically deposit students into *lucrative* careers. What is far likelier is a series of false starts followed by the discovery of a satisfying career. In the Virginia survey, for example, only 16 percent reported being happy with their first jobs.

Willson's advice, the results of the Virginia survey, and my advice to Angela come down to the same thing: Major in getting an education.

 ## Vocabulary

As you think about this essay, these definitions may be helpful to you:
1. **fledgling**   a bird at about the age it learns to fly; here, metaphorically, someone getting ready to start independent living
2. **solar plexus**   a *plexus* is a gathering or network of nerves, and the solar plexus is located in the abdomen; a blow to the solar plexus will cause the victim to double over in pain
3. **entrepreneurs**   people who start and maintain businesses, taking the risk for the sake of possible profit
4. **complemented**   not *complimented* or *flattered* but completed and perfected by something else
5. **lucrative**   profitable

Discussion Questions

1. What reasons does William Raspberry give for his assertion that your choice of a major is not as important as many college students think?
2. How do you react to Raspberry's thesis that any relationship between majors and careers is "largely incidental?" Why is this perceived connection made by so many students?

 How Can These Ideas Apply to You?

1. Find someone (perhaps the parent of one of your friends, or someone who graduated from the college you are attending) who works in the kind of job you think you would like, and ask him or her whether a liberal-arts background is a good basis for the daily work of that position.
2. Raspberry and Burtchaell clearly agree on some important points about selecting a college major. What are they? What argument does Raspberry's article add to the discussion that Burtchaell does not mention? Which author do you find more persuasive? Why?

Fourteen Ways of Looking at Electives*

Thomas L. Minnick

Thomas Minnick is associate dean of University College at Ohio State University, where he completed his bachelor's, master's, and doctoral degrees in English. A specialist in the English Bible and the writings of William Blake, Minnick currently directs an academic advising program that serves about 15,000 students each year. In this essay, he encourages you to think before you schedule your electives, so they can complement your required course work by helping you to achieve some of your goals for college study.

E lectives are what is left over for you to take once you deduct all your required courses.

Typically, a college degree is made up primarily of several kinds of requirements. These may include courses required of all students, no matter what degree they may have decided to seek; such university-wide requirements are often called "core" or "general education" requirements. They are likely to include some basic mathematics, one or more courses in college-level English composition, and several courses distributed among the social sciences, sciences, and humanities. Does everyone at your institution need to take some history? Then history is probably a general education or "core" requirement for your institution, whether you are working toward a bachelor's degree at a university with an extensive graduate program or toward an associate's degree at a community college.

Additionally, you are likely to have to complete some courses that everyone in your degree program needs to take. For example, students working toward a degree in engineering, no matter what area of specialization, all typically need to have at least a year of college physics, mathematics through differential equations, some basic course work in engineering graphics, mechanics, and chemistry. Similarly, business students are all required to study economics (both "micro" and "macro"), accounting, statistics, marketing, finance, and the like. Requirements shared by everyone aiming toward a specific degree are usually called "program requirements" or "degree requirements."

A third kind of required course work is that which you complete for your major. Major requirements might include an introductory survey course (or a series of them), usually taken by first- or second-year students while they learn

---

*With apologies to Wallace Stevens. (Gentle reader, Wallace Stevens wrote a thoughtful poem entitled "Sixteen Ways of Looking at a Blackbird." You might enjoy it.)

the dimensions and variety of the major field. English majors are likely to be required to take a survey of American literature and another of British literature, for example. In some colleges they may be required to have a course in research methods for English majors. And some majors require that everyone in the program complete a senior year "capstone" course that puts—or attempts to put—all their previous major work into a *coherent* perspective.

Once you add up all these kinds of requirements (general education, college, and major), you are likely to find that there are still some classes you need to take to complete your degree. At the university where I work, which follows the quarter system and sets 196 quarter credit hours as the minimum for an undergraduate degree, the university-wide general education core and the college/program requirements usually total about 100 credits. Major programs vary dramatically but average about 45 credit hours. Deduct 145 from 196 and you get 41 credit hours (or eight to ten classes) that are not specified. For these, which are "electives," our students can take just about anything they like. This essay is about some ways you can use these extra classes to your advantage.

1. To explore possible majors. Many students enter college without knowing what they want to study for a major. An undecided student can use elective hours to explore several possible major programs, usually by taking the appropriate introductory survey classes. Do you think you might like Forestry? Sign up for a basic introduction to the field and find out through that class whether you really have an interest and/or an aptitude for it.

2. To serve as a cushion. This use of electives is closely related to (1) above. Suppose you started college as an engineering major and then discovered that you lack the commitment or the focus to be an engineer, so you change programs to business. You will probably have taken some classes in your first term (engineering graphics, for example) that are not required in your new major. Electives allow you to move from one major to another without losing useful credits: in this example, the engineering graphics class will still count toward graduation, and it served the purpose of helping you make a sound decision on a new major. Electives give you flexibility—within reasoned limits—to change from one program to another without losing credits or unduly prolonging your degree work.

3. To develop a focus or cluster outside your major. Perhaps you don't really want to be limited to a single concentration. If your college does not provide for dual majors or minors, or if you don't want to complete *all* the work for a second major but would like an additional focus to your degree, electives can provide the way. Imagine that you have decided to major in Elementary Education but you also have an interest in the History of Art. Using your electives, you can build your own concentration in art history by taking the courses in that area that attract you. In this way you may be able to select your art history classes more freely than a formal major might allow—limiting yourself to national schools (American painting) or individual styles (contemporary art) that you really like, while official majors may need to follow a strictly prescribed *regimen* of courses.

4. To explore your career options. Nationally, one of the most frequently selected electives is the career exploration course. Such courses usually fall into one of two categories—fairly general in approach and scope, or quite specific. A general approach can help you assess your personal characteristics, such as your interests, abilities, values, and goals. It can also help you explore educational and occupational fields that might match your personal interests and strengths. Some courses include information about techniques for writing your resume and for presenting yourself effectively in job interviews. These general career courses can teach you career decision-making strategies that will be useful throughout your life. The other, more specific type of career course is often limited to specific career opportunities in the area (or areas) related to the department teaching the class: "Careers in Agriculture" would be such a course that focuses on, and discusses in very specific detail, the career options available to people with a specific kind of education. Such a course typically provides very helpful information about specific employers who look for and hire graduates with a particular educational and career background. Career information courses—whether general or specific—can help you enhance your understanding of who you are in relation to your academic major and related career opportunities and, in so doing, prepare you for the work world.

5. To enhance your marketability. A popular use many students make of their electives is to build a business focus—even if they are not pursuing a business degree. Suppose you are an English major who likes and knows something about computers. By adding several advanced computer science courses to your English major, you become more competitive for job offers that want a liberally educated student with added skills. Your focus might take the form of several courses from a single department (a number of marketing classes, for example), or several related classes from a variety of departments (a marketing class, a course in beginning accounting, a class in business management, a course in personnel issues). A business major might like to take classes in the language and culture of a specific part of the world in order to be better prepared to do business with that part of the globe.

6. To develop a talent you have neglected. Are you good at singing or playing a musical instrument? Perhaps you don't want to major in that area, but it would be a shame to give up that *expertise* or let it *languish* while you complete your undergraduate studies. Take a class in singing, or join one of your college's choral or instrumental groups. Register for drawing or painting, or making pottery, or creating art on the computer. Sign up for a basic photography class. Electives can allow you to pursue and develop interests and talents that you do not plan to turn into a major, but that you should not neglect. Because the credit you earn with electives counts toward your graduation, you do not need to feel that courses you take just because you want to are wasted.

7. To get, or stay, fit. I am often surprised by the number of college students I talk with who participated strenuously in high school sports. Both men and women find physical exercise and competition to be challenging and exciting. Yet often, when such students get to college, they neglect their interests in being fit, largely, I think, because they equate college courses with "serious" work and sports with play. However, getting fit and staying fit are lifelong activities that help you to work and think better. They also promote a healthful lifestyle because people who have worked to keep fit as a rule avoid destructive activities like drinking alcohol to excess and smoking. If your college has a good physical education facility and offers you courses in activities you have never tried, take a few elective credits to learn and practice some of these activities—oriental martial arts, for example, or caving, or whitewater rafting, or working out on the high ropes. And all these physical activities can be great for helping to cope with the stress of college work.

8. To develop skills in leisure time activities. Once you begin your career, your work will take up much of your life, but it will always be important for you to make time for enriching activities—especially when you are away from the stimulus of a learning environment. Develop the habit of reserving time for thoughtful entertainment. Electives may provide just the opportunity you need to learn more about theater, fine art, music, and similar interests. Do you like jazz? Check your school's course catalogue to see if there are classes in American music, or nonwestern music, that might help you to better understand the origins and history of jazz. Do you like attending plays? Take an introductory theater course, or take an acting class and try out your talents in a learning setting, or sign up to help build scenery and earn college credit while learning more about the technical details of putting on a performance.

9. To learn to help others. Most universities provide courses, often for modest amounts of credit, in such helpful skills as first aid and cardiopulmonary resuscitation (commonly abbreviated to "CPR"). These skills can help you in getting summer work. More important, knowing how to help others in an emergency can actually save a life—maybe even your own. Less dramatic but also very helpful are opportunities to provide tutoring and similar assistance to others at your university or in your neighborhood. Interested? Ask your adviser if there is a program where you can tutor underprivileged kids or read a textbook for a blind student or help in adaptive physical education for handicapped students. These experiences can teach you a great deal about yourself and may provide some of the greatest personal rewards of your college experience.

10. To learn life-skills that will be useful later. For example, many business schools provide a "service course" (so named because they teach it as a service to students from outside their own college) about basic financial matters, like establishing credit, managing your income, buying a home, planning for financial independence, selecting basic insurance, and the like. Courses in family financial planning for nonbusiness majors are likely to accentuate the practical and introduce theory only when absolutely necessary. Many other departments offer the chance to learn material that will have lifelong practical value. Basic courses in public speaking and communicating effectively in small groups apply to almost every later career; go to the Communications Department to find them. Most sociology departments offer a class in the varieties of modern marriage, or the sociology of the family—with obvious utility for later experience.

11. To learn to understand and appreciate different cultures. Studying other cultures can help you prepare for working with people from those cultures in your life after college. Most of your life will be spent in the 21st century, and experts predict that there will be *no* majority culture in America by that time. Many American cities in the south and west—Dallas, Los Angeles, Miami—already have no dominant majority group, only larger or smaller minorities. Even if you plan to live in a largely *homogeneous* small town, chances are you will be doing business with, or your children will need to do business with, the larger multicultural world. If you find that a little frightening, take a class in dealing with other cultures and you may find it exciting instead. Check with the appropriate language departments, and you are likely to find some classes taught in English that will help you understand the patterns and values of cultures different from your own.

12. To learn study and time management skills. Most two- and four-year colleges now provide organized help for students who need better study habits. This need is not restricted to students who did less than well in high school. Often, good students could earn better than average grades in high school with only modest investments of study time—and have consequently developed weak study habits that need to improve in the face of more difficult, more rapid college instruction. Would you like to read with greater comprehension? Could you manage your time better than you do? Check with your adviser for information about classes that teach effective study skills, time management, and related learning skills. Even if these are offered *without* credit, and so are not technically "elective hours," consider them carefully, since they can greatly improve the quality of your work as a student.

13. To develop leadership skills. Usually students turn to their extracurricular experiences (student government, interest clubs, other campus associations) for training in leadership. But there is a significant body of writings about various leadership qualities and styles, and your institution is likely to offer at least one credit-bearing class in leadership. Such courses are often taught as "laboratory courses"—that is, you get practical training in a hands-on way. If you are aiming toward a professional career in a management position, you ought to get some experience in leadership, and such a course may be your best route toward it.

14. To take some courses just because you will enjoy them. In the best of all possible worlds, every class you take would be one that you love to attend, and I hope that many of your required courses—in general education, in classes that relate to your degree program, and certainly in your major—fit this description. But in the real world we are bound to spend our time in, you may find yourself required to take some classes you enroll in only because they are required. If you anticipate that such a course is coming up next term, you may successfully balance it with an elective class that you take just because you want to take it: perhaps you've already had the instructor, and you really enjoyed his or her previous course, or perhaps you've always had a hobby of reading about a specific area, so taking a course in it as an elective would help round out your knowledge of that field.

How can you select classes for Use Number 14? I encourage my advisees to imagine that they have just won the state lottery (tonight at $35 million!) and have spent a chunk of it having fun—traveling the world, buying your parents a mansion and each of your friends an expensive car. Eventually, you tire of doing nothing, however nicely you can now afford to do it, and you realize the permanent attraction of learning. In such a case, what courses would you take? Assuming you do not financially *need* a degree, you could just take the classes you want. If you were free in this way, what classes would you sign up for? Make a list of them, then sign up for them as electives!

Reprinted by permission of the author.

Vocabulary

As you think about this essay, these definitions may be helpful to you:
1. **coherent**   consistent
2. **regimen**   a systematic plan
3. **expertise**   the skill of an expert
4. **languish**   to be or become weak or enervated
5. **homogeneous**   of the same or similar kind or nature

Discussion Questions

1. How are electives defined in this reading? How do they fit into the general structure of degree requirements?
2. What kind of electives can enhance your chances of finding a satisfying career?
3. Through what kind of electives can you acquire skills and knowledge that may be useful for your future leisure time activities?
4. Although taking extra courses in your major is not listed as a way to use elective hours, would this use of courses be a way to increase your mastery of the subject? Why or why not is this a good idea?
5. How can you expand your understanding and appreciation of other cultures through electives? Why is this a particularly good use of electives today?

How Can These Ideas Apply to You?

1. Of the 14 reasons for selecting electives identified by Minnick, which ones appeal to you the most? Why?
2. Selecting electives as "a cushion" (Use Number 2) requires a knowledge of the curricula you are considering. What specific resources on your campus are available to help you with the wise selection of these electives?
3. What kind of life skills would you like to learn while in college? What type of electives can help you to develop these skills?
4. From your college catalogue, list some *specific* elective courses that you would like to take while pursuing your degree. Then identify *specific* terms when you could fit them into your schedule.
5. What elective courses would you like to take "just because you will enjoy them"? Why?

The Right Stuff: Research Strategies for the Internet Age

Nancy O'Hanlon

Nancy O'Hanlon is an associate professor of University Libraries at Ohio State University, where she has taught library research skills and recently developed online courses in using the Internet and other technological tools for beginning and advanced researchers. In the following reading she explains why students need to develop good research strategies, especially given that information defines the age. Books, she reminds us, will also always be an important tool for any research undertaking.

Tom Wolfe describes the unique qualities that enabled the first U.S. astronauts to meet unknown challenges as "the right stuff." For these explorers, "the right stuff" was not simply courage, but a unique combination of daring, skill, experience and a persistent determination to succeed:

> ...the ability to go up in a hurtling piece of machinery and put his hide on the line and then have the moxie, the reflexes, the experience, the coolness, to pull it back in the last yawning moment—and then to go up again the next day, and the next day, and every next day....A career in flying was like climbing one of those ancient Babylonian pyramids made up of a dizzy progression of steps and ledges, a *ziggurat*, a pyramid extraordinarily high and steep; and the idea was to prove at every foot of the way up that pyramid that you were one of the elected and anointed ones who had the right stuff and could move higher and higher....(Wolfe 24)*

Research today challenges us to navigate effectively through Internet space. At one time, knowledge of the library and skill at using printed resources were sufficient preparation for finding useful information. Today, the Internet, particularly the World Wide Web, is the vehicle for most research. The sheer volume of information available through this medium is staggering, like the Babylonian pyramid in Wolfe's vision. To be a successful researcher also requires "the right stuff"—imagination and flexibility, well-developed searching skills, persistence and the ability to evaluate information coming from diverse sources.

Why is it important to learn research skills? During college, students are expected to find information in order to answer academic research questions, understand important societal issues and analyze complex problems. Information supplied by teachers and textbooks is no longer the sole basis for learning. College students are exposed to a wider range of information and must make

---

*O'Hanlon uses a variant of APA (American Psychological Association) style in citing references. She gives an author's last name and a page number within parentheses in the text, and lists her sources in a "Works Cited" section at the end of the article—ED.

judgments about the relevance and credibility of sources. In *The Craft of Research*, Booth, Colomb and Williams state that, "Those who can neither do reliable research nor reliably report the research of others will find themselves on the sidelines of a world that increasingly lives on information" (Booth 6). They also contend that "We are inundated with information, most of it packaged to suit someone else's commercial or political self-interest. More than ever, society needs people with critical minds, people who can look at research, ask their own questions, and find their own answers" (Booth 3).

Too Much Information?

How much information is available to researchers in the Internet age? Consider the following estimates provided by a recent study published online by the University of California, Berkeley:

- The world produces between 1 and 2 exabytes of unique information in all formats (print, digital, broadcast) each year. An exabyte is a billion *gigabytes*. If stored on floppy disks, the stack would be 2 million miles high.
- Digital information comprises the largest amount of this total. The Internet is the youngest and fastest growing medium today. In 2000, the World Wide Web consisted of roughly 2.5 billion static, publicly available Web pages and is growing at a rate of 100 percent per year.
- Another group of Web pages is dynamically generated and stored in Web-accessible databases. This "deep Web" is estimated to be 400 to 550 times larger than the static "surface" Web.
- Taking all kinds of Web information into account, there are 550 billion Web-connected documents, and 95 percent of this information is publicly accessible. 7.3 million new pages are added to the Web per day. (Lyman, Executive Summary)

Much of this Web-accessible information is not available in any other format. For example, *NameBase: A Cumulative Index of Books and Clippings* <http://www.namebase.org> is a database containing information about people, groups and corporations who have been influential in politics, the military, intelligence, crime and the media since World War II. These names have been drawn from various books, articles and government documents recovered using the Freedom of Information Act. Because of the way it is constructed, this database allows users to find other names that appear on the same pages and thus uncover potential relationships or connections between individuals and groups. *NameBase* is a unique part of the "deep Web" that could be useful both to investigative journalists and to students.

How can you locate useful research tools like *NameBase* among billions of Web sites? Some rules of the road for effective searching of the Web information space are described in the next section of this essay.

Smart Search Techniques

In the years since 1994, when the World Wide Web was invented, a number of powerful search tools have become available to help Web users locate information hiding within this mass of billions of documents. These tools fall into two basic categories: Web directories and Web indexes (or search engines). Success hinges on choosing the right tool as well as using it effectively.

Web directories are lists of sites, along with brief descriptions of their content, selected and compiled by knowledgeable editors. Directories can be browsed by topic and are good starting points for most Internet research because they offer quick access to the best known and most useful sites.

For example, the *Internet Movie Database* <http://www.imdb.com> is widely recognized as an excellent site for finding information on film casts, credits, plots and characters. It is relatively easy to identify using a Web directory like the *Britannica.com Internet Guide* <http://www.britannica.com>, which assigns one to five star ratings to sites in each of its topical categories.

If your information need is not met by sources listed in Web directories, you can search one of several large Web indexes to locate relevant documents. Web indexes are created by software programs called "spiders" or "robots" because they work automatically, crawling from one Web page to any others that are linked to it, harvesting information. The spiders collect every word on each Web page and store them in a huge index or list. When you enter a search, this index is what your search words are matched against.

The companies that own these search engines report that most people enter only one or two search words. When you consider the size of these Web indexes (millions of documents, with thousands of words in each document), this search strategy (or lack thereof) seems doomed to failure. You must use more than one or two search terms in Web indexes in order to narrow down search results and make them more relevant to your specific research question.

Search engines are quite literal and don't deal well with words that have multiple meanings. Using a variety of relevant search words can help with this problem as well. For example, a search for the word "spider" might retrieve this essay, since that word is used several times. [But] if you were looking for information about the insect, rather than the Web software program called a spider, you could get better results by including other search words that also describe what you want (such as "insect" or "arachnid").

Three other techniques will help to improve your chance of success when searching in large Web indexes. First, learn to use search qualifiers in order to specify the importance of your search terms and indicate any relationship between them. For example:

- To require that all of your search terms are included in each document found, you may put the plus sign (+) before each term.

  Example: +spider +arachnid +tarantula

- Use the minus sign (-) before each word that should be eliminated from your results.

  Example: +spider -Web -robot

- Use quotation marks to indicate when search words should be treated as a phrase.

  Example: "brown recluse spider"

It is also important to develop intelligent limiting strategies. In many search engines, it is possible to limit or screen search results by different variables, such as type of site (for example, government, military, educational, or commercial). This technique can be especially fruitful when you want to find varying perspectives. For example, you could limit a search for information on campaign finance reform to government Web sites, in order to learn the viewpoints of elected officials on this topic.

Finally, use specialized search tools, ones that focus on a particular topical area, whenever possible. By using specialized resources, like *FindLaw* <http://www.findlaw.com> for legal topics or *Achoo* <http://www.achoo.com> for health-related research, you are searching only the portion of Web space that is relevant for your research topic and are thus more likely to find good results.

Evaluating Information Quality

When we use the phrase "good results" in this context, we really mean search results that appear to be useful based on a quick look at the Web page. Determining the quality of information found on the Web actually takes more effort and some special techniques.

It is relatively easy and inexpensive to "publish" information on the Internet. On one hand, this open environment often permits you to see more sides of a topic than you might when relying only on printed sources. For example, when doing research on sweatshop labor in developing countries, you may be able to locate first person accounts and discussions of working conditions in overseas factories, reports of watchdog groups and other kinds of information sources that are difficult or impossible to find in print.

At the same time, because there is no real filtering mechanism to check accuracy, one cannot accept at face value the information found on the Web. In *Evaluating Internet Research Sources,* Robert Harris notes that on the Internet, information exists on a continuum of reliability and quality:

> Information is everywhere on the Internet, existing in large quantities and continuously being created and revised. This information exists in a large variety of kinds (facts, opinions, stories, interpretations, statistics) and is created for many purposes (to inform, to persuade, to sell, to present a viewpoint, and to create or change an attitude or belief). For each of these various kinds of purposes, information exists on many levels of quality or reliability. It ranges from very good to very bad and includes every shade in between. (Harris, Introduction)

Harris further notes that when evaluating information sources, there is no single perfect indicator of quality. You must make inferences from a collection of clues. Here are three important variables to consider as you review and evaluate sources:

Purpose: Consider both the purpose of the source as well as the purpose of your research when determining which Web sources to use. Sites published by advocacy groups (such as the Sierra Club or the American Civil Liberties Union) may include fact sheets, position papers and findings from scientific research studies. These groups may present evidence to support their cause but ignore contrary findings. If you are attempting to understand an organization's mission or find evidence that is representative of a particular viewpoint, advocacy organization Web sites can be quite useful. Look elsewhere for a balanced treatment of controversial issues.

Authority: The most credible information is provided by writers who have education, training or life experience in a field relevant to the information. You can read the jacket blurb to find out more about the author and the scope of a printed book. On the Web, look for an "About Us" link to find brief information about site authors and their credentials.

For example, the *nationalissues.com* Web site <http://www.nationalissues.com> has an "About Us" page that provides the names and educational/employment backgrounds of the principal staff as well as a statement about this site's intent to provide a balanced viewpoint on issues such as gun control, school reform, and taxes. The authors appear to be individuals with substantial experience in public policy research, government and journalism.

But inquiring minds may want to check credentials or learn more than Web site authors tell us about themselves. If the author is an organization rather than an individual, what is their reputation? You have access to the tools that will help you to locate this kind of information. Search in a Web index to find other documents that the site authors may have published. Use your college library's catalog and online reference databases (of newspaper, magazine and journal articles) to locate works in print written by or about individuals and organizations.

Content: When evaluating the content provided by a Web site, there are a number of questions to consider. These are the same questions that one would ask when evaluating the content of any information source.

- First, does the information appear to be accurate? Factual information may be checked in other sources.
- Is there an attempt by the author to be objective? Opposing viewpoints should be presented in an accurate manner. Harris notes that "there is no such thing as pure objectivity, but a good writer should be able to control his or her biases." Does the author use a calm, reasoned tone or resort to inflammatory language? Does the site author have a vested interest in the topic, one where "the messenger will gain financially if you believe the message …"? (Harris, Objectivity)
- Finally, does the author cite evidence to support claims and then document (provide references to) these sources, so that they are easily available for further research? Harris recommends that you "triangulate" an important information source, finding at least two other sources that support it. References

supplied by an author can help in this process, but you should look for other sources as well.

A World Beyond the Web

Does all important information live on the World Wide Web, somewhere among the exabtyes? In a word, no. Despite its size and scope, not everything useful for research is on the Web. There are numerous holes in this fabric—many important printed books and articles will never be available online, because their conversion to digital format is not cost-effective.

For example, when studying about focus group interviews for a marketing or sociology class, you should read *The Focused Interview*, the seminal work on this subject written by Robert K. Merton, an eminent sociologist who invented the technique. This book was first published in 1956 and a second edition appeared in 1990. Neither work is Web-accessible.

Although it is important to learn how to search effectively on the Web and to evaluate the information found there, it is equally important to understand that there are projects for which Web research will not be sufficient. The college library will continue to be important to successful research, despite the phenomenal growth of online information. It is the place where students can expect to find the most important or influential works on many subjects as well as personal assistance and advice about research problems from librarians. Having "the right stuff" for research in the Internet age involves the willingness to explore all spaces where information and knowledge abide, not just the most obvious ones. Booth states that by learning and practicing the craft of research, you

> ...join the oldest and most esteemed of human conversations—the conversation conducted by Aristotle, Marie Curie, Booker T. Washington, Albert Einstein ... all those who by contributing to human knowledge have freed us from ignorance and misunderstanding. They and countless others once stood where you now stand. Our world today is different because of their research. It is no exaggeration to say that, done well, yours will change the world tomorrow.
> (Booth 7)

Works Cited

Booth, Wayne C., Gregory C. Colomb and Joseph M. Williams. *The Craft of Research*. Chicago: University of Chicago Press, 1995.

Harris, Robert. *Evaluating Internet Research Sources*. Version Date: November 17, 1997. 30 October 2000 <http://www.vanguard. edu/rharris/evalu8it.htm>.

Lyman, Peter and Hal R. Varian. *How Much Information?* University of California, Berkeley: School of Information Management and Systems. 30 October 2000 <http://www.sims.berkeley.edu/how-much-info/>.

Wolfe, Tom. *The Right Stuff*. New York: Farrar, Straus, Giroux, 1979.

• •

Vocabulary

As you think about this essay, these definitions may be helpful to you:

1. **ziggurat** a form of early temple with the general shape of a pyramid but having recessed tiers that appear as huge stairs or ledges around the structure
2. **gigabyte** a unit of computer information. The basic unit is a binomial bit (that is, its value must be either 0 or 1). Eight bits make a byte; 1,048,576 bytes make a megabyte; and 1,024 megabytes make a gigabyte.
3. **inundated** flooded; overwhelmed

 # Discussion Questions

1. What is the difference between a Web index and a Web directory?
2. What does O'Hanlon mean when she talks about a "search strategy"?
3. Explain the use of these signs in searching for information on the Web: +, -, and " ".
4. What kind of questions should you ask when evaluating a Web site? Give some examples that O'Hanlon does *not* provide for evaluating a Web site with respect to its purpose, authority, and content.
5. O'Hanlon says that we still need to consult books for much of our information. Is she right? Explain your answer.

 # How Can These Ideas Apply to You?

1. Select a topic from the following list and explain what steps you would take to find information about it on the Internet: American religious groups, meatloaf, painting and sculpture in Latin America, the origin of jazz, addiction to "designer" drugs.
2. If for any of your classes this term you are writing a paper that requires research, keep a diary in which you record the steps you take to find information for that paper. How did you think about finding that information? Did you rely mostly on books? On the Web? Once the project is complete, comment in your diary about the process you followed: Was it thorough? Efficient? Effective?
3. Sometimes it can be helpful to know what other people think about the books you are reading or the sources you depend on. Select a book or essay from one of your assignments. Then check the Internet for any evaluations you can find—about the author or the author's other writings. Finally, see if

you can locate any criticisms, positive or negative, about the book or essay itself, including how it was received when it was published. Did you locate any other books related to the same subject that might modify how you rely on the first book?

Please! It's Only Seven Minutes Late, Professor

Joel J. Gold

This essay describes Professor Joel J. Gold's "solution" to overdue student papers. However, after recounting a student's experience with a late paper to his classes, he was the recipient of one class's payback.

● ● ● ● ● ● ● ● ● ● ● ● ● ● ● ● ● ●

Toward the bottom of the large *pseudo*-wooden door of my faculty office is a small hand-lettered sign that reads: PAPER SHREDDER. An arrow points to the space under the door where students are always sliding things, such as late papers and requests for letters of reference. My colleagues see the sign and make little jokes, but most of them don't really know the story behind it.

It began simply enough a few years back, when I was telling a class about the next essay. Allowing myself to be jollied away from the usual deadline of class time on Thursday, I told them the papers could be submitted by 5 P.M. Friday, but no later. At 5 o'clock, I would leave and turn on the paper shredder, so that anything slipped under the door later would be automatically shredded.

Now it should be obvious that in these *straitened* times no garden-variety English professor is going to have a paper shredder at his disposal. They all grinned back at me, and I figured we understood each other.

By 4:50 on Friday, all but three papers had been turned in. In a few minutes I heard someone running down the hall, and a young man thrust his paper at me. "Plenty of time," I said. He looked almost disappointed that he was not the last. At 4:57 the next-to-last paper arrived. "Am I the last one?" the young woman wanted to know. Again disappointment.

Well, now it was 5 o'clock, and one paper was still out. It was possible that it would not arrive, but the student was one of my conscientious overachievers. She was probably triple-checking her footnotes. I decided to wait.

I shut my door. I turned out my light. Then I pulled a chair up behind the closed door, gathered a couple of sheets of old ditto paper in my hand, and sat down to wait. At seven minutes past, I heard footsteps hurrying toward my office. Whoever it was stopped right outside. And panted for a few seconds. Then the paper began to come in under the door. There in the dark, I was ready.

With exactly the degree of pull you get when you try to make change for a dollar in one of those airport change machines, I tugged slightly and evenly at the proffered paper. For a moment, the person on the other side gripped the paper more tightly. Then, probably surprised at herself, she let go. Her paper was mine.

I took the ditto paper I had been holding all this time and began as noisily as I could to tear it into bits and pieces. There was dead silence on the other side of the door. Then I said aloud. "Chomp, chomp, CHOMP." Audible gasp outside.

"Please!" she said. "It's only seven minutes late." The thought of what it might look like outside that door to a passerby got me giggling. (I know, I know. It was unworthy of me. But I pictured a stricken young woman, talking to the door: "Please, door, it's only seven minutes late.") Perhaps the muffled giggling or the implication of the "Chomp, chomp, CHOMP" had just registered, but I heard the closest thing to a "Humph!" I have heard in real life before she stalked off down the hall. I suppressed my giggling, collected my papers and my *composure*, and went home.

She wasn't in class the next time it met, and I told the story—without names, of course. The class loved it, "Chomp, chomp, CHOMP!" they kept repeating throughout the hour.

I told the story again the following semester and the one after that—you can get a lot of mileage out of a good story. Students began to ask me about the paper shredder, and that's when I decided on the sign for the bottom of the door.

For a couple of semesters it was Our Joke. But you know how it is—sooner or later the old retired gunslinger is going to have to draw one more time. One of my students actually had the nerve to say, "You're always telling us about what you did to other classes, but you don't ever *do* anything about it." Now it was my turn for a "Humph!"

So amid the groaning about the deadlines for papers in my course, "The Comic Spirit," was born the idea for One More Twist. Essays were due Friday by 5 P.M. "And then the paper shredder," they chortled. "And then the paper shredder," I said.

When 5 P.M. came, and six papers were still missing, I gathered up what I had, turned out the lights, and went home. That weekend I spent much of my spare time tearing paper—all kinds of paper—into tiny bits and dropping them into a brown paper sack.

On class day, I secreted my nearly full shopping sack inside a large book bag and went upstairs. I *surreptitiously* pulled it out and hid it in my reading stand, planning to *discourse* on the papers at the end of the period.

It worked out even better. Halfway through the period, as I was shifting from *Northanger Abbey* to *Alice in Wonderland*, one of my anxious worrywarts raised his hand. "When," he wanted to know, "will you be giving back the papers?"

"I'm glad you asked me that," I said, quite sincerely. The students were now all waiting for the answer, not paying much attention to my hands, which were reaching in behind the reading stand to move the sack into position.

"Those of you who turned your essays in by 5 o'clock last Friday will get them back at the end of next week." A slight groan: They had hoped it would be sooner. They always do. "For the rest, those who slid them under the door some time after 5 P.M.—and I'm afraid I don't know how many of you there actually were . . ." By now, they were hanging on every word. The sack was in ready position. "But those of you who turned your paper in late (I had lifted the sack high above the desk) should come up after class (I turned the sack upside down and thousands—thousands—of little shreds of paper were fluttering down over the reading stand, the desk, the floor) and identify your papers. If you can."

There was an explosion of laughter, stamping feet, pandemonium, as the shower of confetti continued for several seconds. They could not believe that a university professor would do anything so idiotic.

"Now," I said, in my best professional rhythms, "let us consider the scene in which Alice finds the caterpillar sitting on a mushroom."

At the end of the period, while I tried to get as many of the tiny bits of paper into the wastebasket as I could, I saw a few of my students in the doorway, pointing at the debris. They were apparently explaining to friends and passersby what had just happened in the classroom. And I don't think they were discussing the Mad Hatter or the March Hare. At least not directly.

I knew that somewhere down the road the old gunslinger would probably have to draw one last time, but I reckoned I was safe for a couple more semesters.

I didn't have quite that much time.

Given everything else that had gone on in my honors satire class, I might have known they would be the ones. I had, of course, recounted to them the story of the paper shredder.

The day I realized just how closely they had been listening was the day their papers were due. As I unlocked my office door, I saw on the floor a few hundred strips of shredded paper. Without quite understanding what had happened, I gathered up the scraps and carried them to my desk. There, I found that the segments could be fitted together and deciphered. I appeared to be in possession of 10 or 11 (it was a little hard to tell) essays on ". . . andide and Saint Joan," "The Innocents in *Volpone* and *Can* . . . ," and "Satiri . . . *Travels*." Page numbers helped me piece parts of essays together. Then I realized that the scraps were all on copier paper. On a hunch, I went to see the departmental secretaries. Grinning widely, they handed me a large envelope filled with the originals.

Those wags in the honors class had copied their essays, shredded the copies, slid them under my door, and given the originals to the secretaries to whom, obviously, they had explained the whole scam.

And up on Boot Hill, the old gunslinger's tombstone reads: Those Who Live by the Shredder, Die by the Shredder.

Reprinted by permission of the author.

Vocabulary

As you think about this essay, these definitions may be helpful to you:
1. **pseudo**   false
2. **straitened**   hard up, short of money
3. **composure**   calmness of mind, bearing, or appearance
4. **surreptitiously**   secretively, as if afraid of being caught
5. **discourse**   verbal exchange of ideas

 Discussion Questions

1. What happened to the student who turned in her paper seven minutes late?
2. How did Gold get even with the class that began to doubt his story about the paper shredder? What was their reaction?
3. How did one class "get even" with the author? How did Gold react to their prank?

 How Can These Ideas Apply to You?

1. How would you react to Gold's story about late papers if you were in his class?
2. Have you ever turned in a late paper? Was it accepted? What consequences did you expect?
3. What do you think is a professor's fair reaction to students who turn in papers late?
4. What type of relationship do you sense Gold has with the students in his classes?
5. If you turn your papers in on time and others turn theirs in late without penalty, have you been treated fairly?

Why I Don't Let Students Cut My Classes

William R. Brown

William Brown is professor of English at the Philadelphia College of Textiles and
Science. In this essay, he presents his opinions on why students cut classes and
describes how he arrived at his no-cut policy in his course. The positive results from
enforcing his policy are also described.

Last year I announced to my classes my new policy on absences: None would
be allowed, except for illness or personal emergency. Even though this violated the statement on cuts in the student handbook, which allows freshmen
cuts each term up to twice the number of class meetings per week and imposes
no limit for upperclassmen, my students didn't fuss. They didn't fuss even after
they discovered, when I telephoned or sent warning notices through the mail to
students who had missed classes, that I meant business.

Part of their acceptance of the policy may have resulted from the career
orientation of our college, but I don't think that was the main reason. After I explained the policy, most seemed to recognize that it promoted their own academic interests. It was also a requirement that virtually all of them would be
obliged to observe—and would expect others to observe—throughout their
working lives. It had to be Woody Allen who said that a major part of making it
in life is simply showing up.

I told my classes about recent research, by Howard Schuman and others,
indicating that academic success is more closely tied to class attendance than
to the amount of time spent studying. I shared my sense of disappointment and
personal *affront* when I carefully prepare for a class and a substantial number
of students do not attend. I think they got the message that the policy is not ar-
bitrary—that I care about their learning and expect them to care about my professional effort.

I don't claim to have controlled all the variables, but after I instituted the
no-cut rule, student performance in my classes improved markedly, not so much
in the top rank as at the bottom. In fact, the bottom rank almost disappeared,
moving up and swelling the middle range to such an extent that I have reas-
sessed my evaluation methods to differentiate among levels of performance in
that range. The implications of so dramatic an improvement are surely worth
pondering.

Additional benefits of the policy have been those one would expect to
result from a full classroom. Student morale is noticeably higher, as is mine. Dis-

cussions are livelier, assignments are generally turned in on time, and very few students miss quizzes.

The mechanics of maintaining the policy kept me a little busier than usual, especially at first, but the results would have justified a lot more effort. I called or mailed notes to several students about their cuts, some more than once. I eventually advised a few with *invincibly* poor attendance to drop my course when it seemed that an unhappy outcome was likely. They did.

No doubt this kind of shepherding is easier in a small college. But it can work almost anyplace where a teacher cares enough about the educational stakes to make it work. The crucial element is caring.

At the first faculty meeting of the year, I confessed what I was doing. After all, I was defying college policy. I told my colleagues—at least those not cutting the meeting—that it rankled me when I had carefully prepared a class and a fifth, a quarter, or a third of the students didn't show. I thought my classes were good, and I *knew* Faulkner, Austen, and Tolstoy were good. What had been lacking in my classes, I said, was a significant proportion of the students. I told my colleagues that I believed my problem was not unique but was true of college classes everywhere, and that I was doing something about it.

Although no one seemed to attach much importance to my ignoring college policy, few of my colleagues gave me active support. Some were agreed that a 25 percent absence rate in a college class was not alarming. Others felt that college students must take responsibility for their studies, and that we should not feel liable for their losses from cut classes. One implied that if students could bag a lot of classes and still pass the course, it reflected badly on the teacher.

If professors have enough drawing power, another said, students will attend their classes. (How do you *parry* that?) Still another pointed out that if the professor covers enough material, there will be no time to waste taking the roll. In a large lecture, someone said, who knows who is there and who isn't? After the meeting, one *wag* told me I should consider using the acronym PAP for my "professional attendance policy," but congratulated me on at least evoking an interesting discussion in a faculty meeting, something rare indeed. It was easy to conclude that most of them preferred not to see a problem—at least their problem—in spotty class attendance.

Why do students cut so frequently? I can cite the immediate causes, but I first want to note the enabling circumstance: They cut because they are allowed to. They cut because of the climate of acceptance that comes from our belief that responsibility can be developed only when one is free, free even to act against personal best interests. That this is a misapplied belief in this case can be easily demonstrated. When substantial numbers of students do not attend, classroom learning is depreciated, student and teacher morale suffer, and academic standards are compromised. Students who miss classes unnecessarily are hurting more than themselves. With our *complicity,* they are undermining what colleges and universities are all about.

Students cut for two general reasons. They have things to do that appear more important than the class, or they wish to avoid what they fear will be painful consequences if they attend. In regard to the first, nursing an illness or attending family weddings or funerals are good excuses for missing a class. But other excuses—the demands of outside jobs, social engagements (including recovering from the night before), completing assignments for other courses— are, at best, questionable.

The other general reason is more disturbing and perhaps less well recognized. A few years ago, I asked several classes what they most disliked about the way courses were taught, and the answer was plain—anything that produced sustained tension or anxiety. I believe cutting is often a result of that aversion. The response of students to feelings of personal inadequacy, fear of humiliation, or a threatening professorial personality or teaching style is often simply to avoid class. This response feeds on itself, as frequent absences make attending even more threatening.

But what accounts for frequent cutting where the teacher tries to make the material interesting, knows the students by name, and approaches them with respect, help, and affability? I accept that question as unanswerable. I simply tell my students: Attend my classes regularly or drop the course. That's the rule.

Reprinted by permission of the author.

• •

 # Vocabulary

As you think about this essay, these definitions may be helpful to you:
1. **affront**   an insult
2. **invincibly**   incapably of being overcome or subdued
3. **parry**   to evade, to shove aside
4. **wag**   joker, smart-aleck
5. **complicity**   association with or participation in

 # Discussion Questions

1. What, according to Brown, does research indicate about academic success as related to class attendance?
2. What happened after the author instituted his no-cut rule?
3. What benefits did he see after enforcing the policy?
4. What reaction did he get from his colleagues?
5. Why, according to Brown, do students cut classes?

How Can These Ideas Apply to You?

1. Do any of your instructors have a no-cut policy? If so, what effect does the policy have on you?
2. If you put yourself in the place of your instructor, how would you be affected by students cutting your class?
3. Do you think students appreciate the teacher who cares enough about them to institute such a policy?
4. Do you agree with the reasons the author gives for why students cut classes? Have you ever cut for the reasons he gives? Why?
5. Can you answer the author's "unanswerable" question? Why do some students cut classes even when all the positive aspects of a course are in place?

UNIT SUMMARY

The writers in this unit offer many perspectives on how to be a successful student. One defining purpose of college is to learn about our intellectual and cultural heritage. To be intensely involved in learning requires great concentration and many skills. The readings in this unit have offered many suggestions for accomplishing this.

Summary Questions

1. How do the readings in this unit suggest you can become a successful student?
2. What tasks or strategies described in the readings could you adopt to improve your own attitudes or behaviors toward your academic work?
3. What skills do you hope to acquire in college to help you in your future work and in living in general?

Suggested Writing Assignments

1. Write a brief essay describing the qualities of a successful student and why you selected those qualities.
2. Select one reading in this unit and write about your personal experience with the academic concern it describes.
3. Several authors in this unit write about various approaches to learning. Describe how your own approach to learning is the same as or different from the ones they describe.

Suggested Readings

Lawrence, Gordon. *People Types and Tiger Stripes.* Gainesville, FL: Center for the
    Application of Psychological Types, 1982.
Matte, Nancy, and Susan Henderson. *Success, Your Style!* Belmont, CA: Wadsworth, 1995.
Pauk, W. *How to Study in College,* 4th ed. Boston: Houghton Mifflin, 1989.
Uchida, Donna, with Marvin Cetron and Floretta McKenzie. *Preparing Students for the
    21st Century.* Arlington, VA: American Association of School Administrators, 1996.

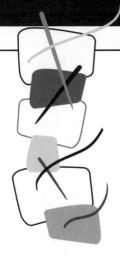

How Should I Expect to Learn?

The act of learning is so ingrained in our everyday life that we usually take it for granted. However, as psychologists who study learning professionally can demonstrate, learning is a complex process that operates differently for many people. Learning can be defined in many ways. It is not only the acquisition of knowledge and skills by instruction or study; it is also an accumulation through experience. Although students enter college after years of "learning," many find that college learning offers new and exciting challenges.

A great deal of research on how people learn has provided important insights and tools to enhance our understanding of the process. David Kolb, a business professor, has suggested that the demands of different academic disciplines require students to use different learning styles or approaches. Howard Gardner takes a multifaceted view when he discusses seven "intelligences" which he describes in terms of a set of abilities, talents, and mental skills (see pp. 107–108). Daniel Goleman writes

I am not young enough to know everything.

—James M. Barrie

about "emotional intelligence," which includes both personal competence and social competence. Goleman suggests that emotional intelligence will be especially important in the future workplace where emotional competencies will be increasingly essential for excellence in every job.

Many researchers believe there is a relationship between the knowledge that exists in the mind and the situations in which it was acquired and used. Successful learning also depends on the individual's past experiences and attitudes toward the learning process. Perhaps the most important factor in successful learning, however, is the motivation or desire to learn.

This unit offers many perspectives about learning. James reviews some newer ideas about intelligence. Siebert and Gilpin provide insights into students' varied approaches to learning. They point out that the learning circumstance or situation for one person may require a different approach than for another. In a practical essay, Twining describes specific methods for approaching "active learning." Service-learning is not a new notion, but is being implemented in new ways in many colleges today. Waterman provides an overview of this experiential form of learning. Distance learning—as described by Governati, Steele, and Carey—is increasingly being viewed by some as the learning mode of the future. To complete this unit, the Illinois Online Network contributes a description of the characteristics of a successful online student—relevant in that, even in very traditional teaching, more and more assignments and other class experiences are being completed online.

Understanding Who Is Smart

Jennifer James

Jennifer James is an urban cultural anthropologist and a highly regarded business speaker. A university professor for 14 years, she is the author of six books and has written a weekly newspaper column. In this essay James writes about a new vision of intelligence and how "system thinking" can help us understand change.

• • • • • • • • • • • • • • • • • •

The debate over intelligence is a debate over higher standards. Over the past forty years, researchers of all kinds have uncovered the weaknesses of our tests and shown new respect for a broader-based definition of intelligence that reflects more than traditional fact retention and computation skills. Educators, in particular, are looking for a battery of tests that is more predictive of real-world success. The designers of a school testing program in California, for example, put a premium on the skills required for "reasonably deciding what to think and do." Among other things, students had to be able to determine the relevance of information, distinguish between fact and opinion, identify unstated assumptions, detect bias or propaganda, come up with reasonable alternatives or solutions, and predict possible consequences. Intelligence is the ability to make adaptive responses in new as well as old situations.

At Harvard, philosopher Nelson Goodman wanted to understand why some people were "creative" and others were not. In his work, Goodman expanded the concept of intelligence from "How smart is he or she?" to "How is he or she smart?" Motivation and interest in the task at hand—along with traits such as concentration, intention, purpose, drive and tenacity—emerged as important influences.

Howard Gardner, a psychologist who helped to conduct this research, thought of intelligence as the ability to solve problems or create products. He devised the following list of eight primary forms of intelligence (to which I have added one of my own):

1. **Verbal/linguistic intelligence.** This form of intelligence is revealed by a sensitivity to the meaning and order of words and the ability to make varied use of the language. Impromptu speaking, story-telling, humor, and joking are natural abilities associated with verbal/linguistic intelligence. So, too, is persuading someone to follow a course of action, or explaining, or teaching. Will Rogers had this form of intelligence. Good journalists also have it.

2. **Logical/mathematical intelligence.** This form of intelligence is easiest to standardize and measure. We usually refer to it as analytical or scientific thinking, and we see it in scientists, computer programmers, accountants, lawyers, bankers, and, of course, mathematicians, people who are problem

solvers and *consummate* game players. They work with abstract symbols and are able to see connections between pieces of information that others might miss. Einstein is one of the best examples of someone with this form of intelligence.

3. **Visual/*spatial* intelligence.** Persons with this form of intelligence are especially deft at *conjuring* up mental images and creating graphic representations. They are able to think in three-dimensional terms, to re-create the visual world. Picasso, whose paintings challenged our view of reality, was especially gifted at visualizing objects from different perspectives and angles. Besides painters and sculptors, this form of intelligence is found in designers and architects.

4. **Body/kinesthetic intelligence.** This form of intelligence makes possible the connections between mind and body that are necessary to succeed in activities such as dance, mime, sports, martial arts, and drama. Martha Graham and Michael Jordan delighted audiences with their explosive and sensitive uses of the body. Because they know how we move, inventors with this form of intelligence understand how to turn function into form. They intuitively feel what is possible in labor-saving devices and processes.

5. **Musical/rhythmic intelligence.** A person with this form of intelligence hears musical patterns and rhythms naturally and can reproduce them. It is an especially desirable form of intelligence because music has the capacity to alter our consciousness, reduce stress, and enhance brain function. For example, students who had just listened to Mozart scored higher on standard IQ tests than those who had spent the same period of time in meditation or silence. Researchers believe that the patterns in musical themes somehow prime the same neural network that the brain employs for complex visual-*spatial* tasks.

6. **Interpersonal intelligence.** Managers, counselors, therapists, politicians, mediators, and human relations specialists display this form of intelligence. It is a must for workplace tasks such as negotiation and providing feedback or evaluation. Individuals with this form of intelligence have strong intuitive skills. They are especially able to read the moods, temperaments, motivations, and intentions of others. Abraham Lincoln, Mohandas Gandhi, and Martin Luther King, Jr., used interpersonal intelligence to change the world.

7. **Intrapersonal intelligence.** Sigmund Freud and Carl Jung demonstrated this form of intelligence, the ability to understand and articulate the inner workings of character and personality. The highest order of thinking and reasoning is present in a person who has intrapersonal intelligence. We often call it wisdom. He or she can see the larger picture and is open to the lure of the future. Within an organization, this ability is invaluable.

8. **Spiritual intelligence.** This form of intelligence is tentative; Gardner has yet to decide whether moral or spiritual intelligence qualifies for his list. It can be considered an *amalgam* of interpersonal and intrapersonal awareness with a "value" component added.

9. **Practical intelligence.** Gardner doesn't list this form of intelligence, but I do. It is the skill that enables some people to take a computer or clock apart

and put it back together. I also think of practical intelligence as organizational intelligence or common sense, the ability to solve all sorts of daily problems without quite knowing how the solutions were reached. People with common sense may or may not test well, but they have a clear understanding of cause and effect. They use intelligence in combination with that understanding.

QUALITIES OF MIND

Rate yourself on each of these forms of intelligence. What are your strengths and weaknesses? How are they reflected in the kind of work you do and your relationships with others?

	Low				Moderate					High
	1	2	3	4	5	6	7	8	9	10

1. Verbal/linguistic
2. Logical/mathematical
3. Visual/spatial
4. Body/kinesthetic
5. Musical/rhythmic
6. Interpersonal
7. Intrapersonal
8. Spiritual
9. Practical

Don't let this list intimidate you. There is increasingly strong evidence that intelligence can be taught, despite ongoing arguments about genetic predetermination. Also, the levels of each of these forms of intelligence can vary from one person to the next. Albert Einstein had a high degree of logical and spatial intelligence, but his lack of personal skills was legendary. He left those details to others.

Regardless of the forms of our intelligence, we also need to know how we think. Researcher Gail Browning studies approaches to problem solving. She identifies four "styles" that people use to process information: analytical, conceptual, structural, and social. She concludes that most of us use more than one of them, depending on the problem before us. Her work helps us visualize thought processes, something that makes communication and negotiation easier. When forming a creative and productive team for problem solving or futuring consider combining different thinking styles.

Analytical thinkers are the most logical. They must have facts, figures, directions and reasons to approach problem solving. They want to design a system. They see themselves as straightforward, clear and purposeful. In a team meeting they ask, "Is this feasible?"

Conceptual thinkers accept information in almost any form. They enjoy a challenge and often plunge into the problem-solving process before considering what direction to take. They want to paint a picture. They don't mind mistakes. They usually suggest, "Let's look at this problem in a different way."

Structural thinkers draw comparisons and look for systematic links to determine the source of a problem. They prefer creating flow charts. They organize the components of the problem and the possible solutions and ask, "How does this apply to our situation?"

Social thinkers are the facilitators of group process. They talk to everyone; they weigh all the solutions equally; they may identify the best solution but not know how they reached it. In a team situation they ask, "What do you think of this idea?"

Review these four styles and combine them with the nine forms of intelligence outlined. Try to identify yourself and imagine how different problems or situations engage different aspects of your intelligence or thinking style. Create a perfect team for a problem you are currently trying to solve. What ideal set of minds would potentially be the most intelligent and the best at processing?

British researcher Edward De Bono, in a series of books on intelligence, believes he has the answer. He adds the term lateral thinking to this mix. He sees it as the most productive thinking process because it is easily taught and allows everyone in a group, regardless of their intelligence frame or thinking style, to operate with the same broad set of thinking tools.

Lateral thinking is similar to what others currently call critical or system thinking. It enables us to view a problem from all sides and understand all the alternatives before devising a solution. It requires us to abandon certainty and security, at least for the moment. De Bono's most useful exercise in lateral thinking is called PMI, an acronym for Plus, Minus, and Interesting. Participants are divided into small groups and are asked to evaluate what is good (plus), what is bad (minus), and what is interesting about an idea. In a session with a group of auto manufacturers, for example, De Bono posed the suggestion that all cars should be painted yellow....

[Table 1 on page 111 shows] how the group reacted.

Exercises in lateral thinking work best if each category (good, bad, and interesting) is considered separately and in order when pondering an idea or a problem rather than brainstorming them in the random fashion preferred by conceptual thinkers. Such exercises can be particularly useful when you are floating some new idea or looking for a solution to some problem. They help people focus their perceptions and articulate their reactions and responses. *Common Ground,* a PBS series designed to bring opposing sides together on several controversial issues, used lateral thinking with powerful results. Participants were able to put aside rhetoric and emotion and find they had far more in common than they realized....

We are all, to one degree or another, system thinkers. (I prefer the term system thinking to De Bono's lateral thinking because we are looking at the whole to understand the parts.) We must also combine disparate parts into coherent wholes to put together the puzzles and solve the problems of daily life. A system

Table 1

Good (Plus)	Bad (Minus)	Interesting
Easier to see on the roads.	Boring.	Interesting to see if shades of yellow arose.
Easier to see at night.	Difficult to recognize your own car.	Interesting to see if people appreciated the safety factor.
No problem in deciding which color you want.	Very difficult to find your car in a parking lot.	Interesting to see whether attitudes toward cars changed.
No waiting to get the color you want.	Easier to steal cars.	Interesting to see if trim acquired a different color.
Easier for the manufacturer.	The abundance of yellow might tire the eyes.	Interesting to see if this were enforceable.
The dealer would need less stock.	Car chases would be difficult for the police.	Interesting to see who would support the suggestion.
It might take the "macho" element out of car ownership.	Accident witnesses would have a harder time.	
Cars would tend to become transport items.	Restriction of your freedom to choose.	
In minor collisions the paint rubbed off onto your car would be the same color.		

thinker believes in cooperation and knows that pooling or combining ideas, skills, and experience improves innovation, efficiency, and performance. I think of system thinking as broadscope intelligence and very much like *synergy,* a buzz-word in business in the 1990s. Companies that practiced synergy did so by buying or developing related businesses or by welding their existing units into a more coherent whole.

Social scientists used system thinking in the 1970s when they began working together to examine the "culture of poverty" as a whole. Edward Deming used it to fine-tune quality processes. The earliest ideas about man and environment as a whole organism represented system thinking. The interrelationship of mind and body in the healing process is another example. When we think about parts of a system, separate from the whole, we cut ourselves off from important information.

System thinking can bridge the gap that sometimes exists between reality and our perception of reality. For example, unproductive workers, falling orders, and sagging profits are indicators of serious problems in any business. Our usual way of thinking may cause us to look at each in isolation. But system thinking helps us understand that all parts of a business or a process are connected, and that when one part is challenged, all the others are as well. We may look for productivity problems on the production line and create new incentives if salespeople are not doing well, but the real "cause" of our problems may be hidden in the system that underlies the entire enterprise. System thinking accepts the inter-relatedness of all things. System thinking is usually the best way to find out what is going on.

System thinking can help all of us understand the zigzags of change. It enables us to see the big picture. From that vantage point we can more easily perceive the changing realities of our work and lives and solve problems. Here are some of the basic characteristics of a system thinker:

- You are physically and intellectually alert.
- You are always wondering how things can be improved.
- You are able to resolve conflict by agreeing to disagree on some points and moving the discussion forward.
- You do not demand perfection from yourself or others.
- You are imaginative and creative.
- You are empathetic and compassionate.
- You are comfortable with chaos.
- You are a nonconformist in one way or another.
- You have a sense of humor.

The future challenges us to question our own minds and how we think, to reexamine our assumptions and see how they connect to the changing realities of our world. Thinking must become a more fluid process; I call it "water logic" because the future will require the development of a fluid, more adaptive level of reaction and response. As humanity evolves, creating ever more complex patterns, the ability to understand, synthesize, and adapt to those patterns will become basic intelligence.

Reprinted with permission of Simon & Schuster from Jennifer James, *Thinking in the Future Tense.*
© 1996 by Jennifer James.

● ●

Vocabulary

As you think about this essay, these definitions may be helpful to you:
1. **consummate**   extremely skilled and accomplished
2. **spatial**   relating to three-dimensional space

3. **conjuring**   imagining
4. **amalgam**   combination of different elements
5. **synergy**   combined action or operation

 ## Discussion Questions

1. In her first paragraph, Jennifer James provides her own definition of intelligence. What is it?
2. What traits seem to be important in Nelson Goodman's expanded concept of intelligence?
3. Why are Howard Gardner's eight basic forms of intelligence important in broadening our concept of intelligence? Is the form that James adds to Gardner's list different from the others? How?
4. Do you agree with the author's addition of "practical intelligence"? Why?
5. What is "lateral thinking"? How can it be used in problem solving?
6. What are the characteristics of "system thinking," according to the author? How can system thinking be used to analyze problem areas?

 ## How Can These Ideas Apply to You?

1. The author says that a broader definition of intelligence is needed as educators look for tests to measure "real world success." Do you agree? Why?
2. On which of Gardner's eight primary forms of intelligence do you rate yourself the highest? The lowest?
3. Which of the eight forms of intelligence do you think are most important for doing successful college work?
4. Which of Browning's four thinking styles most closely describes yours? In what ways?
5. Are you intelligent in some way or ways that Gardner or James has omitted to describe? Be specific.

Learning Styles: They Can Help or Hinder

Al Siebert and Bernadine Gilpin

Al Siebert is a psychologist with more than 20 years of teaching experience in adult education. Bernadine Gilpin started college at age 35 after rearing five children. She has more than 15 years' experience as a teacher, administrator, and counselor.

Siebert and Gilpin believe that understanding how one learns best can help make studying and learning easier. This essay points out how mismatches between teaching and learning styles may cause difficulties and makes suggestions for recognizing and overcoming this common problem.

R esearchers wanting to understand all aspects of success in college asked: "Why do some students do well with one instructor but not another?" Their research uncovered a simple truth about academic life: The way some people teach does not always match up with the way other people learn.

Other research looked at why students show wide differences in the time of day and the circumstances best for learning. This research identified an important truth about studying and learning: The learning circumstances best for one person may not be good for another.

Research findings and experience have identified the following important differences in how people learn.

Auditory Versus Visual Styles

Have you ever noticed that someone can read a note you've left him, but the message doesn't get through to his brain? Or that you can tell a person something, but it doesn't register unless you write it down for her? That's because people differ in how information gets into their conscious mind.

Some people learn best by listening. Information doesn't stick well unless they hear it. Other people learn best by reading. They must see something before they believe it and remember it. Some people learn best by doing. What is your natural style?

Do you remember best what is said to you or what you read?

Do you prefer television or newspapers as your source of news?

Would you rather hear an expert talk on a subject or read what the expert has written?

When you purchase new equipment, do you read the instruction manual carefully or do you rarely read manuals?

Is reading the college catalog your main way of learning about your program and classes, or do you merely skim the catalog and go see an advisor who tells you everything you need to know?

Based on your answers to these questions, which learning style do you prefer, auditory or visual?

Everyone learns both ways, of course. It is not an either/or situation. Yet the differences between people are sometimes extreme enough to cause problems. If you have a visual learning style, you operate mainly on the basis of what you read. You may have difficulty with an instructor who believes that telling people what and how to learn is sufficient.

Auditory Learning Style

If you have an auditory style, you will probably do well with an instructor who says everything to learn and do. You may have difficulty with a visually oriented instructor. Such an instructor hands out a written statement about what to do to pass the course without discussing it and assigns textbook material and outside readings that are never discussed in class.

The solution, if you have an auditory style in a class taught by a visually oriented instructor, is to:

1. Find classmates who will tell you what they learned from the textbook readings.
2. Dictate the main points from the reading assignments and handouts onto cassette tapes and then listen to the tapes.
3. Consciously work at improving your ability to acquire information visually. (Note: For professional help, go to the reading improvement center or the office of disability services at your college.)

Visual Learning Style

If you learn best visually, you may be in trouble with an instructor who doesn't use handouts, emphasizes class discussion, and doesn't write much on the blackboard. The solution with a verbally oriented instructor is to:

1. Take good notes on what the instructor and your classmates say. After class fill in sentences and compare notes with other students.
2. Ask the instructor for suggested articles or books that will let you read the information you need to understand better.
3. Consciously work at listening and remembering what the instructor says. TIP: One woman wrote to us saying that she types her lecture notes immediately after each class.
4. If you are confused about a point, ask the instructor to tell you again and write down what you hear.

External Versus Internal Learning Styles

Psychologists have done extensive research on a significant personality variable. It is called the "external and internal *locus of control.*"

Externally oriented students believe information when it comes from an authority or expert. Information or suggestions from other sources aren't trusted as accurate.

If you prefer to get the guidance from expert sources and your instructor enjoys being an expert, then you have a good match. The more you need an instructor who tells the class exactly what to learn, the better you will do with this type of instructor. If you need clear guidelines from instructors but take a course from someone who provides little direction, you may flounder. You may be sitting in class waiting for the instructor to tell you what the answer to a problem is, only to have him or her ask the class, "What do you think?" After the class talks for a while, the instructor may refuse to say what the right answer is. He or she might say, "You may be right," or "There is some truth to that."

Some students react negatively to classes in which the instructor encourages discussion and encourages students to develop their own views and answers. These students protest, "I didn't pay good money to sit and listen to a bunch of uninformed people express their opinions. I can get that in the coffee shop." This attitude is legitimate. It is also narrow-minded.

The word *education* means to "draw out of." It does not mean "shovel into." A good education teaches you to think for yourself. It teaches you to ask good questions and then how to find the answers on your own. A good education does not give you a diploma for learning how to seek out an expert for any question you have. It teaches you how to both listen to authorities and come to your own conclusions.

Self-motivated, internally oriented students appreciate an instructor who allows them freedom to follow their own paths. Such students get upset with instructors who tell them exactly what they must learn, and in what way. For them, too much course structure is *abrasive*. They feel handicapped more than helped. Such reactions are legitimate and narrow-minded.

In every field of study, certain basics must be mastered. There are basic terms and concepts that must be understood. There are some techniques fundamental to the mastery of the subject even though the reasons why may not be given.

Being Both Internal and External in Learning

Students who get the most out of school are able to follow the tightly controlled steps used by some teachers and, at the same time, organize their own learning experiences when in a class taught by someone who gives few guidelines. Can you learn to do both?

Differences in Temperament

Isabel Myers and her mother Katharine Briggs developed a test to measure four dimensions of *temperament* identified by psychotherapist Carl Jung. Myers-Briggs tests are probably the most popular personality tests in the country because many people benefit from seeing how differences in temperament explain misunderstandings between people.

This means that differences in *how* you and an instructor think are more important than differences in *what* you think. Here's how the four temperaments influence your learning style.

Extroversion Versus Introversion

Instructors and students vary widely in how friendly they want to be and how much emotional distance they need to have. A friendly, *extroverted* instructor enjoys after-class contact with students. He or she will ask students to coffee or out for pizza. If you are similarly friendly, you will have a great year.

If you are a more *introverted* person, however, you may suffer from too much personal attention and closeness. You would much rather have a quiet, tactful instructor who respects your need to be left alone. Such an instructor understands how embarrassing it is to be called on to talk in class or to be openly praised for getting a high score on an exam.

On the other hand, if you are an extroverted person with a more introverted instructor, you may find it puzzling to have him or her pulling away from you after class. After all, what are instructors for if not to be available for students? Yet your desire to be friendly may cause the instructor to stare at you and make excuses to get away. After that, you may feel avoided.

When it comes to studying, the introverted person needs a private, quiet place where everyone stays away. The extroverted person likes to study in the kitchen, in a student lounge, or with classmates. Don't hesitate to tell friends, relatives, and classmates with temperaments different from yours what you need.

Thinking Versus Feeling

Descriptions of this dimension of temperament match up closely with left-brain/right-brain research findings. The left brain is where the speech center develops in most humans. The left brain is where you remember words, use logic, and think analytically. It gives you your ability to think rationally and unemotionally. The left brain thinks in a linear fashion. It is time oriented.

The right brain carries your memory for music. You think visually, emotionally, and irrationally in the right brain. It is the source of creativity and intuition. Right-brain thinking follows emotional logic. Using it, you can visualize and think in patterns jumping from one spot in a pattern to another without apparent logic or reason.

If you tend to be left-brained, you will be well matched to an instructor who gives you thorough, unemotional listings of facts, data, analytic explorations, hypotheses, logic, evidence, numbers, definition of terms, and rational conclusions.

If you tend to be left-brained and get an instructor who teaches in a right-brained way, you may find the course to be a bewildering experience. You may experience the instructor as weird, too emotional, disorganized, and a bit nutty.

If you tend to be right-brained with a left-brained teacher, the course will be painful for you. You'll feel like a thirsty person handed a glass of water only to find it is filled with sand.

To resolve personality conflicts such as these, avoid indulging in the attitude, "If only other people would change, my world would be a better place for me." When you have a mismatch, you can try to find someone (perhaps even the instructor) who will translate the material into a form you understand better. More important, however, make an effort to gain more use of your other brain.

The situation may not be easy at first, but it does give you a chance to add another dimension to yourself. And isn't this why you're in school?

You do not have to give up your more natural and preferred way of thinking, feeling, and talking. What you can do is add more to what you already have.

Sensation Versus Intuition

Sensation-oriented people like to be sensible. They are guided by experience. Intuitive people like fantasy. They are creative dreamers. According to David Keirsey and Marilyn Bates, authors of *Please Understand Me*, differences on this dimension cause the widest gulf between people.

The sensation-oriented student is practical, wanting facts and evidence. An intuitive instructor can fill the lecture hour with hypothetical explanations, theories, concepts, and a long list of views held by others.

A sensation-oriented instructor gives practical instructions on what to do. An intuitive student wants to know what the underlying theories and concepts are, and asks "but what if?"

What to do about this sort of conflict? Stretch your understanding. Ask for what you need. Try to minimize the judging dimension of the next pair of traits.

Judging Versus Perceiving

If you remember Archie Bunker from the television series "All in the Family," you have seen an excellent example of the judging temperament. Such people make up their minds quickly. They judge others and situations as good or bad, right or wrong.

The perceiving style is to observe without judgment. Such people can watch world events, movies, and sports events without taking sides or having an opinion.

A judgmental style instructor believes the purpose for being in college is to work hard to become qualified for an occupation where hard work will get you ahead. The instructor works hard, expects the same from every student, and privately judges students as good ones or bad ones.

A perceiving instructor looks for ways to make learning fun, tries to minimize office work, and sees all students as learners. This instructor is frustrating for a judging style student who wants serious homework and wants to know how he or she compares to the other students.

Practical Suggestions

What do you do when a teacher is less than ideal? Do you get distressed? Complain?

By now we hope you have realized that finding a really good match between yourself and an instructor does not happen all the time. In fact, if you are an experienced victim, then the college will provide you with many chances to be upset, complain to classmates, and criticize instructors you judge to be imperfect.

As an alternative to being a victim, we have the following suggestions:

1. Before registration ask around to find out about various instructors. If you have a choice between instructors, you'll know which one to choose.
2. Try to get as much out of every course as you can, regardless of who your instructor is or how much the teaching style does not fit your preferred learning style. Be open to try a new way of learning.
3. When you have difficulty understanding what is happening in a course, make an appointment to talk with the instructor. Be prepared to ask for what you want.
4. If you still have problems, go to the office or center that teaches studying and reading skills. The specialists there can be very helpful.

Learn to Appreciate Human Differences
When you experience conflicts with others at school, at work, or in your family, question your attitudes about what other people should be like. If you experience an irritating difference, use that as an opportunity to learn more about human nature. You might as well, because you won't change other people by criticizing them!

We humans are all born with different temperaments and different ways of functioning in life. That is simply the way things work.

Do You Know Where and When?
Several final suggestions: If you grew up in a large family you may study best in a noisy place with lots of people around. Experiment with locations to see what works best for you.

Time of day is another learning style difference. If you are a morning person, get up and study for an hour before others get up. Leave chores for evening when your brain is disengaging. If you are an evening person go ahead and study until one or two in the morning.

The better you know yourself, the more skillfully you will manage your learning style and the easier it will be to succeed in college!

From *The Adult Student's Guide to Survival and Success: Time for College* by Al Siebert and Bernadine Gilpin. Copyright © 1992, Practical Psychology Press. Reprinted by permission.

• •

 Vocabulary

As you think about this essay, these definitions may be helpful to you:
1. **locus of control**   center of self-control, either by internal or external influences

2. **abrasive** causing irritation
3. **temperament** characteristic or habitual inclination
4. **extroverted** being predominantly influenced by what is outside of the self
5. **introverted** being wholly or predominantly concerned with one's own mental life

 ## Discussion Questions

1. What is a learning style?
2. What is the difference between the auditory and visual style of learning?
3. How does temperament affect your approaches to learning?
4. What aspects of learning does the left brain control? What aspects does the right brain control?
5. What four temperaments can influence your learning style? Describe them and how they affect the way you learn.

 ## How Can These Ideas Apply to You?

1. Have you ever experienced a class in which the instructor does not seem to teach the way you learn best? What happened?
2. Are you more comfortable learning visually or auditorily? How do you know?
3. Why is incorporating both internal and external temperaments the best way to learn?
4. How do the authors' suggestions for learning more effectively pertain to you?
5. Describe the learning situations that are best for you.

Active Learning

James Twining

James E. Twining is on the faculty at the Community College of Rhode Island. This essay is from his book *Strategies for Active Learning*. In this essay he presents an overview of learning that has a very practical application.

● ● ● ● ● ● ● ● ● ● ● ● ● ● ● ● ●

How people learn is an intriguing subject. Ask a group of students what they do when given a reading assignment, and most will respond, quite logically, "I read it." If you then ask, "How do you know when you've completed the assignment?" the answer is typically, "I've completed it when I'm finished reading." Neither response says much about how learning takes place.

Knowing when an assignment is complete is at the heart of the learning process. It suggests that the purpose of the assignment is clearly understood and that the activities necessary to complete the work are also known. More important, this knowledge suggests that each of us is responsible for our own learning, for taking charge of the learning process. Think about what that means.

Studies done by psychologists and others show that active learners— those who take charge of their learning—are successful learners. One result their research demonstrates is that students who use appropriate study methods, such as underlining key ideas and taking notes, remember more from a study period than those who do not. Furthermore, the research shows that those students who search for ways to improve their methods of study and who further develop their skills are much more likely to become successful learners. But most of all, these studies show that active and successful learners are aware of how to think about a learning situation, such as studying a textbook chapter in preparing for an exam, and how to regulate the learning process, such as making specific plans to pass a test successfully....

As people grow, they learn many things that are quite difficult to grasp at first but eventually become so familiar that they are done automatically. Learning to ride a bicycle is one of these tasks. Think of how many rules riding a bike requires us to know: Keep the wheel straight, keep pedaling, hold your balance, watch where you're going, and so on. Yet once bike riding is learned, you do it automatically. You don't think about holding your balance; you just do it, naturally.

Learning how to learn is a bit like learning how to ride a bike. It is not always easy, it is sometimes confusing, and it doesn't guarantee success, particularly in the beginning. But knowing how to learn, how to use specific strategies, and to make good study habits a routine practice improves the likelihood of success.

Learning is also like problem solving. Each course assignment is essentially a problem to be solved. Your job is to get from point X, an assignment to learn a subject about which you have little or no knowledge, to point Y, a thorough understanding of the material and the increased potential for success on an examination. But to get from point X to point Y, to solve the problem, means moving in steps—doing things first, second, and so forth until completion. And because of the many steps to learning, it is useful to think about grouping them in three major stages: planning, monitoring, and evaluating.

Active learners plan how they will accomplish a task. They monitor their work carefully to make sure things are working as they had planned. And they evaluate their results to be sure they have accomplished the task, to be sure that they are now successful learners. That's why you need to look closely at how this learning process works....

Planning is the first step in successful learning. Planning is, in fact, an integral part of everyday life. People make plans to go out. They make plans to see friends. They make plans for the weekend. It seems quite reasonable, therefore, that people also make plans for learning.

One approach to planning ... considers four types of information: the characteristics of the learner, the critical tasks or specific assignments, the nature of the materials, and the learning strategies necessary to complete the task....

Good planning requires first that you know yourself, know your characteristics as a learner.... The more aware you are of how you learn, of your strengths and weaknesses, and of how you can build your strengths, the more successful you are likely to be in learning how to learn....

Do you take good notes, or should you learn how to take better notes? Are you able to retain much that you study, or should you learn more efficient memory techniques? These are the issues of self-awareness. To accomplish any task, you must be aware of how best to guide your learning.

You must also plan with purpose. What is the critical task, the specific assignment to be completed? How will you be evaluated? What method of testing will the instructor use? How will you know before the exam whether your efforts are succeeding?

Imagine, for instance, that your assignment is to read a chapter in your sociology text on socialization (how people become a part of their community) and to prepare for a quiz on the difference between socialization in highly developed urban communities and in more traditional rural communities. The assignment is the critical task; it creates the purpose for your study: (1) what you need to do—read the chapter on socialization; (2) what you need to know—the differences between the two communities; and (3) how to judge when you are done—to test your knowledge of the differences. You fulfill your purpose, and you are done when you know those differences....

Next, consider the nature of the study material. What type of material is it? Is it typical of a textbook chapter or a magazine article? How is it organized? Differences, for example, are frequently presented with comparison and contrast patterns. Is there a plan of action most appropriate to this type of material? These questions suggest a couple of important points.

On the one hand, you need to be aware of how different reading materials are organized. Recognize, for instance, the difference between the organization of textbook chapters, which are very explicit (new ideas are both explained and illustrated) and the organization of short stories, which are less explicit (new ideas are introduced via the interaction of character, plot, and setting). These differences influence your choice of method to study the material.

On the other hand, different types of study material present different organizational clues. Textbook authors frequently signal important parts of the text with phrases like "the key point here" and "to summarize." The clues in the short story are more general. Understand the characters—how they are presented, how they behave, what the consequences of their thoughts and actions are— and you will understand the story. Reading materials differ in their purpose and structure, and these differences determine how best to study them....

Next, good planning requires that you determine which learning strategies are most useful for the task, the material, and your strengths as a learner. What strategies will make you an efficient and effective learner? ... But for the moment, look again at the hypothetical sociology assignment.

The task is to know the differences in socialization for urban and rural communities. Because the material follows standard textbook organizations, the information should be fairly explicit. As you think about your reading habits, you realize that you sometimes lose your concentration while reading textbooks and that careful underlining helps you stay alert and keep track of important facts. Imagine then that the strategy you choose may look something like this:

- My purpose is to know the differences in socialization between urban and rural societies.
- I will read the text to answer this question: "What is the difference between rural and urban patterns of socialization?"
- I will underline important ideas as I read to keep track of the information.
- Once I have completed my reading, I will review my underlined points to be sure I understand them and that they help answer the question.
- I will also reread sections I find confusing.
- To evaluate my understanding, I will give myself a written self-test to see if I know the differences and can explain them.
- Reviews and additional self-tests will depend on my previous successes. My success on my self-test will determine when I'm done.

This, of course, is just one example, but it does suggest how planning works. To be successful, you should consider (1) your characteristics as a learner, (2) the critical tasks of learning, (3) the nature of the materials to be learned, and (4) the variety of learning strategies available....

As soon as you put your plan into play, begin monitoring. Start by observing your activities to see if your plan and your strategies are working successfully. Try to decide if the material you are studying makes sense, if your approach is appropriate to the assigned task, and if your progress is proceeding efficiently. Remember that learning always carries time limits.

Self-Questioning

You might think of the monitoring process, at least initially, as a self-questioning procedure. You can examine your progress by asking a series of questions about your purpose, your task, and your response. You might consider checking your work with these questions:

_____ Is my purpose clear?
_____ Am I able to identify important ideas?
_____ Does my underlining and note-taking aid my comprehension?
_____ Are the questions I ask about the subject being answered by the text?
_____ Can I summarize the main points in the material I've studied?
_____ Am I using effective memory techniques to help me retain the information? ...

Also consider the importance of monitoring your reading comprehension, because reading is such an integral part of all study. Reading is a continuous process of interpreting what is happening in the text and predicting what will happen next. To the extent you understand—comprehend—the material, you will succeed in learning it. To the extent you don't, your comprehension will break down....

Three basic strategies are generally suggested to help you monitor your comprehension in the reading for study: note-taking, questioning, and summarizing.

Note-Taking

Note-taking has long been considered an effective strategy for learning because it requires the learner to pay close attention to the text and to construct, through notes, a meaningful interpretation of the text. *Paraphrasing*—rewriting in your own words—the important information from the text also helps clarify its meaning. Note-taking creates the opportunity for you to think about the material you are reading, thereby increasing your ability to understand and remember its most important points.

Questioning

Questioning strategies work much like note-taking strategies in that questioning also requires the learner to pay close attention to the text. Specifically, questioning helps you to identify important ideas in the text, to use those ideas to ask further questions, and to think of possible answers to those questions.

For example, thinking about the note-taking paragraph above, you might ask, "How can note-taking increase my comprehension?" Then your recall of the details of the paragraph—"Notes help me think about what I'm reading"— answers the question and checks your understanding. Furthermore, self-generated questions increase your awareness of the learning process and your potential for success because they make you a more active learner....

Summarizing

Summarizing is another useful technique for monitoring comprehension. Summarizing helps organize large quantities of information into a condensed, more easily remembered version and tests your understanding. Effective summarizing aids learning by making you identify key elements of a text once again and restate, or reorganize, that information in a meaningful fashion.

Good summaries focus on the main point of a reading selection, identify major supporting points, and eliminate all unnecessary information. Imagine yourself writing a summary of a short article about the negative influence of television on children's reading habits. An effective summary requires that you:

- Ignore unnecessary material. For example, exclude issues other than reading habits.
- Delete *redundant,* or repeated, points. For example, eliminate repeated examples or additional statements making similar points about the negative influence of television.
- Use general statements to consolidate details. For example, summarize the conclusions from different examples of television watching.
- Select important topic sentences. For example, find statements in the text that explain the negative influence of television.
- Invent topic sentences where necessary to focus on key information. For example, create a sentence that links heavy viewing and low reading scores.

Summarizing helps you to monitor your comprehension by keeping you alert to important points and it helps you to comprehend by requiring you to organize information in a meaningful way....

Evaluating your success in learning means judging whether or not you have achieved your purpose and are able to retain what you have learned. In practice, it is a continuous cycle of self-testing and review. Regular self-testing promotes successful academic performance.

Self-Testing

Self-testing is a natural part of learning in everyday life as in academic life. Imagine that you are having some friends over for dinner and you want to prepare something very special. You decide first to look for a fancy seafood dish in your favorite cookbook. But once you find a recipe, study it carefully, and imagine how tasty it is, you realize you have no experience with such a dish. What if the recipe is a flop with your guests?

The answer for many people is to cook the new dish ahead of time to gain practice before it's time to cook for friends. That first cooking is not simply practice; it is also a self-test. It is one way to judge your ability to handle the job ahead of the actual test. The same is true of self-tests in academic life (the cooking example is somewhat similar to the way laboratory classes promote understanding in science courses). The test provides you with an opportunity to judge your understanding of a subject prior to a formal examination. Self-testing prepares you for the actual experience....

Review and Memory

Evaluation also contains a review component. All students recognize the hazardous effects of forgetting. In fact, it is not uncommon for students to find themselves staring blankly at a test question, searching for an answer they know they studied but have completely forgotten.

Why does memory fail? There are many reasons. You may, for instance, not understand the material and, therefore, not remember it. Understanding is probably the most important element of good memory. You may very well understand the material while you are reading, but the information may seem so obvious that it is merely included in your short-term memory and quickly lost as you continue reading....

To your benefit, a few basic study strategies will increase your memory and support your continuous review. The strategies are spaced study, active rehearsal or recitation, *overlearning*, and relearning....

Spaced study means simply: Don't try to learn everything at once. Fatigue undermines learning and remembering primarily because of a loss in concentration. To study for three or four 45-minute periods with a 5- or 10-minute break between is much better for learning than to study for three or four hours straight. Smaller units of time with clear purpose, good concentration, and effective strategies will aid learning and memory, especially if supported by follow-up reviews. A good sequence, for instance, might be to study for three 45-minute periods and then to review that material in the fourth period....

Active rehearsal or recitation of material studied is an excellent technique for storing information in your long-term memory. Practicing your knowledge by thinking aloud is also a good method for regular review. You can "rehearse" material—talk it over with yourself—at any time, and then use self-tests to judge your accuracy. The point is to give yourself repeated practice through verbal rehearsal....

Another useful technique is "overlearning." Common sense may suggest that once you learn something, the job is complete. It is learned. Overlearning seems a waste of time. But the fact of the matter is that once you learn something, it can still be rather quickly forgotten. Therefore, it is frequently worth your time to overlearn important information. Overlearning gives you more practice, and learners who give themselves more practice remember more of what they learn. When you think you're done with analyzing or memorizing some material, practice it a few more times; you'll do much better in the long run....

A final aid to memory is relearning—sometimes referred to as the savings technique. Simply stated, it is easier to learn—or relearn—information previously studied than it is to learn new information. That idea is probably obvious to you. It's a bit like riding a bicycle. Even if you haven't been on a bike in years, riding quickly comes back to you if you once learn how. The benefit of ease in relearning lends further support to the review process. Once something is learned, it is much easier to relearn or retain if it is reviewed from time to time. And once you have thoroughly reviewed, you can evaluate the accuracy of your knowledge through self-testing....

Planning, monitoring, and evaluating each are critical stages in the learning process (see Figure 1). They are not always easy to apply and they don't guarantee success. They do give the learner a sense of direction and allow active learners to take charge of their learning. Each stage offers you the opportunity to think about your learning and to direct and control it. The goal is for you to establish habits for learning, to develop automatic approaches to thinking about learning, approaches that allow you to decide for yourself how to get from point X to point Y most effectively, most efficiently, and most successfully.

Figure 1

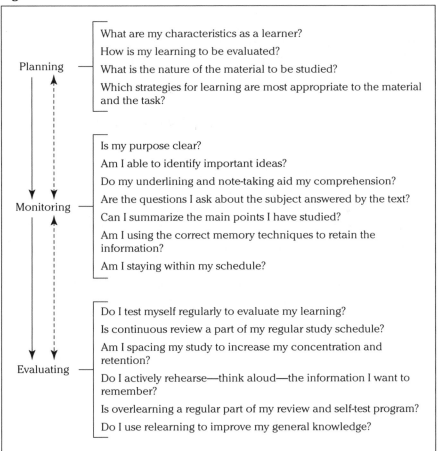

Planning	What are my characteristics as a learner?
	How is my learning to be evaluated?
	What is the nature of the material to be studied?
	Which strategies for learning are most appropriate to the material and the task?

Monitoring	Is my purpose clear?
	Am I able to identify important ideas?
	Do my underlining and note-taking aid my comprehension?
	Are the questions I ask about the subject answered by the text?
	Can I summarize the main points I have studied?
	Am I using the correct memory techniques to retain the information?
	Am I staying within my schedule?

Evaluating	Do I test myself regularly to evaluate my learning?
	Is continuous review a part of my regular study schedule?
	Am I spacing my study to increase my concentration and retention?
	Do I actively rehearse—think aloud—the information I want to remember?
	Is overlearning a regular part of my review and self-test program?
	Do I use relearning to improve my general knowledge?

From *Strategies for Active Learning* by James E. Twining. Reprinted by permission of Allyn & Bacon.

Vocabulary

James Twining tries to help readers by defining complex words within his text. How does he define each of the following?

1. **paraphrasing**
2. **redundant**
3. **overlearning**

Discussion Questions

1. What do some research studies indicate about successful learners, as cited by the author?
2. What does Twining mean by "learning to learn"?
3. What are the four types of information you must have to formulate a plan for learning, according to the author?
4. What three basic strategies does Twining suggest for monitoring your comprehension in reading?
5. How can you evaluate whether your learning is successful?

How Can These Ideas Apply to You?

1. How do you approach a learning task? How are your techniques the same as, or different from, those suggested by the author?
2. What approaches do you use when learning different subjects (e.g., foreign language, English, math)?
3. How do you know when you have successfully learned something—even before you get your grade on a test?

An Overview of Service-Learning

Alan S. Waterman

Alan S. Waterman is professor of psychology at The College of New Jersey. He has been
associated with service-learning for over twenty years. This essay provides an overview
of service-learning from a book he edited on the subject.

. . . .

We have been doing "service-learning" in our society for far longer than we
have applied the label to this approach to experiential education. We
have involved our children, adolescents, and young adults in service to the
community through our schools, our religious institutions, and youth organizations (e.g., scouting). We have expected service experiences to promote responsibility, caring, citizenship, competence, and a practical knowledge of our communities, our nation, and our world. We have believed that service promotes
these goals more effectively than other means, particularly standard classroom
instruction. And we have found that in doing service, many of our students
come to feel quite differently about that standard classroom instruction as a
function of seeing its application in ways that make a difference in the lives of
others. . . .

The term service-learning has come to be applied to a very wide range of
activities with students from kindergarten through higher education. As the use
of the term has expanded, there has risen a lively debate about what should
and should not be considered educational practices under this label. Although
there is potentially much to be gained from this debate in terms of the identification of parameters potentially necessary for effective practice, this is not the
forum to review the sometimes broad, but often subtle, distinctions offered from
competing perspectives. Still, it is appropriate to provide some formal definition
of service-learning, so as to identify the major defining features of this approach
to education.

The Commission on National and Community Service has defined service-
learning as follows: Service-learning is a method

(A) under which students learn and develop through active participation
in thoughtfully organized service experiences that meet actual community needs and that are coordinated in collaboration with the school and
community;

(B) that is integrated into the students' academic curriculum or provides structured time for the student to think, talk, or write about what the student did
and saw during the actual service activity;

(C) that provides students with opportunities to use newly acquired skills and
knowledge in real-life situations in their own communities; and

(D) that enhances what is taught in school by extending student learning beyond the classroom and into the community and helps to foster the development of a sense of caring for others. (National and Community Service
Act of 1990) . . .

Contemporary programs in service-learning represent the *confluence* of
two important historical traditions: (a) the American tradition of service to the
community, and (b) the experiential approach to *pedagogy*. The value and importance of service to the community is reflected in the writings of Thomas
Jefferson and in the works of the American philosopher William James. James
(1910) called for a program of national service for youth that would function as
"the moral equivalent for war." The circumstances of the economic depression
of the 1930s spurred the creation of community service programs such as the
Civilian Conservation Corps that involved millions of unemployed youth with
benefits to the environment, the society, and the participants. More recently,
John F. Kennedy and Bill Clinton promoted national and community service as
a means of tapping the best potentials within individuals and integrating youth
into the community and the nation.

The philosopher and educator John Dewey advanced the view that active
student involvement in learning was an essential element in effective education. Through experiential education, students are challenged to discover relationships among ideas for themselves, rather than merely receiving the information about such relationships from the authorities around them. Dewey viewed
the community as an integral part of educational experiences, because what is
learned in the school must be taken and utilized beyond its bounds, both for
the advancement of the student and the betterment of future societies.

Participants in the field of service-learning make an important distinction
between service-learning and volunteer service. In both activities, individuals
become involved in service projects that are believed to be of benefit to others,
their community, or their environment and from which they derive no direct
monetary or material benefits. In volunteer service there is no explicit focus on
the educational value to be gained through involvement in the particular
projects. In the case of service-learning, the projects are designed, enacted, su-
pervised and evaluated with the educational benefits of the experiences as one
of the consciously held goals. Consistent with the objectives of experiential
learning, practitioners in service-learning endeavor to have the students develop expectations of what can or should be learned as a result of involvement
in the project. Both during and after the activities that constitute the service
project, attention is called to the learning objectives as a means of fostering the
educational outcomes. Both during and after the service activities, time may be
devoted toward having the students and others involved in the project reflect
on the nature of what is taking place (or has taken place), and the reasons that
events have transpired as they have. Further, explicit efforts are made to integrate what is taking place during the service project with elements of the more
traditional in-class curriculum. Although there is a great deal that individuals
may learn on their own from their personal involvement in volunteer service,

the absence of a systematic focus on the educational possibilities of such service inevitably results in less utilization of those possibilities than can be achieved through service-learning....

It is a fundamental assumption underlying the practice of service-learning, as well as other forms of experiential learning, that students will develop a better understanding and appreciation of academic material if they are able to put that material into practice in ways that make a difference in their own lives and/ or in the lives of other people. There is an abstract quality to the subject matter of most courses in which the academic material appears only in classroom and textbook contexts. Students quite naturally respond to the classroom-based curriculum with questions about its relevance for their lives outside of school. By integrating academic material from the classroom with service activities in the community, the relevance and application value of the class content become more readily evident. As important, the hands-on application of skills taught in the classroom provides a clearer, yet simultaneously more complex, perspective regarding those skills. What is experienced through action will be remembered more vividly than what is merely read, or heard in a teacher's class presentation....

In seeking to use service-learning as a means of promoting personal development, it should be recognized that there is a wide range of outcomes that are included under such a heading. Many of the personal development outcomes will be a direct function of the particular nature of the service projects in which students participate, whereas others may be more generic outcomes of such experiences. Furthermore, in a classroom, students participating in the same project may respond to it in a wide range of ways resulting in diversity of developmental outcomes.

The attitudes and values held by students participating in service-learning projects will tend to be specific to the nature of the project itself. We would expect students involved in environmental clean-up projects to become more reflective concerning issues pertaining to pollution, littering, and civic pride, whereas students involved in a project in a retirement or nursing home will become more reflective with respect to attitudes toward the elderly, and about abilities and disabilities. But both groups may experience developments regarding issues about the role of governments, and what can and cannot be realistically achieved through governmental efforts. It should be noted here that from an educational perspective, the goal is to promote a reflective development of attitudes and values, not the forming of particular attitude or value contents.

Service-learning experiences at the high school and college levels may also contribute to students' thinking about their career preparation. One of the difficulties of school-based education is that career decisions are often made without any extensive information about how day-to-day activities in the work environment are actually carried out. By getting students into the community for service projects, they are likely to receive exposure to a wider array of work environments than might otherwise be possible. For some students this might suggest possible career directions, whereas for others it may confirm or disconfirm decisions previously made.

Another type of personal development outcome that is likely to occur across different types of service-learning experiences involves increases in feelings of self-efficacy and self-esteem. Self-efficacy refers to the perception that one has the ability to bring about desired outcomes. Service-learning programs have as one of their points of focus the development of those skills necessary for the conduct of the service projects; skills that are then enacted to make a difference in the lives of other people or in the quality of the community or environment. Students are thus in a position to appreciate the value of their contributions in a way that is generally not available in the classroom. Self-esteem is a somewhat broader concept involving the overall value assessment one makes regarding oneself. Although there are educational programs that are designed to increase feelings of self-esteem apart from the behaviors one enacts, the effects of service-learning on self-esteem are mediated through self-efficacy. If students have a perception of higher levels of skills and competencies that contribute to desired outcomes, the level of their overall self-assessment will be increased. Of course, higher levels of self-efficacy and self-esteem will only result if the students experience themselves as making useful contributions to projects they believe are worth their efforts. . . .

An integral part of service-learning as an educational framework is that the students are providing real service to their communities. Whereas it could be argued that benefits to the community are not, strictly speaking, educational outcomes, it is not likely that positive outcomes in the other categories could be achieved in the absence of evidence that the students' efforts result in contributions to the community. . . .

Reprinted by permission of Lawrence Erlbaum Associates, Inc.

Vocabulary

As you think about this essay, these definitions may be helpful to you:
1. **confluence**   coming or flowing together
2. **pedagogy**   the art or profession of teaching

Discussion Questions

1. What is service-learning? How is it different from volunteer service?
2. Identify some of the historical roots of service-learning.
3. How does Waterman define and distinguish between "self-efficacy" and "self-esteem"?

4. How, according to Waterman, can service-learning lead to better career choices?
5. Waterman argues that service-learning can teach civic responsibility. Do you agree?

 ## How Can These Ideas Apply to You?

1. Have you ever taken part in a service-learning project? If so, what was your experience? Would you have learned the same lessons without the service component?
2. If you have never experienced service-learning, would you be interested in taking a course where this method is incorporated? Why or why not?
3. How could a service-learning experience help you in your job search after college? What actions might you take with this in mind?

Distance Learning

Michael P. Governati, George Steele, and Kate Carey

Michael P. Governati, Ph.D., is the executive director of Miami University Middletown
Campus in Middletown, Ohio. Kate Carey, Ph.D., and George Steele, Ph.D., are
respectively the executive director and director of Degree Completion Programs for the
Ohio Learning Network. The Ohio Learning Network is an organization dedicated to
significantly expanding access to learning opportunities for the citizens of the state of
Ohio. It is also charged with enhancing the capacity and effectiveness of colleges and
universities in their use of technology in instruction and research, as well as collaborating with similar organizations.

I magine going back in time, to a place where the Internet is still more of
a dream rather than a reality, and to a place where all types of Web interactions are limited or do not exist. Imagine going back to the early 1990s!
The speed of the technological revolution that surrounds us is sometimes difficult to comprehend in all of its influences. All sections of our society, culture,
and economy are being transformed by it. Commenting about its impact on
commerce, futurist Peter F. Drucker describes the perceptual and intellectual
change from the industrial age to the technological age: "In the new mental geography created by the railroads, humanity mastered distance. In the mental
geography of e-commerce, distance has been eliminated. There is only one market. The competition is not local anymore; it knows no boundaries."

Just as new telecommunication, computer, and multimedia technologies
have changed the business sector and spurred the development of e-business,
they are also creating a new approach in education called distance learning.
Distance learning uses a variety of computing, telecommunication, and multimedia technologies to provide interactive learning experiences and to deliver
these experiences to students in both synchronous and asynchronous learning.
Synchronous learning is that which occurs in the same time and place. This traditional type of learning is illustrated when teachers and students are located in
the same place (a classroom) and time (periods within a schedule such as
quarters or semesters).

Asynchronous learning is learning that can occur anywhere and at any
time. Logging on to a computer and taking a course when it best fits your schedule is an example of this. Asynchronous learning did not begin with the Internet.
The attempt to remove distance and increase access to higher education in the
United States can be traced back at least to the development of correspondence courses by the private sector and public institutions at the beginning of
the 20th century. Before e-mail, correspondence courses relied on text-based in-
terchanges between teacher and student through the postal system. Asynchro-

nous learning, however, has blossomed with the advent of affordable computers and the new technologies. In the last decade of the past century, the share of U.S. households with personal computers rose from 22 percent to 53 percent. Households with access to the Internet went from 0 percent to 52 percent, and by the end of the decade 95 percent of public schools in the United States had Internet access. Higher education in the United States responded too. From 1995 to 1998, there was a 72 percent increase in distance education programs, from 690 to 1,190 with over 1.6 million students enrolled. The rate of acquisition and utilization of computer and Internet technologies compared to that of other innovative technology in the past, such as color TV, has been astounding. While it took TV nearly four decades from invention to mass-market acquisition, the personal computer enhanced by Internet access will be as *ubiquitous* as televisions in American households by 2010, only twenty years after the emergence of the World Wide Web.

Changes for Higher Education

These changes are creating a new context for higher education and providing new opportunities to different types of students. Yesterday's context for higher education shared many of the characteristics of the industrial age itself. The organizational emphasis was based on standardization of delivery (courses) that emphasized specialization of learning (majors) supported by an elaborate bureaucratic structure. The purpose of education fit neatly into one of the three boxes of life—education, work, and retirement. Education prepared people for work from which they planned to eventually retire. Education, work, and retirement created a pattern of life that was linear and easily understood. Throughout most of the last century, participation in the first box of life was limited, particularly at the higher education level. Access to higher education was dependent on socioeconomic status, geographic proximity to campuses, congruency of time available and schedules of course offerings, and one's age. The predominant pedagogy and delivery systems were synchronous teacher-centered lecture-and-discussion formats supplemented by low-tech support such as chalk and blackboards, motion pictures, overhead projectors, audio tapes, and slides. The focus of teaching centered on providing the "basics" or the "essentials" to students to prepare them for the next box of life—work. Although differences of opinion about the need for and nature of the "basics" or the "essentials" existed, society believed that education prepared individuals for work.

In the twenty-first century, new technologies will radically change the context for higher education. The greatest change will be the emergence of a life span model for education that will replace the "three boxes of life" *paradigm*. Educational emphasis will shift from preparing students for a lifetime of work in predominantly one career area, to a focus on acquisition of tailored knowledge and skill sets for people who change jobs and careers more frequently over an extended period of time. For students, learning how to learn will become more critical as continued education and learning throughout one's life will become the norm. The focus of teaching will become more student-centered as the barriers of time and place diminish and asynchronous learning becomes more quickly accessible. These efforts will be supported by the continuous development of information technology and electronic delivery systems that will make learning anywhere any time a reality. We will see a convergence of technologies—the merging of computing, telecommunications, and multimedia technologies. This convergence will draw upon the worldwide resources of both materials and people for teaching and learning.

How much will traditional higher education be affected by this? One school of thought says higher educational institutions' stakeholders will determine the impact of these changes. For example, traditional residential colleges and universities that focus on students in their late teens and early twenties will not be as radically affected as those institutions that serve commuter and adult students. Some form of traditional education will always exist for most young adults leaving home every autumn to live on campus. Classroom and social learning are equally important in this view of higher education. The new technologies will change the way teachers teach, but the difference will be more subtle, rather than revolutionary.

Another school of thought sees all of higher education being impacted by distance learning. Technological change will continuously and radically alter social, political, and business structures. These powerful forces will create an expectation and demand for information age responsiveness from all of higher education. As learning needs for the great majority of the population is spread out over their lifetimes, both personal and social costs will seriously question the value of the personal four-to-five year moratorium higher education currently exacts. This moratorium might well be an educational and pleasant experience, but is it worth the current debt often incurred to achieve it? With the barrier of distance broken, students can seek exceptional educational offerings to acquire a degree or upgrade their skills while continuing to engage in other social roles whether it is leisure pursuits, parenting, or career interests.

Types of Technology

Several new technologies will link teachers and students in both synchronous (same time) and asynchronous (anytime and anyplace) ways in the twenty-first century. The distinguishing characteristics of these technologies relate to how they permit learners to access learning opportunities anywhere and at any time. All these technologies will be Internet applicable. Today, most Internet access is limited to hard-wired networks. Tomorrow, wireless connections will greatly increase the meaning of anywhere access for distance learning. Some of the technologies used in learning will still be synchronously based: for example, instant messages, chat room discussions, and streaming video. Technologies that will enhance asynchronous learning will include e-mail, captured video, and CD-ROMs. The important difference between these two groups is that anytime/anyplace (asynchronous) technologies can more easily support learning designed to be same time (synchronous). Conversely, synchronous technologies do not adapt well to asynchronously designed learning.

Perhaps the most serious issue facing distance learning is the *digital divide*. This term refers to the unequal access to the use of technology based on primarily socio-economic factors, but also geographic factors. Computers and Internet access are seen as items that are unaffordable to many disadvantaged individuals and families. Additionally, some rural areas do not have reliable, fast Internet service.

Access to computing and information can be compounded by the rate of technological change. Moore's Law (so termed by Intel co-founder Gordon Moore) proposes that computer capabilities as measured by computer memory will double every 18 months while costs hold constant. This means that you can buy a faster computer with more memory at about the same price as your last computer. This technological advance is great, but most of us have tired of using "old" computers for "new" things. While this experience would certainly frustrate someone trying to take a course over the Internet, having no computer and no Internet access precludes this even as a possibility. Public libraries offer computer and Internet access but users are often limited so that others can share that resource.

Needed: A New Type of Learner

Although distance learning offers a more convenient and flexible way to take courses and complete a degree, it may not necessarily fit all students' learning styles or needs. Just as the current lecture and discussion approach that is predominantly used in traditional higher educational settings is better adapted to some students' learning styles (auditory and verbal learners who can commit large blocks of time to attend campus), Internet-based distance learning creates its own preferences. Some students will find it difficult to study as independently as distance learning requires and will feel more comfortable with the daily contact with an instructor and other students found in more traditional learning. Self-motivated adult learners with strong reading and writing skills have the best success with distance learning modes of instruction.

Hence, just as traditional approaches to learning have not met the needs of everyone, the challenge for distance learning educators is to design learning opportunities that have greater access, flexibility, and scope than that which is currently available. The challenge, though, must be met soon. The world is moving fast. More and more households have computers and Internet service. A new, more computer-literate generation of students is coming of age. And a new adult learner computer-literate market is emerging. Technology-enhanced learning in the classroom or offered via distance is here. Given the exponential changes in telecommunications and multimedia technologies, reliance on traditional modes of time- and place-bound education may be viewed in this century not only as quaint, but as a relic of a bygone industrial age.

Vocabulary

As you think about this essay, these definitions may be helpful to you:
1. **synchronous learning**   learning that occurs in the same time and place
2. **asynchronous learning**   learning that occurs anywhere, anytime
3. **ubiquitous**   widespread
4. **paradigm**   an outstandingly clear or typical example; theoretical framework
5. **digital divide**   unequal access to the use of technology

Discussion Questions

1. What is the difference between synchronous and asynchronous learning?
2. Should economic considerations be the primary way to evaluate the value of higher education?
3. Can society afford to let some of its members not participate in distance learning? What would be the costs?

How Can These Ideas Apply to You?

1. How would you describe yourself as a learner? What type of courses does your style fit with best? What type of courses do you have difficulty with because of your learning style?
2. How would you describe your technology skills? What computer software programs are you comfortable using? What other technologies do you know how to use? Video camera? DVD player? How did you learn to use these technologies?
3. Would you feel comfortable taking a distance-learning course? Have you taken one already? What was your experience?

What Makes a Successful Online Student?

Illinois Online Network

• • • • • • • • • • • • • • • • • •

[T] he successful online student possesses unique qualities. The online students of today consist primarily of working people who are trying to better their opportunities. . . . The traditional school will never go away, but the virtual classroom is a significant player in today's educational community. Corporations are using the online model to train technical professionals while private and public universities redefine the world as their markets. In general, the online student should possess the following qualities:

1. **Be open minded about sharing life, work, and educational experiences as part of the learning process.** *Introverts* as well as *extroverts* find that the online process requires them to utilize their experiences. This forum for communication eliminates the visual barriers that hinder some individuals in expressing themselves. In addition, the student is given time to reflect on the information before responding. The online environment should be open and friendly.

2. **Be able to communicate through writing.** In the virtual classroom, nearly all communication is written, so it is critical that students feel comfortable in expressing themselves in writing. Many students have limited writing abilities, which should be addressed before or as part of the online experience. This may require remedial efforts on the part of the student.

3. **Be self-motivated and self-disciplined.** With the freedom and flexibility of the online environment comes responsibility. The online process takes a real commitment and discipline to keep up with the flow of the process.

4. **Be willing to "speak up" if problems arise.** Many of the non-verbal communication mechanisms that instructors use in determining whether students are having problems (confusion, frustration, boredom, absence, etc.) are not possible in the online paradigm. If a student is experiencing difficulty on any level (either with the technology or with the course content), he or she must communicate this immediately. Otherwise the instructor will never know what is wrong.

5. **Be willing and able to commit to 4 to 15 hours per week per course.** Online is not easier than the traditional educational process. In fact, many students will say it requires much more time and commitment.

6. **Be able to meet the minimum requirements for the program.** The requirements for online are no less than that of any other quality educational

program. The successful student will view online as a convenient way to receive their education—not an easier way.

7. **Accept critical thinking and decision making as part of the learning process.** The learning process requires the student to make decisions based on facts as well as experience. Assimilating information and executing the right decisions require critical thought; case analysis does this very effectively.

8. **Have access to a computer and a modem.** The communication medium is a computer, phone line, and modem; the student must have access to the necessary equipment.

9. **Be able to think ideas through before responding.** Meaningful and quality input into the virtual classroom is an essential part of the learning process. Time is given in the process to allow for the careful consideration of responses. The testing and challenging of ideas is encouraged; you will not always be right, just be prepared to accept a challenge.

10. **Feel that high quality learning can take place without going to a traditional classroom.** If the student feels that a traditional classroom is a prerequisite to learning, he or she may be more comfortable in the traditional classroom. Online is not for everybody. A student that wants to be on a traditional campus attending a traditional classroom is probably not going to be happy online. While the level of social interaction can be very high in the virtual classroom given that many barriers come down in the online format, it is not the same as living in a dorm on a campus. This should be made known. An online student is expected to:

- Participate in the virtual classroom 5–7 days a week
- Be able to work with others in completing projects
- Be able to use the technology properly
- Be able to meet the minimum standards as set forth by the institution ...

The online learning process is normally accelerated and requires commitment on the student's part. Staying up with the class and completing all work on time is vital. Once a student gets behind, it is almost impossible to catch up. Basically, the student needs to want to be there, and needs to want the experience. The instructor may have to contact students personally to offer assistance and remind the student of the need to keep up.

Just as many excellent instructors may not be effective online facilitators, not all students possess the necessary qualities to perform well online. [In an] online course, ... reference links to resources and tips [may be used] to help students be more successful. ... [Online students need to] understand if the online environment will be a productive learning environment for them.

Vocabulary

As you think about this essay, these definitions may be helpful to you:
1. **introvert**   one whose attention and interests are directed inwardly
2. **extrovert**   one whose attention and interests are directed outside one's self

 # Discussion Questions

1. Why is commitment critical to the success of an online student?
2. How do you think social interaction might differ in doing a class project from an online course versus a traditional classroom version?

 # How Can These Ideas Apply to You?

1. Suppose that all courses are offered online, and only online. Use the model of "Good, Bad, Interesting" from the essay by Jennifer James (p. 107) to analyze the possible outcomes of such a different way of learning.
2. Of the ten qualities listed as important for effective online learners, which ones might be the most difficult for you to develop? The most comfortable?

UNIT SUMMARY

The writers in this unit describe the learning process from many different perspectives. Because learning is the central mission of the college experience, understanding learning is essential to college success. The readings in this unit have offered an overview of different learning approaches, from which every student can benefit.

Summary Questions

1. What specific approaches to learning do the readings in this unit describe? Which ones would you like to experience in more depth? Why?
2. What tasks or strategies described in the readings could you adopt to improve the learning skills needed in your academic work?
3. What implications for your own life-long learning are suggested in these readings?

Suggested Writing Assignments

1. Write a brief essay describing the advantages and disadvantages of either service-learning or distance learning.
2. Select one reading in this unit and write about how your personal experience has been the same as or different from what the writer describes.
3. Has the use of the Internet influenced how you learn? In what ways?

Suggested Readings

Gershenfeld, Neil. *When Things Start to Think.* New York: Henry Holt, 1999.

Goleman, Daniel. *Working with Emotional Intelligence.* New York: Bantam Books, 1998.

Kolb, D. A. "Learning Styles and Disciplinary Differences." In A. W. Chickering and Associates (eds.), *The Modern American College.* San Francisco: Jossey-Bass, 1981.

Tapscott, Don. *Growing Up Digital: The Rise of the Net Generation.* New York: McGraw-Hill, 1998.

What About Technology?

Higher education is in transition, and technology is a major force driving the change. As the essay on distance learning in Unit 4 (pp. 134–138) suggests, some colleges are expanding beyond their traditional buildings and campuses into cyberspace in order to reach out to students who want or need to study in nontraditional ways. Technology will not replace colleges, but it is already affecting how we learn. In the next decades, many new information technologies will emerge. As a result, students will experience new and exciting methods of teaching and learning.

As you begin your college experience, you will witness many of these changes. How you adapt to and learn about technology in college will have an impact on how well you later adapt and learn in the workplace. Information technology is changing the nature of jobs and how workers do those jobs. It is projected that by 2010, 90 percent of all workers will be affected.

This unit touches on some interesting facts, applications, and

The information revolution has changed people's perception of wealth. We originally said that land was wealth. Then we thought it was industrial production. Now we realize it is intellectual capital.

—WALTER WRISTON,
FORMER CEO OF CITICORP

opinions about technology and the influence it has on our lives. Mortimer Zuckerman traces how technology changed the world in the 20th century and how it is now repeating its effect. In an interview with Larry King, John Seely Brown speculates on the office of the future and how it will affect not only our work lives but our private and family lives as well.

Steven McDonald deals with practical implications of using the Internet, especially your legal rights and responsibilities in using it. Clifford Stoll offers a different perspective as he writes about how libraries and librarians are reinventing themselves. Ellen Goodman describes her foray into the new technological age by recounting her past experience with old systems. She points out how, much to her sorrow, new technology is changing the way we communicate, or fail to communicate, with each other.

The Times of Our Lives

Mortimer B. Zuckerman

Mortimer B. Zuckerman is editor-in-chief of *U.S. News & World Report* magazine. In this essay, he traces the history of the 20th century and how certain historical events have influenced current technology. He discusses the global economy as the new frontier and how we enter the new century dynamically and oriented to the future.

• • • • • • • • • • • • • • • •

A few years into the 20th century a couple of bicycle makers named Wright got a heavier-than-air machine 15 feet in the air for a whopping 59 seconds. Few newspapers bothered to report the news. That seems surprising to us today. Surely it was obvious that aviation was going to shrink the world, if not the galaxy? But wait. It would have taken a Leonardo da Vinci to imagine how even a few of the innovations of the early 20th century would work out by the millennium—which makes these profound changes so *beguiling*.

Edison's incandescent light and Bell's telephone arrived by 1900, Marconi's radio telegraph fired up a year later. But who could conceive how these inventions might begin to lay the foundation of our modern world? A Nebraska farmer in 1900 might, if he were lucky, learn news of the outside world from an out-of-date newspaper. Today's farmer, by contrast, thinks nothing of punching up satellite weather pictures on his cable television or of getting a download from the Web to check on the wheat crop in Russia.

The Faces of Change

We have gotten used to having more for less. More than a third of Americans began the century working on farms to feed some 76 million people. Now just over 2 percent grow the food to feed 270 million people—and there's plenty left over. The number of hours Americans worked annually has dropped from about 2,700 at the beginning of the century to about 1,800 today; average life expectancy has gone from about 45 years to 80. The children who [once would have] died of whooping cough, scarlet fever, or diphtheria can now expect to grow up as parents of their own families. Or think of the millions laid off in the Great Depression, simply because we did not understand how capitalism works.

That's not surprising. We changed so rapidly—from a rural agricultural society, to an industrial economy, to a service economy. Today, we inhabit an information-based economy that spans the globe. Change, as is its wont, took many forms: Henry Ford's vision of automobiles for the masses, Ike's interstate highway system, mass transit, the suburbs.

Who could have guessed how radio and television would transform politics? We grumble about the tube, but we ought to remember that it was television's gift to enable all of us to share a common experience without being there, a vital element in the movement—in Arthur Schlesinger Jr's apt phrase—from exclusion to inclusion. It was that movement that paved the way for the expansion of the democratic franchise to women, young people, and blacks.

The movement occurred in phases. As the century developed, the middle class exploded, blurring the nation's 19th century class distinction between blue- and white-collar workers, between men and women. In the second half of the century, blacks entered the middle class at the fastest pace of any group in our country's history. All this despite fighting two world wars, Korea, Vietnam, and the Cold War.

Amazingly, we came to the end of the century in a vastly more positive mood than anyone could have thought just 20 years ago. The nation is confident that it can handle the staggering acceleration of change that is propelling us into the next century. In just the past four decades, we have amassed more scientific knowledge than was generated in the previous 5,000 years. Indeed, 90 percent of all the scientists who ever lived are alive today, and they are using more powerful instruments than ever existed before.

What does it all mean for the future? Scientific information is now increasing twofold about every five years. Information doubles every $2\frac{1}{2}$ years. New knowledge makes most technology obsolete in just five to seven years. Even computers are out of date in less than two years. Recently, IBM announced that it is going to build a supercomputer working 500 times faster than the fastest computer today. "Blue Gene" it is called, and its target speed is a thousand trillion calculations each second!

The potential benefits defy imagining. Today, the Human Genome Project promises to map every gene, but before too long, we may be able to prescribe gene therapies for individual disorders. We should be able to measure the human impact on climate, learn more about how the brain works, and postpone human aging. Looking to our past, we may be able to reconstruct the genetic history of the human race, unravel the mystery of the birth of our universe, and perhaps learn once and for all whether other universes really exist. We may even find out that the big bang is only one of many, raising the possibility of life elsewhere in space.

One thing we know for sure. Whatever we discover will be transmitted around the world, not in 80 days, but in seconds, giving us little time to adjust psychologically to the new knowledge. It took five months for the news of the discovery of the New World by Columbus to reach Spain. It took just 1.3 seconds for Neil Armstrong's historic step on the moon to reach millions of viewers through television.

Magic?

But we must be humble about prognostications. Many *gray eminences* have failed to anticipate developments within their fields of expertise. In 1932, Albert Einstein concluded that there was not the slightest indication that nuclear energy would ever be obtainable. A decade and change later, Tom Watson, the chief of IBM, surveyed the potential world market for computers, pondered, and concluded that there was a demand "for about five."

Nor can we expect just more of the same. For as one wit said of Thomas Edison, if he had just extrapolated, we would have had better oil lamps. There is another thing that we know. America will lead the world in its openness and receptivity to new discoveries, information, and innovation. Undoubtedly, we will play a leading role in all the key sciences; we now lead the world in virtually all of them. The progress of America these past 100 years was founded on an uncanny ability to turn knowledge of the physical world into economic and military advantage. We created a vast network of research institutions, private and public universities, specialized institutes of technology, corporate laboratories, and private and public foundations. Then we integrated the new knowledge yielded by these creations into our daily life, especially our economic life.

It didn't happen by magic. To fill one end of the pipeline of human skills flowing into our country and into higher education that was providing business with the engineers, scientists, and managers it needed, our forebears invented that unique American institution—a free, universal, public high school. The results have been astounding. Just think. At the beginning of the 20th century, only 6.4 percent of young Americans graduated from high school. By the middle of the century, that figure had reached 59 percent. Today, it is 83 percent. Then look at our colleges. After the GI Bill of Rights was passed in 1944, college education surged. (Contrast this to the veterans of the American Revolution, rewarded with land grants.) By the end of the century, over 27 percent of the population, ages 25 to 29, had completed four or more years of college—up from 1 percent at the beginning of the century and 16.4 percent in 1970. Since 1970, black students with four years of college have doubled to approximately 15 percent. Education became not just for the privileged elite but for ever broader segments of our population. Today, a far higher percentage of Americans attend college than in any other nation in the world.

This says a lot about the American philosophy of *pragmatism,* whose intellectual seeds first took root 100 years ago. Few outside academia noticed the ferment created by turn-of-the-century philosophers like William James, Lester Ward, and John Dewey. They assaulted the ideology of Social Darwinism with the revolutionary thought that the uncivilized masses could learn and that the most mediocre, properly taught, could double or triple their achievements; that life, liberty, and the pursuit of happiness required government to free the people to do the best they could by providing opportunities for education, welfare, and health.

Essentially, the expanding opportunities made possible by education were the keys to the upward mobility that liberated so many from the artificial barriers of wealth and class. Education has proved a surer base for the creation of the middle class than organization. Human skills make up about 75 percent of the energy behind our economic growth. Jobs based on muscle power that could support the accouterments of middle-class life have shrunk dramatically in the past several decades.

In fact, by the end of the century, Americans had concluded that not just an education, but a higher education, was the right of every American for without it, an individual is cheated out of his or her maximum growth potential.

The people given their chance have more than met expectations. It is because of our embrace of science, and learning, and technology that we have surpassed the rest of the world in equipping ourselves and our businesses with the new information technologies at a rate, as a percentage of GDP, twice that of Europe and Japan. Today, roughly 50 percent of all business fixed investment in the United States is in information technologies. We lead the world in building the new infrastructure of the information world. An estimated two thirds of the world's top technology producers—the Microsofts, the Intels, Ciscos, IBMs, Dells, AOLs—are U.S. companies. Of the 48 information technology companies that Morgan Stanley Dean Witter believes will enjoy a sustainable competitive advantage over the next number of years, 31 are American. Only 6 are European. . . .

The United States is at a point reminiscent of its entry into the 20th century. In 1893 Frederick Jackson Turner pronounced the end of the American frontier. The West had been won; there were no new lands to conquer. Turner thought this might mean the end of American adventure and individualism. But he was wrong. The newly settled continent, linked by rail, lay open as a vast, tariff-free marketplace conducive to the sale of mass-produced products at prices more and more Americans could afford. Unimpeded access to those burgeoning marketplaces was the critical condition for the flowering of American enterprise.

Today, of course, the new frontier is the global economy. And the evidence is clear that the United States is as well placed to exploit that as it was the new continental marketplace of a century ago. We have demonstrated a unique ability to move financial capital, human capital, and management capital in massive amounts to the cutting edges of technology and economics. Our democratized capital markets allocate money to the future, not the past, to the new, not the old. New technologies make it increasingly feasible to set up small businesses, even at home, enhancing a deeply rooted American tradition, for, in this country, there are more small business owners than there are union members. We established 1.8 million new businesses in the 1990s, exceeding the 1.5 million of the 1980s. We are natural managers and organizers of our lives and our own careers.

America's culture is a perfect fit for this new world. The legacy of our individualism, entrepreneurialism, and pragmatism has outlived the passing of the frontier and continues to inspire millions. American culture nourishes its *heretics,* mavericks, and oddballs, celebrates its young, welcomes the newly arrived, and is dramatically open to the energy and talent rising from the bottom. No other country has the capacity to organize and respond to a huge market, vast and diverse populations, and rapidly changing economic conditions. No other country has met the requirements of an emerging industrial system in an information era that needs people to be mobile and flexible both physically and psychologically. No other country shares the American belief in science and in statistics as the basis for decision making and classification. We have a giant information-processing system that improves our capacity to enhance, absorb, and manage the ongoing revolutions in today's technology, information, and logistics that are too dynamic, rapidly changing, and complex to be processed in any top-down system, no matter how talented the bureaucracy, government, or corporate *oligopoly*. No other country so highly values the organizer, the discoverer of new opportunities, and the risk taker. No other country has a population so prone to self-help, self-improvement, even self-renovation, and certainly self-education. We encourage innovations through patent protection and a tax system that enables the successful innovator and investor to keep a large share of the value he has created. We tend to choose people for jobs by competence and relative merit, demote and promote primarily on the basis of performance. We value the new against the old, youth against experience, change and risk against safety, and making money over inheriting it.

That is why we entered the century dynamic and future-oriented, and ended it in the same way. We are thus perpetually a modern and not a traditional society, based on the concept type known as the self-made man—a social type who has flourished more in this society than in any other before or since. It reflects in that we ask a person not who he is but what he does. Collectively it has made up the American dream—the opportunity to achieve, to ascend the ladder, to transcend our origins, however humble. We began the century living the dream of our ancestors, and end it even more so.

As the poet Ovid once said, "Let others praise ancient times. I am glad to be alive in these."

Reprinted by permission of the author.

● ● ● ● ● ● ● ● ● ● ● ● ● ● ● ● ● ● ● ●

Vocabulary

As you think about this essay, these definitions may be helpful to you:
1. **beguiling**   persuasive by use of wiles
2. **grey eminences**   a person who exercises power from behind the scenes (from the French, *éminence grise*)
3. **pragmatism**   a practical approach to problems or affairs
4. **heretic**   one who dissents from an accepted belief or doctrine
5. **oligopoly**   a market situation in which each of a few producers affects but does not control the market

Discussion Questions

1. What inventions does Zuckerman say laid the foundation for our modern world? What others, if any, would you add to the list?
2. What are the four societies that have emerged in this country? What makes the latest one different from the other three?
3. How have "free and universal" educational opportunities affected American progress? How has the role of public education changed over time?
4. According to Zuckerman, the United States is uniquely suited to dominate the information age. Why is this so?

 ## How Can These Ideas Apply to You?

1. Do you ever feel the "staggering acceleration of change" that the author describes? If so, in what way?
2. What specific actions can you take during your college years to prepare you for the information age?

An Interview with John Seely Brown

Larry King

Larry King has been a talk-show host for more than four decades. In his book *Future Talk,* he interviews many individuals who represent the top of their fields. In this essay he interviews John Seely Brown, chief scientist at Xerox Corporation and director of the Palo Alto Research Center. Brown describes how technology will change the office of the future.

First, learn how to learn and learn how to love learning new things. Second, be open to new ideas no matter how bizarre they first seem because a lot of ideas are going to come at you and many will challenge certain background assumptions you hold. But if you give them the time of day you might find ways to use them.

LK: What are we going to find in an office in the twenty-first century?

Brown: I question whether we'll have "offices" as we currently think of offices. We're moving into an era where, instead of thinking about the office, we think about the "workscape." Most of us probably spend a tiny fraction of our time in our offices. We spend as much time around coffeepots, conference rooms, hallways, airports, home, highways, and so forth, so we should break away from the frame of thinking most work gets done in offices; rather, work becomes distributed over the entire physical space that we traverse through or occupy during any eight- or twelve-hour period of our day.

LK: So we will still have an office building?

Brown: We'll still have office buildings but I think you'll find offices will take more the shape of social gathering spaces where you can come together to have high-powered, high-performance conferences and informal meetings.

LK: No more conference rooms?

Brown: There will be an increase in electronic-based conference rooms where you have powerful meeting capture tools that facilitate the streamlining of meetings and the ability to capture everything that is being decided at the meeting without the extra work of having to prepare minutes after that. There will be things like electronic white boards where anything that you write will be automatically captured and transformed into a document for you without any additional work. Video and audio can be captured for later replay if you want, perhaps indexed by what you've been writing on the white boards and so on. So you'll see more emphasis on the social spaces of office buildings which facilitate coming together and having not just high-powered meetings but very productive, informal conversations.

LK: This sounds like we're going to be taped.

Brown: I think you'll find meeting capture rooms have facilities for recording anything that's going on for later replay or transcription if you want. Think of a tape loop that records everything that's been said for one minute and then erases it after that one minute, so if somebody says a brilliant idea, others in the rooms won't have to say, "Oh, can you say it again?" You won't have to. You hit the replay button and the last thirty seconds will be replayed and the ingenious thought will be there. You can set it for thirty seconds or a minute or whatever you want.

LK: Let's go back to the office.

Brown: The workscape.

LK: Sorry. There will be a desk and a fax machine and a computer screen?

Brown: The type of equipment you think about today will be history. There won't be personal computers, there won't be telephones, there won't be fax machines. I doubt there will be pagers. Instead you'll see some kind of totally integrated communication appliances that will facilitate all your communication needs in one device. You will see a smart input-output basket that is a portal for taking any document in the physical world and immediately converting it into the digital world or taking anything in the digital space and converting it into the analog physical paper space. You'll see personal desks going away and see desks crafted for two or three people to sit around and be able to share information on the screen. The screen will also become part of the woodwork.

LK: It sounds like there will be many group projects and not a lot of individual working.

Brown: There's a lot more collaborative work going on than the architects of office buildings today understand or the architects of informational systems understand. Most real work happens collaboratively. We need to find ways to honor how knowledge and ideas are actually created.

LK: Will secretaries be necessary in the workscape?

Brown: There will definitely be a blurring of distinction between administrative assistants and executive assistants, and we may find ourselves going back to the original notion of secretaries. Those are the people who are really orchestrating the events that you find behind the scenes. So there will be secretaries, but not in the way we currently view them or pay them. It will be an evolutionary change, a gradual change. Right now secretaries do a lot of this and aren't recognized for what they do, and there will come a point where we will recognize their skills and problem-solving abilities and they will become full-blooded participants in the workscape as opposed to these subservient roles.

LK: You were talking earlier of integrated appliances which will sit in an office—

Brown: A workscape.

LK: Workscape. What will these be like?

Brown: You'll carry them with you. I think you'll carry a wireless device that is your phone and is your fax machine and is also a small window onto the World Wide Web and so on. Every device you have will be "IP addressable" (Internet addressable), so every artifact that we have will actually sit on the Internet, and many will be highly integrated so they can carry on multiple functions all at the same time.

LK: What is it going to look like?

Brown: Something like digital paper, which is the size of an eight-by-eleven pad of paper. It may be a quarter-inch to a half-inch thick. It will have high-resolution displays and wireless communication, a virtual keyboard (if you still use keyboards), and it would be something which connects into a set of almost-personal Web sites behind the scenes sitting on the Internet, which carry out the assistant tasks which you have created.

LK: This sounds like we're not going to need those yellow Post-it Notes anymore.

Brown: Each of us wants to be able to have the opportunity to craft the workspace as we want. We all work differently. We actually all think differently, and what you want to be able to do is have each person craft his or her digital workscape as he really wants. And the key property of the Post-it Note is it allows you to put your persona on anything you want at a particular moment. Now, walk into ten people's offices and you'll see just how different each office really is. One person puts huge stacks of paper all over the place, another has a very pristine desk—

LK: And that always has been the case.

Brown: Always been the case. So as we move more into the digital world that same ability to tailor the workscape as you want, to match your particular cognitive style of work, is going to become even more important.

LK: Do you expect employees will be in their homes for the most part and just show up at the office, excuse me, workscape, once a week?

Brown: The key notion of a workscape is, it blurs the distinction between the office, the home, the road, and so on. The workscape is like a *manifold* which spreads over all of these places. I think you'll find that people are doing some work at home, some work at clients' workspaces, some work in the conference rooms, so work will happen all over the place. The key is going to be able to connect, or disconnect, or stay connected to your own workscape as you move around from these physical places without having to worry about "What did I leave over here?" or "If I update a file here is it also updated over there?" and so on.

LK: Will it matter where a headquarters is located and will cities like New York and Los Angeles still be big business centers?

Brown: Yeah, I think they will. Out here in Silicon Valley you can't help but go to a restaurant, listen to a conversation at the next table, and wonder, "My God, is my company ready to do that?" You hear the buzz, and in the buzz you not only pick up ideas but you get a sense of what everyone else is doing and you start thinking about yourself relative to that. So I think the physical locale is actually going to be very important in terms of providing one kind of grounding in terms of your intuitions about what's going on in the world and how good you are relative to other people.

LK: Tell me about the office staff.

Brown: There will be an increasing necessity to have someone around who understands multiculturalism, be it bilingual or bicultural, because translation is only part of the game, and there has to be understanding of what that utterance might have meant from that conversation. When you move to a global economy it becomes increasingly challenging to see the world from the other person's point of view.

LK: Will we still commute, and will there still be a rush hour in the twenty-first century?

Brown: Commuting doesn't necessarily mean rush hours. If you are working wherever it makes sense at that particular moment there's no reason to believe it makes sense for everybody to jump on the road at eight A.M. to go to some centralized office buildings. You may go there anytime during the day and you may stay home. So I think you'll find a much more uniform distribution of travel. You won't find these burst modes of travel at eight A.M. and five P.M. I don't even think we'll have an eight-hour day anymore.

LK: Let's talk about travel. Are we still going to travel to meet a client and do business, or will we do it by teleconferencing?

Brown: I think you'll find meetings where you get a chance to look the other person in the eye. Having some physical and social contact will always be important. Cyberspace will not replace physical space. But once you've established connections physically, you'll be able to extend that into cyberspace. At the same time, you will, no doubt, make connections in cyberspace that will lead to getting together in the physical space. So I see these as two complementary structures, each one aiding the other.

LK: A follow-up on the conference room where we're having a meeting. Will there be screens there so we can have John Seely Brown in his Palo Alto—

Brown: Workscape.

LK: Yeah, and then someone in Bangor, Maine, on another screen, and everyone else at the table in a conference room someplace else?

Brown: Every reasonably equipped conference room will have at least those capabilities. You want to blur the distinction between who's physically in the conference room and who's virtually in the conference room. This is what I've been talking about: blurring the boundaries between physical space and cyberspace.

LK: The move toward a workscape will begin with a small business or a large corporation?

Brown: It could go a number of ways. A large corporation has the constant need to attract publicity, so they may be the first to change. On the other hand, if you look at the industry that does construction or the industry that makes movies, both are already well out in front in terms of being able to bring vast collections of tiny companies and teams together for brief moments to get the job done. That hints at a new kind of workscape. You will see, because of digital form and the Internet, the movie industry come together in virtual space as opposed to just physical space. So you may find an industry as opposed to just a firm doing it. The third possibility is a state. I've been thinking how California could actually experiment with building a new kind of fabric that brings commerce and learning together in this virtual space. There could be huge webs of mom-and-pop shops coming together to get products done but the same thing could be done for a university. Soon you will see these webs serving the dual purpose of work and learning, and you might see a state putting in the infrastructure that allows new ways to work and learn. We're twenty years away from the third possibility.

LK: Companies now are doing a lot of *outsourcing* such as hiring an independent contractor to do the payroll rather than have someone on staff doing it. Is security a concern?

Brown: It already is a concern, and one of the challenges we face in the cyberspace age is how to really create a moderate sense of security. You'll be seeing some major progress within the next few years on this. It is a false hope to believe computer systems can be totally secure because it has as much to do with social-political practices as it does with technological practices.

LK: So there's going to be problems?

Brown: There are always going to be problems, and especially if we don't address the social side of work and if we don't live in a civil society and if we don't have some moderate amount of trust. Work without trust is always going to be highly inefficient and without a technical solution.

LK: Will the workscape become more family-friendly?

Brown: Absolutely. Remember, we are blurring the boundaries between living, working, and learning, so it stands to reason we will blur how families impinge on the workscape itself. A lot of times you may be working with a lot of your family members around you or in your *periphery*. You may find kids in the workscape. When you engage in knowledge-work you aren't going to have dangerous equipment around, so many of the reasons for barring families from being around the workscape or workplace are no longer quite so valid.

LK: Will there be opportunities for employees to get together in the workscape?

Brown: I think as businesses go beyond the pure business process (engineering craze), they'll begin to realize knowledge-work gets done in a social fabric, and as much attention has to be paid for the social fabric as is paid to the business processes which structure the work. You will see increased attention to an understanding of trust and of each other, and a willingness to listen to highly diverse points of view. We need to find ways to enrich the social fabric of work as opposed to just the *syntactical* business processes of work. We are going to blur the distinctions of what we think of as work, what we think of as learning, what we think of as entertainment, and what we think of as living. You are going to see yourself doing several things simultaneously where you can see a movie, have a conversation, and then have a flash about how to finish the painting. The distinction of when we had an idea and where it came from will blur.

LK: And one way to enrich the social fabric of work is how?

Brown: Provide more opportunities to have informal conversations in meetings and to find ways to honor the multiple points of view that will be brought forth in trying to understand something. As we look at the chaos around us, we recognize that no one person is an expert all the time. You will find the value of cultural, intellectual, gender diversity is going to play out in very major ways as we move forward. Again, this is a way to *triangulate* on the best possible interpretation of something in that particular moment.

LK: If I call an off—Wait, if I call a workscape will a human being answer or will it be one of those voice mail systems where I punch "1" to talk to somebody?

Brown: In calling other businesses you will encounter more intelligent but nevertheless automated voice dispatch systems. On the other hand, in the workscape of your colleagues (the community or practice that you happen to be a part of) there will be new technology to enhance your awareness of "the periphery." In other words, you'll know what's happening in everyone else's workspace that you are connected with. This, then, allows you to have a sense of whether that person is in or is busy, so you'll have the ability to pick the right time to place a call.

LK: And this is done by my calling them first and going through this with them?

Brown: No. What you'll probably find is going through some kind of multicast technology on the Internet and you'll have an increased awareness of where others are at that moment and what others are doing. It may be, for example, a low-quality video stamp that says, "Yes, he's in the office," or "No, she's not in the office," so you know whether or not to place a call.

LK: You paint a picture of efficiency.

Brown: Well, it's effective not just efficient. What we're looking at is how to decrease the deadtime when you're doing useless work, like trying to find a document you created a week ago. And how to increase the "live time" when you actually are creating value in the workplace, creating more time to think creatively, more time to actually collaborate with each other. Here at the Palo Alto Research Center, one of the goals is to design technology that is sufficiently powerful that it can get the hell out of the way and just basically disappear. We're looking at bringing calmness back to the office so that the things which really matter are the things you are focusing on, not the technology you are using. We need technology that fits the way an old shoe fits: so perfectly that you never rub up against it and it enables you to focus on the work rather than finding the right document finding the right format, being able to scribble the right kinds of comments for the right kind of person, shipping them off, remembering addresses, and all of that. It will disappear.

LK: We are going through this now because the technology is still new, correct?

Brown: In part yes, but also because the vendors of the technology add more features to the technology. The easiest thing in the world is to say, "I've added more memory, so I can add twenty-five new features." I'd like to say if you add twenty-five new ones, take fifty old ones away. Adding feature after feature requires no taste. It requires taste to step back and say, "What are the minimal features that are needed that can be crafted by the user on the fly?"

LK: What worries you?

Brown: In the twenty-first century we're going to find change even more than it's happening now. This means the competitive edge of the individual, the competitive edge of an organization, actually turns on one's ability to learn. So what worries me is we're not putting enough attention on creating a learning culture. And that's the learning culture in the workscape, at home, and in the schools. So I think if you don't feel comfortable picking up fundamentally new skills every three to five years you're going to be in bad shape. That may cause an increase between the haves and the have-nots which will be determined primarily on whether you have a willingness or even an interest in learning. I think learning is quite different from being educated because if you look at most of us now many years out of college, what we've learned, we've learned from and with each other. Learning is fundamentally social. We learn in groups, from groups, in relationships, from relationships, and so on and so forth. I'll guess that twenty-five years from now we're not going to be talking about organizational architectures, but rather learning architectures. Corporations are going to have to think primarily in terms of how to redraft the physical spaces, the social spaces, and the informational spaces together in a way that enhances our employees and ourselves to engage in learning.

LK: Will fewer people be expected to do more work, or might we see more people in the workscape?

Brown: My guess is you will see more people and they will be engaged in more creative activities that actually create content that gets consumed in leisure as well as in business. An example is Web sites. There are new ones coming on and there will be so many that a new kind of media will be formed that will employ huge numbers of people who are artistically inclined. There will be new jobs which blend the artistic component with the content component. Here at PARC (Palo Alto Research Center), I'm thinking about giving someone this job title: knowledge artist. I'm not sure what it means yet but it brings the artistic sensibilities to try to get to the essence of what some complex knowledge domain is about. We have a hard time getting something that is wonderfully simple but actually captures and honors the complexities of the idea. Picasso could take a pencil and sketch three lines and capture the full-blooded wonder of some person's personality. That's what I want in a knowledge artist. We're going to need more skills like that.

LK: What other job titles will we have in the next century?

Brown: Knowledge architect. Organizational architect who can design structures that enable productive, effective work to happen. We have sacrificed creativity in the push for efficiency, and efficiency is what mattered most in the old
economy. In the new economy we are walking into, creating new rules of the
game is going to be very important. I see it in the shift from making products to
making sense. We are going to find more work in the interpretive role: How do
you make sense out of what is going on? You're doing this right now because
you hear my words and try to figure out what needs to be explained further,
which becomes the next question. You are engaged in sense-making.

LK: The next question is more of an observation than a sentence: You use the
words "blend" and "blur" a lot.

Brown: We have tended to see the world broken up into categories that actually aren't going to help us make sense out of where the world is going, so those
categories are going to have to change or we're always going to be confused
about what is going on. We have to be freer to explore and to think out of the
box. The value of thinking out of the box is going to be increasingly important
as we try to gain competitive edges.

LK: In this century we were thinking within the box?

Brown: We were thinking about constant improvement within the box, and
now we have to worry about effectiveness out of the box.

LK: Because effectiveness out of the box will eventually come back and change
what's in the box?

Brown: Yes.

LK: I don't even know what I just said.

Brown: It's a good metaphor.

LK: To be a good boss in the next century, what will someone have to bring to
the table?

Brown: There are two critical things a boss has to do: (1) be incredibly good at
listening and listen to what is not being said as much as to what is being said,
and (2) ensure that an open and honest communication is actually taking
place. The boss has to communicate with clarity and simplicity without sacrific-
ing the authenticity or the idea.

LK: Will future bosses have to be different than they are now?

Brown: Yes. The boss has to be very skilled at both learning and unlearning. We
have to be willing to challenge our own background assumptions and be capable of giving them up when they don't do the work they used to do. That requires the capability of learning and unlearning, and it's a terrifying thing for
most of us. We tend to hear things over and over again in the same way and we
get stuck in our own "box," if you will. We need to unlearn the assumptions in
that box to see the world afresh.

LK: What's going to happen to paper?

Brown: I don't believe the paperless office will happen anytime in our collective lifetimes. Clutter will still be around, but there are certain forms of paper that will go away. For example, I'm sure you won't find reference books any longer in paper form, you may find novels and you'll find new kinds of paper that are reusable. That is, the paper—we call it digital paper—can be first printed on with a special and very inexpensive new kind of printer or stylus and then, once you're done reading it and marking it up, you drop it into the input-output basket I was talking about earlier and—

LK: Let me guess, it comes out blank?

Brown: It will suck all the annotations off of it and add those annotations to the original digital document as a new layer of information and then erase the paper for immediate reuse.

LK: So you can use the same sheet of paper for a year or something?

Brown: Yes.

LK: One more question: Will we still lift pens from our office?

Brown: Workscape. Yes.

• •

Vocabulary

As you think about this essay, these definitions may be helpful to you:
1. **manifold**   a whole that unites diverse features; complex
2. **outsourcing**   the practice of purchasing goods or services from an exterior provider; for example, a company may contract with an exterior provider for (or "outsource") the task of cleaning the workspaces at night.
3. **periphery**   a boundary line
4. **syntactical**   a connected or orderly system
5. **triangulate**   a method (used in making maps) that finds an area or location by taking several simultaneous measurements from different perspectives

Discussion Questions

1. Why does John Seely Brown use the term "workscape" instead of "office" for describing the 21st century workplace? What does he mean by "meeting capture tools"?
2. What is "IP addressable," and how will it be different from what we use now?

3. How will the global economy affect the type of staff needed in the new workscape?
4. How might the new workscape affect the family?
5. How does the author describe a "learning culture," and why is it so important? What is a "knowledge artist," and how could you become one?

 ## How Can These Ideas Apply to You?

1. What can you do during your college years to prepare for the new workplace that Brown describes?
2. Do you think you will enjoy working in this new workscape? Why or why not?
3. Do you agree with Brown that the new workscape will be more family-friendly? How will it be different from when you were growing up?
4. Brown says you will need to acquire new skills every three to five years if you are to remain competitive. How would you assess your openness and ability to learn new skills at this point in your life?
5. Do you believe, as Brown does, that "most real work happens collaboratively"? If so, what does this imply for your educators?
6. Brown says, "Adding feature after feature requires no taste." What does he mean by "taste"? How can you develop it in yourself?

Virtual Legality: An Overview of Your Rights and Responsibilities in Cyberspace

Steven J. McDonald

Steven McDonald is an associate legal counsel in the Office of Legal Affairs at The Ohio State University. In this essay he discusses legal implications important to those who use the Internet. His focus is especially on college students.

• • • • • • • • • • • • • • • • •

The Internet is a powerful and revolutionary tool for communication—powerful in its ability to reach a global audience and revolutionary in its accessibility to those who formerly were only at the receiving end of mass communications. With access to the Internet, *anyone,* even a preschool child, can now effectively be an international publisher and broadcaster. By posting to Usenet or establishing a web page, for example, an Internet user can speak to a larger and wider audience than does the *New York Times,* NBC or National Public Radio. Many Internet users, however, do not realize that that is what they are doing.

Not surprisingly, given these facts, the Internet also has a powerful and revolutionary potential for misuse. Such misuse is particularly prevalent on college and university campuses, where free *access* to computing resources is often mistakenly thought to be the equivalent of free *speech,* and where free speech rights are in turn often mistakenly thought to include the right to do whatever is technically possible.

The rights of academic freedom and freedom of expression do apply to the use of college and university computing resources. So, too, however, do the responsibilities and limitations associated with those rights. Thus, legitimate use of institutional computing resources does *not* extend to whatever is technically possible. In addition, while some restrictions are built into the institution's computer operating systems and networks, those restrictions are not the only restrictions on what is permissible. Users of college and university computing resources must abide by all applicable restrictions, whether or not they are built into the operating system or network and whether or not they can be *circumvented* by technical means. Moreover, it is not the responsibility of a college or university to prevent computer users from exceeding those restrictions; rather, it is the computer user's responsibility to know and comply with them. When you're pulled over to the side of the Information Superhighway, "I'm sorry, officer—I didn't realize I was over the speed limit" is not a valid defense.

So just what are the applicable restrictions? The same laws and policies that apply in every other context. "Cyberspace" is not a separate legal jurisdiction, and it is not exempt from the normal requirements of legal and ethical behavior within the college or university community. *A good rule of thumb to keep in mind is that conduct that would be illegal or a violation of institutional policy in the "offline" world will still be illegal or a violation of institutional policy when it occurs online.* Remember, too, that the online world is not limited to your college or university, to the state in which it is located, or even to the United States. *Computer users who engage in electronic communications with persons in other states or countries or on other systems or networks may also be subject to the laws of those other states and countries and the rules and policies of those other systems and networks.*

It is impossible to list and describe every law and policy that applies to the use of college and university computing resources and the Internet—since, by and large, they all do—but the following are some of the ones that most frequently cause problems.

Copyright

Copyright law generally gives authors, artists, composers, and other such creators the exclusive right to copy, distribute, modify, and display their works or to authorize other people to do so. Moreover, their works are protected by copyright law from the very moment that they are created—regardless of whether they are registered with the Copyright Office and regardless of whether they are marked with a copyright notice or symbol (©). That means that virtually every e-mail message, Usenet posting, web page, or other computer work you have ever created—or seen—is copyrighted. That also means that, if you are not the copyright owner of a particular e-mail message, Usenet posting, web page, or other computer work, you may not copy, distribute, modify, or display it unless:

- its copyright owner has given you permission to do so, or
- it is in the "*public domain*," or
- doing so would constitute "fair use," or
- you have an "implied license" to do so.

If none of these exceptions applies, your use of the work constitutes copyright infringement, and you could be liable for as much as $100,000 in damages for each use. In addition, if you reproduce or distribute copies of a copyrighted work having a total retail value of at least $1,000 (which could include, for example, posting a $50 software program on a web page or newsgroup from which it is downloaded 20 times), your action may also be criminal, even if you do it for free.

It's usually easy to tell whether you have permission to make a particular use of a work: The copyright owner will have told you so expressly, either in writing or orally. However, it is not always so easy to tell whether the work is in the public domain or whether what you want to do constitutes fair use or is covered by an implied license.

Placing a work on the Internet is not the same thing as granting that work to the public domain. Generally speaking, a work found on the Internet, like a work found anywhere else, is in the public domain only if (a) its creator has expressly disclaimed any copyright interest in the work, or (b) it was created by the federal government, or (c) it is very old. Unfortunately, how old a particular work must be to be "in the public domain" depends in part upon when the work was created, in part upon whether and when it was formally published, in part upon whether and when its creator died, and in part on still other factors. Consequently, there is no one specific cutoff date that you can use for all works to determine whether or not they are in the public domain. As a rule of thumb, however, works that were created *and published* before 1923 are now in the public domain.... Works that have never been published *might* be in the public domain, but if you don't know for sure, it is best to assume that they are not.

In very general terms, a particular use of a work is considered "fair use" if it involves only a relatively small portion of the work, is for educational or other noncommercial purposes, and is unlikely to interfere with the copyright owner's ability to market the original work. A classic example is quoting a few sentences or paragraphs of a book in a class paper. Other uses may also be fair, but it is almost never fair to use an entire work, and it is not enough that you aren't charging anyone for your particular use. It also is not enough simply to cite your source (though it may be *plagiarism* if you don't).

An implied license may exist if the copyright owner has acted in such a way that it is reasonable for you to assume that you may make a particular use. For example, if you are the moderator of a mailing list and someone sends you a message for that list, it's reasonable to assume that you may post the message to the list, even if its author didn't expressly say that you may do so. The copyright owner can always "revoke" an implied license, however, simply by saying that further use is prohibited.

In addition, facts and ideas cannot be copyrighted. Copyright law protects only the expression of the creator's idea—the specific words or notes or brushstrokes or computer code that the creator used—and not the underlying idea itself. Thus, for example, it is not copyright infringement to state in a history paper that the Declaration of Independence was actually signed on August 2, 1776, or to argue in an English paper that Francis Bacon is the real author of Shakespeare's plays, even though someone else has already done so, as long as you use your own words. (Again, however, if you don't cite your sources, it may still be plagiarism even if you paraphrase.)

Exactly how copyright law applies to the Internet is still not entirely clear, but there are some rules of thumb:

- You *may* look at another person's web page, even though your computer makes a temporary copy when you do so, but you may not redistribute it or incorporate it into your own web page without permission, except as fair use may allow.

- You *probably may* quote all or part of another person's Usenet or listserv message in your response to that message, unless the original message says that copying is prohibited.
- You *probably may not* copy and redistribute a private e-mail message you have received without the author's permission, except as fair use may allow.
- You *probably may* print out a single copy of a web page or of a Usenet, listserv, or private e-mail message for your own, personal, noncommercial use.
- You *may not* post another person's book, article, graphic, image, music, or other such material on your web page or use them in your Usenet, listserv, or private e-mail messages without permission, except as fair use may allow.
- You *may not* download materials from Lexis-Nexis, the Clarinet news service, or other such services and copy or redistribute them without permission, unless the applicable license agreement expressly permits you to do so or unless your particular use would constitute fair use.
- You *may not* copy or redistribute software without permission, unless the applicable license agreement expressly permits you to do so.

Libel

Libel is the "publication" of a false statement of fact that harms another person's reputation. For example, it is libel to say that "John beat up his roommate" or "Mary is a thief" if these statements are not true. If a statement doesn't harm the other person's reputation—for example, "Joe got an 'A' on the test"—it is not libel even if it's false. In addition, a statement of pure opinion—for example, "I don't like John"—cannot be libelous. But you cannot turn a statement of fact into an opinion simply by adding "I think" or "in my opinion" to it. "IMHO [In my honest opinion], John beat up his roommate" is still libelous if John didn't beat up his roommate. If you honestly believed that what you said was true, however, you *might* not be liable if it later turns out that you were wrong.

A libel is "published" whenever it is communicated to a third person. In other words, if you say "Mary is a thief" to anyone other than Mary, you have "published" that libel. That means that almost anything you post or send on the Internet, except an e-mail that you send *only to the person about whom you are talking,* is "published" for purposes of libel law.

A person who has been libeled can sue for whatever damages are caused by the publication of the libel. Since a libel on the Internet could potentially reach millions of people, the damages could be quite large.

A good rule of thumb to follow: If you would be upset if someone else made the same statement about you, think carefully before you send or post that statement to the Internet, because it might be libelous.

Invasion of Privacy

There are a number of different laws that protect the "right to privacy" in a number of different ways. For example, under the Electronic Communications Privacy Act, which is a federal statute, it generally is a crime to intercept someone else's private e-mail message or to look into someone else's private computer account without appropriate authorization. The fact that you may have the technical ability to do so, or that the other person may not have properly safeguarded his or her account, does not mean that you have authorization. If you don't know for sure whether you have authorization, you probably don't.

Invasion of privacy, like libel, is also a "*tort*," which means that you can also be sued for monetary damages. In addition to the sorts of things prohibited by the Electronic Communications Privacy Act, it can be an invasion of privacy to disclose intensely personal information about another person that that person has chosen not to make public and that the public has no legitimate need or reason to know: for example, the fact that someone has AIDS, if he or she has not revealed that information publicly. Unlike with libel, a statement can be an invasion of privacy even if it is true.

Obscenity, Child Pornography, and "Indecency"

Under both state and federal law, it is a crime to publish, sell, distribute, display, or, in some cases, merely possess obscene materials or child pornography. These laws also apply equally to the Internet, and a number of people have been prosecuted and convicted for violating them in that context.

The line between what is obscene and what is not is hard to draw with any precision—as one Supreme Court Justice said, "I could never succeed in intelligibly" defining obscenity, "[b]ut I know it when I see it"—but the term basically means hardcore pornography that has no literary, artistic, political, or other socially redeeming value. One reason that it is so hard to define obscenity is that it depends in part on local community standards; what is considered obscene in one community may not be considered obscene in another. That makes it particularly difficult to determine whether materials on the Internet are obscene, since such materials are, in a sense, everywhere, and it is therefore not enough that the materials are legal wherever you are. In one case, the operators of a bulletin board service in California posted materials that were not considered obscene there, but [they] were convicted of violating the obscenity statutes in Tennessee when the materials were downloaded there.

Child pornography is the visual depiction of minors engaged in sexually explicit activity. Unlike obscenity, child pornography is illegal regardless of whether it has any literary, artistic, political, or other socially redeeming value.

Sexually oriented materials that do not constitute either obscenity or child pornography generally are legal. Still, it is illegal in most cases to provide such materials to minors, and displaying or sending such materials to people who do not wish to see them may be a violation of your college or university's sexual harassment policy.

"Hacking," "Cracking," and Similar Activities

Under the federal Computer Fraud and Abuse Act, and under a variety of similar other state and federal statutes, it can also be a crime to access or use a computer without authorization, to alter data in a computer without authorization, to transmit computer viruses and "worms" over computer networks, to conduct "e-mail bombing," and to engage in other such activities. Engaging in such activities can also make you liable for monetary damages to any person who is harmed by your activities. Again, the fact that you may have the technical ability to do any of these things, or that another computer owner may not have properly safeguarded his or her computer, does not mean that you have authorization. If you don't know for sure whether you have authorization, you probably don't.

Institutional Policies

Use of college and university computing resources is also normally subject to the institution's rules and regulations—for example, its code of student conduct, policy on academic misconduct, sexual harassment policy, and all other generally applicable institutional policies. In addition, institutional computer use policies often contain the following types of additional, specific prohibitions:

- Institutional computer accounts and passwords may not, under any circumstances, be shared with, or used by, persons other than those to whom they have been assigned by the institution—even family and friends. Users are responsible for all use of their accounts.
- Users must limit their use of institutional computing resources so as not to consume an unreasonable amount of those resources or to interfere with the activity of other users.
- Institutional computing resources are intended for institution-related use and therefore may not be used for personal commercial or business purposes or for other personal gain. Personal use of institutional computing resources for *other* purposes may be permitted when it does not consume a significant amount of those resources, does not interfere with the performance of the user's job or other institutional responsibilities, and is otherwise in compliance with institutional policies.
- Users of institutional computing resources may not state or imply that they are speaking on behalf of the institution and may not use institutional trademarks and logos in connection with their use of those resources without specific authorization to do so.

For Further Information

If you have questions about the legality of your specific use of institutional computing resources, it is best to ask before proceeding. *The resolution of specific legal issues requires an analysis of all the facts and circumstances; the general guidelines in this document do not constitute, and should not be relied upon as, specific legal advice.* You may be able to get general advice (but, again, not specific legal advice) from your academic advisor, from computer lab site managers, or from your institution's computer help desk.

In addition, you can find more information on these and related topics at the following web sites:

- "Cyberspace Law for Non-Lawyers," which is located at:
  http://www.ssrn.com/update/lsn/cyberspace/csl-lessons.html

- "Law and the Web," which is located at:
  http://www.Cnet.com/Content/Features/Dlife/Law/index.html
- "10 Big Myths About Copyright Explained," which is located at:
  http://www.clari.net/brad/copymyths.html
- "Soundbyting: Music on the Internet," which is located at:
  http://www.soundbyting,com

Reprinted by permission of The Ohio State University Office of Legal Affairs.

 # Vocabulary

As you think about this essay, these definitions may be helpful to you:
1. **circumvent**   to get around, evade
2. **public domain**   the legal realm embracing property that belongs to the community at large
3. **plagiarism**   to steal or pass off words or ideas of another as one's own
4. **libel**   defamation of a person by written or presentational means
5. **tort**   a wrongful act that may lead to legal action

 # Discussion Questions

1. Why, according to the author, does the Internet have such potential for misuse?
2. How does the author suggest you can judge what is legal or illegal in cyberspace?
3. How do copyright laws affect the Internet?
4. Why is your online "right to privacy" so important?
5. Why are "hacking," "cracking," and similar activities illegal?

 # How Can These Ideas Apply to You?

1. What legal responsibilities have you been unaware of when using cyberspace in the past?
2. How can copyright laws affect how you use the Internet?
3. Can you give an example of how libel laws might affect your use of the Internet?
4. Are you concerned about your privacy when using cyberspace? What can you do to protect yourself?

The Connected Library

Clifford Stoll

Clifford Stoll, an MSNBC commentator, lecturer, and Berkeley astronomer, is the author of many best-selling books. In this essay, he describes his reactions to the changes taking place in libraries today because of automation and other technological advances.

· · · · · · · · · · · · · · · · · ·

Sandi Webb, a councilperson in Simi Valley, California, wants to close the community library system: "We need to rip out those useless bookcases, filled with outdated books that are seldom opened, and replace them with low-cost computers and CD-ROMs and high-speed Internet access lines."

Yee-haw! Computers will eliminate those pesky libraries. Get rid of them books. After the book-burning festival, let's eliminate local politicians, now that computers and telephones let us instantly vote on issues.

Alongside churches and day-care centers, libraries are about the most underfunded and underappreciated of our society's institutions. The field receives so little respect that library schools are changing their names to "schools of information management." Apparently embarrassed by their lack of status, many librarians now call themselves information specialists.

Of course, practically every person is an information specialist. A baker specializes in information about breads and cakes. A historian is certainly an information specialist. So is a doctor. Taxicab drivers, too. "Information specialist" is a meaningless, generic title.

I may not know what an information specialist does, but I sure know what a librarian oughta do. For two millennia, they've been stewards of books, charged with organizing, cataloging, preserving, and making books available. Our *cornucopia* of historical appreciation, technological progress, and cultural awareness isn't the result of a team of information specialists; rather it's due to centuries of rarely thanked librarians.

Yet as librarians turn away from their heritage and toward computers, our book collections become less well preserved, less organized, and less available. Their name change symbolizes a transformation of librarians from stewards of our cultural endowment to professional information handlers. They're now at home answering e-mail, reading Internet mailing lists, and surfing the Web. Can't blame them: I'd rather check out some Usenet scuttlebutt than deal with a confused patron at the reference desk.

Libraries, of course, are riding the information age bandwagon. With great fanfare, the University of California opened their version of the library of the future, a brand-new library facility. The official reason for moving the library was seismic strengthening—Berkeley's in earthquake territory and someone worried about books falling off shelves. But pretty quickly, the library reconstruction got hijacked by library automation folks. These are information management types—typically with degrees in computer science—who feel they know more about how libraries should be run than librarians.

The old friendly library of stacks and study tables morphed into an information-age *monolith*, sprouting hundreds of computers. A cumbersome spiral staircase showcases the importance of appearance over function. It's admired by administrators, architects, and technologists. Of course—they don't have to use it.

To make room for the computers and spiral staircase, half the books were shipped ten miles off campus, into a book warehouse. The books available at the actual library are just an echo of the entire collection. Sandi Webb's wishes have come true: Any book that hasn't been checked out in a year gets warehoused. Thus, there's a complete set of Tom Clancy novels on the shelf, but if you're searching for anything over twenty years old, your book has to be hauled in on tomorrow's bus.

And don't think that you can go to the warehouse to read. You'll discover that you can't browse the shelves—books aren't filed by subject, title, or author. They're warehoused by size. Perfect for a computer call system. Impossible for the researcher.

Ever hear of a bookshelf that has stopped working? I've witnessed it. To save space, my library put its shelves on rollers, called compact shelving. To get a book, you turn a wheel and roll several bookshelves, in order to open up an aisle to reach your volume. Nice idea, so long as the mechanism works. When a wheel gets jammed, you can't move the shelves, so your book's out of reach. If several people want books, they wait in line for an aisle to open up. Wait in an aisle next to a bookshelf and nobody can get to any other shelf. It's a storage system designed to provide only the book you're hunting for. Nothing else.

Library administrators love compact shelving; open shelves take up more space than rolling bookcases. Combined with offsite warehousing of books, research libraries are becoming systems which will deliver only the book which you request ... a fiendish way to prevent both browsing and serendipitous research.

Of course, the big library improvement is universal Internet availability. Not just dozens of workstations. My university's library of the future features four Ethernet ports at every table. Sprouting from some study carrels are eight computer ports and sixteen power outlets. Every work space has a high-speed link to the Internet.

These connections let you hook up your laptop computer to the Internet. Of course, you have to supply the computer, cable, software, and account. That's never a problem for the information specialists who'll happily give you a tour.

Who's using all those library ports? At the University of California library, almost nobody. Walking past carrels and tables, I've seen about five students linking their laptops to the network. Practically everyone at the library is reading books. Curiously, all of the library's public terminals are in use—often by students playing Internet games—but the hundreds of computer connections remain unused.

Well, not quite unused. About half of the library Ethernet ports have been broken. Some outlets have pencils stuffed into them. Others show broken faceplates or have been pried apart. Many connectors are missing, leaving a rectangular hole and a colorful bouquet of Class-V communications wires.

Maybe I'm seeing the effect of bored students, curious to see how connectors work. Maybe campus lowlifes infest the library, seeking to vandalize pricey computer networks. Perhaps it's the result of a conspiracy of *Luddite* librarians who object to technology pushing aside their jobs.

Whatever the explanation, so far the electronically wired library has been a dud for students, researchers, and librarians. The only ones who really celebrate this boondoggle are the library automation promoters. They, of course, call it a model for future libraries.

Once, the University of California's library ranked second only to Harvard. But since the library renovation and computerization, the Association of Research Libraries dropped its ranking from second to fifth place. Local librarians feel it will drop another few notches next year, since it is no longer adding as many books as it once did. Sad news for library automation hucksters: College ratings bureaus take into account such outmoded ideas as how many books a library has, how available they are, and the staffing of the library. They don't count unused Ethernet ports.

What about public libraries? Worried that I was just considering the needs of researchers, I conducted a spur of-the-moment, utterly unsystematic survey in Berkeley. I stood on a street corner and asked a dozen passersby, "What do you want in a public library?"

Fully half of those questioned replied, "I don't have any money to give you," and kept walking.

Of the half dozen who took me seriously, the most common answer was "I want books in the library. Lots of books." A few asked for magazines, newspapers, and journals. Several insisted on a good librarian. Evening hours. A harried mom wanted Saturday morning storytelling. Nobody mentioned . . . CD-ROMs, multimedia software, and network connections. Which is odd, given that these are expensive and quickly become obsolete. And, at least in my limited survey, hardly in demand.

According to a survey in *School Library Journal*, 1994 school expenditures on audiovisual and computer equipment roughly equaled book costs . . . each about five thousand dollars. By 1998, computers were way ahead of books.

For some reason, librarians—oops, I mean information specialists—feel that their library isn't doing a good job unless it has plenty of electronic *gizmos* and a flashy Web site. American Library Association conferences hold dozens of sessions on how to make library Web pages. Does this serve library patrons? Local communities? Or does it mainly advertise to distant Internet surfers, who never visit the library and only rarely read books?

Moreover, as librarians get replaced by techno-literate infospecs, you'll find fewer helpful faces behind the library counter. Rhonda Neagle is a library media specialist and technology facilitator at Logan High School in New Haven, California. "It's only the rare moment in any day when I'm on the floor helping kids," she reports. The rest of the time, she's troubleshooting laser printers and VCRs, serving on committees, and overseeing networks, according to the June 1997 *Electronic Learning* magazine.

Rapid *obsolescence* hits libraries hard. Twenty-five years ago, Fort Worth installed the newest and most expensive computers in their library. The modern replacements cost three million dollars, so they dipped into their endowment. A decade from now, there will be no nest egg to replace the obsolete 1997 computers.

Compare a well-cataloged collection of books, magazines, and newspapers with two dozen high-tech Internet workstations, complete with multimedia software. Which will last longer? Which better serves a neighborhood of children, young adults, adults, and elderly? Which promotes reading, study, and reflection? Which is more likely to be seen as a toy? Which will better preserve our heritage and foster a sense of scholarship and friendship?

Library bureaucrats adopt a gee-whiz attitude toward the Internet: "Libraries must develop a new paradigm," writes Brown University library administrator Brian Hawkins. He wants more computers, more networks, and fewer books.

Meanwhile, librarians politely yawn at traditional library tasks, such as cataloging works, storing books, and staffing reference desks. Berkeley's library committee seeks a "fundamental shift in emphasis from being a warehouse to becoming a gateway for information." Translation: Give 'em computers and get rid of books.

The result of this technolust is that libraries—public and private—are hiring lots of computer specialists. Meanwhile, they're laying off librarians. They're spending money on new databases, but not new books. There's no librarian to help you figure out the thousands of available databases. Gateway to information, indeed.

It's odd to read articles in *Forbes* and *Fortune* on how information is the career of the future. Yet librarians, who have taken care of information for millennia, can't find jobs.

During the 1960s, libraries spent zillions on what was then new media: 16mm films, phonograph records, and filmstrips. Then, as now, the stuff was expensive, quickly went out of date, and [was] tough to archive. What happened to all those phonograph records purchased by your library in 1965?

Today, the closest thing we have to a digital archive medium is the CD-ROM. Yet it has a life span of thirty to fifty years. Within a few decades, newer devices will make CD-ROM readers obsolete. And when manufacturers no longer build reading devices, libraries won't be able to access their collection of CD-ROMs. They'll wind up in a landfill. But a book? It's universally accessible, easily stored, immediately readable, completely portable. Thousands of years have demonstrated the book's importance and permanence.

And that's what the high-tech library reformers are out to gut. As librarians get laid off, branches run understaffed. They're open perhaps one or two nights a week. They don't subscribe to out-of-town papers. They quietly cancel story hours. Instead of a librarian helping you look up a book, you're pointed to a computer.

Our technologists are working to change our libraries into sterile information warehouses, filled with workstations yet devoid of books. What'll happen when the Internet is universally available and nobody needs to visit the library to search for information? Will libraries close up because trendy "information gateway" grants aren't available and they no longer have any books?

I can't think of a more effective way to eliminate libraries. Burning books won't work—centuries of fanatics, censors, and dictators have tried and failed. And you can't close down libraries by political fiat: They're far too popular in neighborhoods.

No, the best way to gut our libraries is to ship the books off to distant warehouses, supplant librarians with generic information specialists, and replace bookshelves with gleaming computer workstations. Donate computers and software which will quickly become obsolete. Provide patrons with CD-ROMs and high-speed Internet ports. Encourage kids to surf the Web rather than read books. Count hits on your Web page instead of visitors to the stacks. Pretty soon, traffic to the stacks will evaporate and the library will fossilize.

In the struggle for liberty and literacy, books and libraries are the best weapons we've got. Use them. Appreciate them. Support them.

From *High Tech Heretic* by Clifford Stoll, © 1999 by Clifford Stoll. Used by permission of Doubleday, a division of Random House, Inc.

Vocabulary

As you think about this essay, these definitions may be helpful to you:
1. **cornucopia**   a symbol of abundance
2. **monolith**   an organized whole that acts as a unified powerful force
3. **Luddite**   someone who fights technological change
4. **gizmos**   gadgets
5. **obsolescence**   the process of going out of use or losing usefulness

Discussion Questions

1. What do you think of the writing style the author uses to share his view of the current direction of libraries?
2. What does the author claim is happening to our library systems in general?

3. The author is assessing his library system based on his need for research functions. Are there other functions for which the automated library might be more useful and effective?
4. Upon what does the author base his opinion about the obsolescence of tomorrow's libraries?

 How Can These Ideas Apply to You?

1. Do you agree with the author about the changing role of librarians from "stewards of culture" to "professional information handlers"? Why or why not?
2. Does the author's description of the changes in his university's library in any way reflect yours? If so, in what ways?
3. When you are researching a paper, do you prefer to use books as source material or the Internet? Why?

Technology Eliminating Conversation

Ellen Goodman

Ellen Goodman, a columnist whose essays regularly appear in more than 200 newspapers across the country, began her journalistic career as a reporter for *Newsweek* and the *Detroit Free Press,* then joined the *Boston Globe.* She has won a Pulitzer Prize for distinguished commentary and is the author of several books. In this essay she describes her initiation into new telephone technology and how it has affected face-to-face conversation.

W e are at lunch when my friend leans over the table to share his latest encounter with telephone technology.

It all began with a voice mail message, which wasn't in itself so startling. But my friend was at his desk when the phone didn't ring. A colleague, it seems, had learned how to dial directly into voice mail—avoiding the middleman, or middle ear, entirely.

Was my friend, a man who *parses* moral dilemmas for a living, insulted that this caller didn't want to speak to the real, live and available him? Were either of us aghast at some new techno-wrinkle of rudeness? Appalled by the state of the art of message-dropping?

No, we were delighted, curious, envious. How on Earth did he do that?

I am old enough to remember black rotary phones, the Model T of this technology. I remember when the telephone was a beloved instrument of conversation. Furthermore, I was raised to believe in courtesy as one of the cardinal virtues.

But we are in the middle of a communications revolution that feels increasingly like guerrilla warfare. Everywhere you turn in this revolution, machines are pointed at you. Today, anyone near a phone can end up feeling like the target of snipers.

Half a dozen years ago when I read that Martha Stewart had something like six or seven voice mail numbers, I was bug-eyed in astonishment. Now I have three voice mails, three e-mails, three fax machines all collecting messages in assorted buildings that are nowhere nearly as well decorated as Martha's, but you get the point.

To understand how the world has changed, think back to the warm and fuzzy telephone ads that once encouraged us to reach out and touch someone. Compare that to my favorite telephone ad of this season. It features Paul Revere in his full midnight ride *regalia* trying to reach John Adams, who is of course screening his calls: "John, John, this is Paul. Pick up. It's important."

In this revolutionary atmosphere, it isn't a new communications weapon that is lusted over by patriots seeking their personal freedom. It's an anti-communications weapon.

We want technology that enhances our ability to not talk to people. We want a personal Star Wars defense system to screen and shoot down, avert and disarm the incoming missives. We long for the ability to be out of touch.

This has created a whole new etiquette called "etiquette be damned." The dirty little secret of corporate America is the number of people for whom phone tag is actually dodge ball. All over the various midtowns of our country, people wait to return calls until they are pretty sure the other person is at lunch. Who hasn't picked up a phone to have a startled caller exhale: "Oh, I just wanted to leave a message"?

Of course, the invasion of the dinner snatchers has created an additional wrinkle. People who know the words to "Solidarity Forever" and are generally sympathetic to the plight of the new working class now greet marketing callers by snarling, "Why don't you give me your home number since you have mine?"

This is now leading to a high-tech arms race, a kind of mutually assured destruction. First you pay to put a phone in your house-office-car. Now you can also pay to keep the calls out.

Just last month, Ameritech announced a service to let customers reject the sort of unwanted telephone calls that come from telemarketers. "Customers are screaming for this," said the company's chief executive officer.

We are also "screaming" for what I would call, in *oxymoronic* fashion, one-way conversations. The linguistic types call this *asynchronous* talk. In that sense the phone is becoming more and more like e-mail. One person leaves a message for the other who leaves a message—look ma, no hands. It's like playing virtual tennis.

But such is the reality of modern life. All the advances have *ratcheted* up the number of "exchanges" we're expected to make until our own circuits are overloaded. Efficiency trumps courtesy. We don't just talk, we use the phone as a drop-off center.

Remember Alexander Graham Bell's first words over the newfangled phone? "Mr. Watson, come here, I want you." What would he say today? "Watson old boy, when you get a minute, have your voice mail call my voice mail."

● ● ● ● ● ● ● ● ● ● ● ● ● ● ● ● ● ● ● ●

Vocabulary

As you think about this essay, these definitions may be helpful to you:
1. **parses**   resolves component parts of speech and describes them grammatically

2. **regalia**   special dress, generally very formal, like an Admiral's best uniform or a priest's robes for conducting a high mass
3. **oxymoron**   a figure of speech that combines apparently contradictory or incongruous ideas
4. **asynchronous**   happening at different times
5. **ratcheted**   changed by stages

 ## Discussion Questions

1. How does Ellen Goodman compare her current involvement with technology with her past experiences?
2. What is the "new etiquette" associated with increased telephone technology, according to the author?
3. What does the author mean by "efficiency trumps courtesy"?

 ## How Can These Ideas Apply to You?

1. Have you ever felt frustration over telephone technology described by Goodwin? Under what circumstances?
2. Do you agree that technology is eliminating conversation? Why or why not?

UNIT SUMMARY

The readings in this unit have covered a wide variety of topics and ideas about technology and how it is changing our school, work, and personal lives.

Summary Questions

1. When you enter your campus library, do you encounter the situations that Stoll writes about in his essay? How are they the same? Different?
2. How has technology influenced your role as a student? How is it different from past generations' experiences?
3. What skills described in this unit's readings can you learn while in college?

Suggested Writing Assignments

1. Zuckerman says that the United States is "at a point reminiscent of its entry into the 20th century." Write an essay about the global economy and why you think it is or is not the "new future" as he claims.
2. Visualize the world 25 years from now and write an essay about how you think technology will have changed the college campus and its students' ways of learning.

Suggested Readings

1. Canter, Lawrence, and Martha Siegel. *How to Make a Fortune on the Information Superhighway: Everyone's Guerrilla Guide to Marketing on the Internet and Other On-Line Services.* New York: Harper Reference, 1994.
2. Celente, Gerald. *Trends 2000.* New York: Time Warner, 1997.
3. Levine, John, Carol Baroudi, and Margaret Levine Young. *The Internet for Dummies.* Foster City, CA: IDG Books, 1997.

What Should I Know About Careers?

According to many students, one of the main purposes of acquiring a college degree is to prepare for a career. And yet this process remains a mystery to many students. The concepts of work, job, and career, although often used interchangeably, are very different. Work can be defined as an activity that accomplishes a task. Career is a lifelong process that usually includes many jobs. Work in our culture is often synonymous with one's identity. Even small children are asked what they "want to do" when they grow up. By the time students enter college, they have some idea of general areas of study they might want to explore or pursue. How work is valued by the individual shapes the perceptions of and attitudes about the meaning of a career as the exploration and planning process is engaged.

In their book *Careerism and Intellectualism Among College Students,* Katchadourian and Boli state that there has been an increase in careerism among college students

Our road to success is currently under construction.

—Anonymous

since the late 1970s. This trend has been documented in surveys of entering first-year students who indicated that "becoming an authority in my field" and "being well off financially" were of greater importance to them than other nonwork-related goals. Students' choices of major have also changed. Whereas students wanting business degrees peaked in the late 1980s, other majors, such as the health professions and computer science, have increased.

Students entering college in the 21st century face a bewildering array of issues concerning their choice of career. Economic shifts, societal and environmental concerns, and the increased complexities of business because of new technologies create a volatile job market. Career-planning professionals encourage students to assess their personal strengths and limitations and base their choices on this knowledge rather than rely on external forces over which they have little control.

The readings in this unit represent a wide array of opinions and attitudes toward work and related issues. In a philosophical tone, Thoreau offers his views on the value of working to make a living versus working for its own rewards. Sherry and Ballard both write about searching for a job. Sherry writes about the process and Ballard provides some practical insights into how to prepare throughout the college years for the day after graduation.

Samuel Bleecker describes the "virtual" organization, in which computers and communications technology are changing old corporate structures into collaborative networks. Peggy Simonsen, also looking ahead, points out that traditional career paths no longer dominate the future of new graduates. She describes career patterns for the new century that will require different strategies for success.

All these thought-provoking ideas about work will offer a sense of how important identifying one's work values and purpose is. The college years are a time to explore, gather information, test alternatives, and finally make the first of many career decisions. Although most students approach this process from a very practical perspective, the readings in this unit should also help you think about your personal definition of work and how it will influence your ultimate career decisions.

Getting a Living

Henry David Thoreau

Henry David Thoreau was born in Concord, Massachusetts, where he worked as a
surveyor and housepainter, as well as, for a time, a helper in his father's pencil factory.
He is perhaps best known for his book *Walden,* which describes his completely self-
sustaining life at Walden Pond. In his journal at Walden Pond, he wrote: "What may a
man do and not be ashamed of it?"—a question that preoccupied him for much of
his life.

A lecture Thoreau gave in 1861 sums up his thinking about gainful work. In it he offers
his philosophy on how earning an honest and honorable living can affect living an
honorable life.

Let us consider the way in which we spend our lives.
This world is a place of business. What an infinite bustle! I am awaked almost every night by the panting of the locomotive. It interrupts my dreams.
There is no sabbath. It would be glorious to see mankind at leisure for once. It
is nothing but work, work, work. I cannot easily buy a blank book to write
thoughts in; they are commonly ruled for dollars and cents. An Irishman, seeing me *making a minute* in the fields, took it for granted that I was calculating
my wages. If a man was tossed out of a window when an infant, and so made a
cripple for life, or scared out of his wits by the Indians, it is regretted chiefly because he was thus incapacitated for—business! I think that there is nothing, not
even crime, more opposed to poetry, to philosophy, nay to life itself, than this in-
cessant business.

There is a coarse and boisterous money-making fellow in the outskirts of
our town, who is going to build a bank-wall under the hill along the edge of his
meadow. The powers have put this into his head to keep him out of mischief,
and he wishes me to spend three weeks digging there with him. The result will
be that he will perhaps get some more money to hoard and leave for his heirs
to spend foolishly. If I do this, most will commend me as an industrious and
hard-working man; but if I choose to devote myself to certain labors that yield
more real profit, though but little money, they may be inclined to look on me as
an idler. Nevertheless, as I do not need the police of meaningless labor to regulate me and do not see anything absolutely praiseworthy in this fellow's undertaking, any more than in many an enterprise of our own or foreign governments,
however amusing it may be to him or them, I prefer to finish my education at a
different school.

If a man walk in the woods for love of them half of each day, he is in danger of being regarded as a loafer; but if he spends his whole day as a *speculator,*

shearing off those woods and making earth bald before time, he is esteemed an industrious and enterprising citizen. As if a town had no interest in its forests but to cut them down!

Most men would feel insulted, if it were proposed to employ them in throwing stones over a wall, and then in throwing them back, merely that they might earn their wages. But many are no more worthily employed now. For instance: just after sunrise, one summer morning, I noticed one of my neighbors walking beside his team, which was slowly drawing a heavy *hewn* stone swung under the axle, surrounded by an atmosphere of industry—his day's work begun—his brow commenced to sweat—a reproach to all *sluggards* and idlers—pausing abreast the shoulders of his oxen, and half turning round with a flourish of his merciful whip, while they gained their length on him. And I thought, Such is the labor that the American Congress exists to protect—honest, manly toil, honest as the day is long—that makes his bread taste sweet, and keeps society sweet—which all men respect and have consecrated: one of the sacred band, doing the needful, but irksome drudgery. Indeed, I felt a slight reproach, because I observed this from the window, and was not abroad and stirring about a similar business. The day went by, and at evening I passed the yard of another neighbor, who keeps many servants and spends much money foolishly, while he adds nothing to the common stock, and there I saw the stone of the morning lying beside a whimsical structure intended to adorn this Lord Timothy Dexter's premises, and the dignity forthwith departed from the teamster's labor, in my eyes. In my opinion, the sun was to light worthier toil than this. I may add that his employer has since run off, in debt to a good part of the town, and after passing through *Chancery,* has settled somewhere else, there to become once more a patron of the arts.

The ways by which you may get money almost without exception lead downward. To have done anything by which you earned money merely is to have been truly idle or worse. If the laborer gets no more than the wages that his employer pays him, he is cheated, he cheats himself. If you would get money as a writer or lecturer, you must be popular, which is to go down perpendicularly. Those services that the community will most readily pay for, it is most disagreeable to render. You are paid for being something less than a man. The State does not commonly reward a genius any more wisely. Even the poet-laureate would rather not have to celebrate the accidents of royalty. He must be bribed with a pipe of wine; and perhaps another poet is called away from his muse to gauge that very pipe. As for my own business, even that kind of surveying which I could do with most satisfaction, my employers do not want. They would prefer that I should do my work coarsely and not too well, nay, not well enough. When I observe that there are different ways of surveying, my employer commonly asks which will give him the most land, not which is most correct. I once invented a rule for measuring cord-wood and tried to introduce it in Boston; but the measurer there told me that the sellers did not wish to have their wood measured correctly—that he was already too accurate for them, and therefore they commonly got their wood measured in Charlestown before crossing the bridge.

The aim of the laborer should be, not to get his living, to get "a good job," but to perform well a certain work; and, even in a pecuniary sense, it would be economy for a town to pay its laborers so well that they would not feel that they were working for low ends, as for a livelihood merely, but for scientific, or even moral ends. Do not hire a man who does your work for money, but him who does it for love of it.

• •

Vocabulary

As you think about this essay, these definitions may be helpful to you:
1. **making a minute**   writing brief notes
2. **speculator**   one who assumes a business risk, rather than accept small profits from safe investments
3. **hewn**   cut or shaped with a heavy instrument, usually an ax
4. **sluggard**   a habitually lazy person
5. **Chancery**   a court of equity that settles the claims of creditors

Discussion Questions

1. How does Thoreau define meaningless labor?
2. How is his perception of work different from the others in his town?
3. What is Thoreau's opinion of money?
4. What does Thoreau say about work that is performed well versus work that provides a living?
5. How does Thoreau's admonition to hire a man who works for the love of it, rather than for money, fit in today's work society?

How Can These Ideas Apply to You?

1. Do you agree with Thoreau's ideas about work? Explain.
2. If you lived in Thoreau's town and time, would your ideas about "getting a living" be different than they are today?
3. How do you think getting a living honestly and honorably is tied to living itself?
4. Do you agree with Thoreau's statement that the ways by which we earn money can only "lead downward"? Why?
5. If Thoreau were to give a lecture on his views of work today on a college campus, how do you think he would be received?

Job Search: Chance or Plan?

Mark R. Ballard

Formerly the director of career services in a liberal arts college, Mark Ballard is currently director of human resources development at Victoria's Secret Catalogue, where he continues his work in career planning and organizational career development. In this essay, Ballard offers some excellent advice for initiating the job-search process and delineates specific career-planning tasks for each year of student life. He believes his advice, if followed, will generate good job prospects upon graduation.

• • • • • • • • • • • • • • • • • •

I want to tell you about Terry—the alumnus who "chanced" his career. His story can provide important insights for your own career planning.

Terry was a popular student in high school, was involved in many activities, and graduated in the top 25 percent of his class. Terry could hardly wait to leave his hometown to become a college student at the university. His academic performance was quite respectable. He could not believe how quickly the years passed. They elapsed so fast that he did not get involved in any structured *co-curricular* activities because he was "too busy" with school, sports, and friends. For spending money, Terry worked, but his employment experience, for the most part, consisted of being a lifeguard during the summers at his hometown pool and a cashier in a fast-food restaurant.

The quarter before Terry was slated to graduate, he decided to visit the Career Services Office. (He remembered hearing about this resource in his freshman orientation class.) Terry eagerly signed up for several on-campus interviews with companies that came to campus to interview students.

Terry bought a suit, had someone prepare a resume for him, and interviewed with several company representatives. He was confident that he presented himself well in the interviews and would most assuredly get an offer from one of the employers with whom he interviewed. After all, he had never had difficulty finding part-time jobs.

Graduation came and went for Terry. Summer came, and Terry began to panic. Mid-summer, Terry returned to Career Services since the anticipated job offers did not materialize out of his interviews. Terry came back to the office looking for additional companies who were coming on campus to interview students and alumni. But there were none during the summer, since companies who do come to college campuses to interview students generally complete their hiring visits during April. Terry was unaware of this fact since he did not attend the on-campus interviewing orientation session: he was "too busy." Terry left the office disappointed, failing to take advantage of the many other employment resources. He vowed to return "sometime," but he never got around to it.

In the follow-up questionnaire mailed to alumni six months after graduation, we received a letter from Terry. Good news: he had landed a job! Well, maybe not good news. The job, which he stumbled on by "accident," was not the kind of position Terry thought he would land with a college degree. Sadly, his college education would not be fully utilized, and his salary was not comparable to similar college graduates.

Here's the moral of Terry's tale: Finding meaningful employment *commensurate* with one's educational level is not an event that occurs at the end of one's final term in college. It is a process that begins early in one's collegiate career. Making the transition from academics to the work world does not begin with writing a resume, buying a new suit, or getting that first job interview. It begins with thought, research, and goal setting.

To secure employment upon graduation, begin with the process of self-assessment. As a part of this process, you need to be able to answer such questions as, "What do I want to do for work?" and "Where do I want to do it?" In other words, what are your abilities, strengths, assets, gifts, talents? What is it that you are interested in, enjoy, are curious about, are motivated by, or get pleasure from? What are your values—those needs that you want satisfied by your work (recognition, independence, money, prestige, social status, uncovering knowledge)? What are the job tasks or activities of the careers that you are considering, the types of organizations that employ individuals in these occupations, the job outlook/forecast, salary ranges, entrance requirements, and lifestyle issues associated with the vocations you are considering? What are the steps necessary to undertake the decision-making process related to your career? Do you know where to go to find out how to write a resume, interview for job offers, and to learn strategies to find jobs? If you can answer these questions, you will increase your prospects for success in the job search.

As an entering student, you may find it easy to say: "I'll deal with those job-related questions and issues during my senior year, or when I'm ready to graduate." "It's too early now." "I don't have time." "I'm just a freshman." "I'll figure it out. After all, I figured out how to apply to and get accepted to college."

But consider the following. Suppose you were to interview today for the job of your dreams, and the interviewer said to you, "Tell me about yourself and why you want this job. You have thirty minutes. I'll begin timing when you begin talking." How would you respond? What would you say? That is a common opening statement for an employer to make in a job interview.

To land the job of your dreams, you will first need to know about yourself. Do not confuse starting the process with implementing your career decision. You don't need to choose a career now, just to begin to think about, and to get actively involved in, the process during your early years of college. That way, early in your senior year, you can reflect on the self-assessment and the career exploration tasks that you addressed and the career decision that you made early in your college years. Your senior year is also the time for you to focus attention on *transitional* issues that will take you from academics to the work world, or on to graduate or professional school. Career planning is working through the many tasks associated with finding employment through planning—rather than through chance.

Career planning is the developmental, systematic process of

1. learning about yourself (for example, your interests, abilities, and values),
2. identifying occupations that correspond to your assessment of self,
3. exploring the occupations that you are considering,
4. selecting an occupation to pursue,
5. readying yourself for the job search process (resume and application letter writing, job interview skill development, job finding techniques and strategy knowledge), and
6. securing satisfying employment.

Does it seem that the process of career planning could be simplified by proceeding directly to step six—finding a job upon graduation? If so, remember Terry. That is exactly what he did. He jumped into the job search without establishing the foundation of the first five stages. He landed a job, but a job in the ranks of the underemployed, and that can have *ramifications* for a lifetime.

Your career process will be easier if you fully use the career planning and placement services provided at your university. There, staff members can help you answer the all too familiar question, "What can I do with a major in ...?" and assist you in finding purposeful, gratifying employment.

As a career services professional, I have worked with thousands of students, employers, and alumni. When I survey employers and alumni for their perspective on how students can best prepare themselves to make the transition from academics to the work world, they usually give five recommendations for students entering a university.

1. Choose a major in a subject that interests you—one that really gets you excited. Do not rely on your parents, peers, or counselors to make the choice for you regarding your academic major or the occupation to pursue. Make the decision yourself. As a related note, given the difficulty of predicting which skills will be in demand even five years from now, not to mention in a lifetime, your best career preparation is one that emphasizes broad skills (for example, social, communication, analytical, logical, leadership, human relations), intellectual curiosity, and knowledge of how to learn.
2. Strive for a rigorous academic program and high grades. Yes, grades are important to employers. Job candidates are often rejected from interviews due to low GPAs.
3. Develop your leadership, communication, human relations, and time management skills by taking active roles of responsibility in student organizations and activities. This involvement will provide you with an opportunity to put knowledge from the classroom into practice.
4. Get career-related experience prior to graduation (through part-time positions, *cooperative education,* internships, and volunteer work). The benefits of such experience go well beyond making money. You will have a chance

to sample a variety of jobs and work settings, make valuable contacts with professionals for future networking, develop self-confidence, and gain insight when choosing elective courses in your academic program.

5. Use the career planning and placement services on campus early in your academic experience to help you with your career decision making and your job search. By doing so, you can get a head start on your employment future.

You can take the above recommendations a step further by following a year-by-year plan for your job search. Use this scheme as a general strategy to increase the likelihood of your landing the job of your dreams upon graduation.

As a Freshman . . .

The goal of your freshman year should be to learn as much as you can about yourself and the relationship this information has to careers. Consider the following:

In your academic course work, use the required general education courses and other college courses to help you explore your potential. You might wish to take courses and explore subjects that have always been of interest to you but that you never before had an opportunity to take.

Visit the career services office (sometimes referred to as the Placement Office) on your campus and get acquainted with the services and resources of that office. Your academic adviser can direct you to the right place.

Explore your interests, abilities, and values. Identify appropriate career choices by using the computerized career guidance systems (DISCOVER and SIGI-PLUS are two that are commonly available), meeting with a staff member of the career services office for a career counseling session, attending any career awareness workshops offered on campus and sharing your goals with your academic adviser.

Find out about cooperative education and internship opportunities through your intended college of graduation.

Analyze job descriptions in the career services office and ask yourself how these positions fit with your identity profile.

Begin investigating and getting involved in at least one of the student organizations and activities on campus to develop your leadership, communication, human relations, and time management skills.

Find a summer job that will provide you with an opportunity to learn or refine skills that will be attractive to a prospective employer (e.g., communication, responsibility, ethical decision making, and human relations—learning to work with individuals of differing backgrounds).

As a Sophomore . . .

During your sophomore year, your goal should be to concentrate on identifying careers that appeal to you and to begin testing them out.

Use the career books and other references in the career office and elsewhere on campus to research career options.

Learn to begin the process of informational interviewing—contacting and talking with people employed in fields you are considering. For example, if you are interested in chemistry, dietetics, or nutrition as a major, consider conducting an informational interview with a nutritional researcher at an area business or hospital. Career services staff members can help you identify professionals working in occupations that are of interest to you.

Take active roles of responsibility in clubs, organizations, and activities.

Cultivate relationships with faculty, counselors, and others who can help in answering questions that relate to careers and the relationship of course work to careers.

Take time to attend the "career days" held on campus and in the area. These events provide you with the opportunity to meet representatives from major U.S. organizations. Be sure to ask about cooperative education and internship opportunities.

Find out about summer internships and cooperative education opportunities through the career services office.

Begin developing a resume as well as job interviewing skills. Workshops on these topics are conducted regularly through many career services offices.

As a Junior . . .

During your junior year, your goal should be to obtain career-related experience.

Prepare for the job search by attending workshops and individual counseling sessions on resume writing, application letter writing, job search strategies, and interviewing skills.

Develop a network of contacts in the field of your choice through continued informational interviewing, involvement in professional associations, and cooperative education or internships.

Continue to attend the "career days" held on the campus and in the area. Continue to ask the company representatives about internships and cooperative education opportunities.

Research job leads and make initial contacts early in winter for sources of possible employment that have some relationship to your tentative career choice. Gather letters of recommendation written on your behalf from past employers, current employers, professors, teaching associates—professionals who can vouch for your skills and abilities. Open a credentials file if your career services office has such a service.

As a Senior . . .

Your senior year is the culmination of your college education and is the launching pad for your future. Your goal is to secure satisfying employment or to get accepted to graduate or professional school if your career interest indicates the need for an advanced degree.

Learn the procedures for interviewing with the various career placement offices on campus should you wish to interview with organizations that come on campus to interview graduating students.

Research the organizations with which you wish to interview by using the career services office's company literature libraries.

Attend "career day" events that are held on the campus and in the area and actively participate by distributing resumes to the company representatives and telling them about who you are and the type of position you are seeking.

Interview for jobs during the year with employers who come on campus through the career services office. Note: they are not likely to be there during the summer. (Remember Terry's disappointment?)

Continue collecting letters of recommendation written on your behalf by people who can attest to your skills and abilities. Keep these letters on file in your college's career services office.

Explore, in consultation with career services personnel, other strategies to find employment for your field of interest, such as using the many job listings that are published through career services offices, making use of computerized listings of positions, enrolling in national employment databases through career services offices, and learning the process of networking (getting involved with professionals in the field you wish to enter and learning where the hidden job market is). **The best job search strategy is to use a variety of job search strategies simultaneously; do not rely solely on one strategy to find employment.**

Choosing a career and finding a professional job take a lot of time and effort. You need to find out as much as you can about what interests you, what you do well, and what you want out of life. Even after you have decided on your career direction, you will find a wide range of job options available to you. There may be occupations that you have never even heard of that would suit your education, interests, values, and abilities perfectly. It is important to find out about them as early as possible. By waiting too long to begin proper planning and preparation for a successful career, you run the risk of embarking on the job search scene unaware of what field to pursue, getting frustrated, giving in, giving up, and taking any job you are offered.

The staff members of your career services office can help you with every phase of the career planning and employment process. It is not a magical, quick process, and the staff will not find a job for you. What you can expect, however, are informed professionals who will guide your career decision making and your job search process.

The valuable information you will receive from these offices will prove beneficial to you for the rest of your life. Make a commitment to get a head start on your career. Visit your career services office today. You owe it to yourself.

Vocabulary

As you think about this essay, these definitions may be helpful to you:
1. **co-curricular** being outside of but complementary to the regular curriculum
2. **commensurate** equal in measure or extent
3. **transitional** in the process of passing from one state, stage, or place to another
4. **ramifications** consequences or outgrowths
5. **cooperative education** a program that combines academic studies with actual work experience

Discussion Questions

1. What is the first important step in the job search process, according to Ballard?
2. What would you tell an employer about yourself in thirty minutes during a job interview?
3. What are the six steps that Ballard outlines to systematically begin the career planning process?
4. What type of work experiences can students engage in prior to graduation?
5. What are some strategies students can use during their first year to enhance the career planning process? As sophomores? Juniors? Seniors?

How Can These Ideas Apply to You?

1. What have you done to determine your interests, abilities, and values as part of the self-assessment step in career planning?
2. Describe your dream job.
3. Which of the six steps in career planning that Ballard outlines have you accomplished? How and when will you accomplish the rest?
4. Which of the tasks that Ballard lists under "As a Freshman" have you completed? Have you completed any of the tasks listed under the other three years?
5. What resources on your campus will help you with the job-search process during each of these years?

Postgraduate Paralysis

Mary Sherry

Mary Sherry owns a firm that publishes research reports for architects and real estate developers. In this essay, which first appeared in *Newsweek* magazine, Sherry offers a parent's perspective on an offspring's job search. When she realized her daughter was looking for a career, not a job, her perspective on how to help changed.

Thousands of college graduates took their diplomas this year in fear or even embarrassment. They were not proud of themselves, nor eager to take on the real world. Instead, they thought of themselves as failures. These are the graduates who have not been offered fat salaries and generous benefits. They are the ones who won't be going to work as lawyers, investment bankers and engineers. They have taken the right courses, gotten good grades and gone through some on-campus job interviews. But because they weren't offered the perfect job—no, that exciting career—seemingly guaranteed to all those who make the right moves, they are sitting at home, victims of postgraduate paralysis.

This may come as a surprise to anyone who has read about the fabulous job offers tendered to recent graduates. However, those of us who are parents of children in this age group know that such offers are relatively rare and that many liberal-arts students graduate with the belief that the work world may not have a place for them.

Consider my daughter; she graduated from college with a degree in economics two years ago. She was offered a job by a *recruiter* who came to her campus—but it was with a trucking firm in South Carolina, as a dispatch-management trainee. She turned it down. It was her parents' first clue that she had a problem.

It seems economists don't work for trucking firms. Nor do Midwestern children want to live in the South before they become arthritic. Yet even at home in Minneapolis, our daughter couldn't seem to find anything to apply for. Her father told her to make the rounds of the personnel agencies. But she was so horrified by the *demeaning* atmosphere at one that she refused to visit any others.

Then one day, when she was looking at the Sunday paper and complaining that there was nothing in it, I told her that there had to be something. "Look at this," I commanded. "And this! And this!" I circled a number of jobs in the first two columns I skimmed. But Maureen protested: "I don't want to be an administrative assistant."

It was then that her father and I realized that she had been looking in the paper for a career, not a job. And ever since, we have watched the children of friends suffer from this same *delusion.* No one, it seems, has told them that a career is an *evolutionary* process.

When I graduated from college 25 years ago, I never expected to find a job that was in itself a career. In those days, we were told we knew nothing, but that upon graduation we would have the tools to learn. And learn we did—on the job. I began by doing grunt work in the customer-service department at *National Geographic* magazine. In due time, I wound up with a career, indeed, owning and running a firm that publishes research reports for architects and real-estate developers.

Apparently, schools have changed their approach. Today's students are told they know everything in order to succeed in a career. Career talk often begins in seventh grade or earlier, and the career is offered as the reward one receives upon graduation. No one is satisfied with this system. Businesses complain that they get new graduates who are unhappy with anything less than high-level, decision-making jobs as their first assignments. And parents are shocked that the child without a job can graduate traumatized by the fear of rejection.

As I see it, parents are a principal cause of the problem. Who among us hasn't thought, "What's wrong with that kid?" when we hear that a recent college graduate is a checker at a grocery store because "he can't find a job." At the same time, how many of us can put the screws on a recruiter's reject and convince him that he must abandon his idea of a career and take up the idea of finding work?

This is a distasteful task, especially when we have shipped our children off to expensive colleges, believing that simply by footing the tuition bill we are making them economically secure. The kids believe this, too, but the reality is that when they graduate, they are no more prepared for careers than we were.

Entry-level positions: It is not a disgrace to go out and pound the pavement. I used just this expression the other day with a friend of my son who, though he had graduated in December with a degree in philosophy, has not yet found a job. He had never heard the saying before. He is bright, personable and would do well in almost any kind of business. But he complains that he can't find work in the want ads—he has not visited any personnel agencies—and so he talks about going to law school instead. He was crushed by not having been recruited before graduation.

Which brings me back to my daughter. After some yelling and screaming by her parents, she did make the rounds of *headhunters* and found one who specialized in entry-level positions. This gentleman was wonderful; he helped her assess her skills and prepared her for interviews. She also read the newspapers and answered different types of ads. Not surprisingly, she got many responses. After a few weeks she had the exhilarating experience of having three job offers at once. Two were the products of answering newspaper ads and one came through the headhunter's efforts. She landed an excellent position as an insurance underwriter—a job she didn't even know existed when she graduated.

Happy in her job, Maureen also fell in love; and when she began to look for employment in Chicago where she and her husband will live, she needed no help from her parents. She was confident and aggressive. She used headhunters, the want ads, her friends and ours. She had a new resource—business contacts. Yet as she was typing letters one day, I offered some sympathy about how hard it is to hunt for a job.

"It's OK, Mom," she said. "This isn't like the first time. Now I know how to look for a job!"

And she found one as a senior underwriter. She'll make more money and more decisions.

It's beginning to look like a career.

Reprinted from *Newsweek* by permission of the author.

• •

 # Vocabulary

As you think about this essay, these definitions may be helpful to you:
1. **recruiter**   a representative of a company or organization who is seeking to secure the services of or hire individuals to work for that organization
2. **demeaning**   degrading
3. **delusion**   something that is falsely believed
4. **evolutionary**   characterized by a process of change in a certain direction
5. **headhunters**   paid recruiters of personnel

 # Discussion Questions

1. Why do some students feel like failures if they do not have a job at graduation, according to Sherry?
2. How did Sherry's daughter approach the job-search process?
3. What is the difference between a job and a career?
4. What advice does Sherry give for finding entry-level jobs?
5. How did Sherry's daughter finally find her first job? Subsequent jobs?

 # How Can These Ideas Apply to You?

1. Have you known any college graduates who were still searching for a job after graduation? What were their circumstances?
2. What type of entry-level job will you be seeking at graduation? Where on your campus can you obtain information about entry-level jobs related to your major?

3. Have you known students who have approached the job search as Sherry's daughter did? How were their experiences similar or different?
4. When do you think you should start preparing for the job search? How will you go about it?
5. Are you aware of the resources on your campus to help you explore and select a career field? How have you used them?

Virtual Organization

Samuel E. Bleecker

Samuel E. Bleecker is a technology consultant specializing in the office of the future. In
this essay, he describes a new form of an evolving corporation that uses information
technologies to collapse time and space.

· · · · · · · · · · · · · · · · · ·

L ook around. The corporations you see today on the business landscape are
changing rapidly in structure and function and will be, within a few decades, almost entirely new entities.

What is evolving are virtual enterprises. Using integrated computer and
communications technologies, corporations will increasingly be defined not by
concrete walls or physical space, but by collaborative networks linking hundreds, thousands, even tens of thousands of people together.

These collaborative, or consultative, networks—combinations of local-area
and wide-area computer and communications networks—allow businesses to
form and dissolve relationships at an instant's notice and thus create new corporate ecologies. They also allow a single worker to seem like an army of workers and for work to collapse time and space.

For example, let's suppose you head a large company. It's Christmas time,
and you need to add 100 customer representatives to the payroll. It doesn't
make sense to keep 100 offices with 100 computers open all year long just to
accommodate one month's rush of business. Instead, it makes sense to hire 100
people who work at home and have their own computers. These "virtual workers" can be in Hong Kong or Singapore or Cincinnati. It makes no difference.
They dial into the company's database and become an extension of the company. When a customer calls in, all information about that person is flashed on
the computer screen of the temporary worker, wherever located. The widely
scattered workers can operate as if they were all at company headquarters.

A prelude to virtual enterprising appeared in one state's efforts to find
jobs for the homeless. Colorado's dilemma was this: How do you locate a homeless person to tell him or her that a job interview has been scheduled or an opportunity for work has opened up? After all, the homeless have no addresses, no
telephones. The state decided to establish individual voice mailboxes accessible by toll-free telephone numbers for each homeless person in the program.
The individuals simply call their personalized numbers to get their messages.
And it works: So far, more than 75 percent of the homeless people enrolled in
this program have found jobs.

In the future, virtual enterprising will follow Colorado's example by
operating without walls. These collaborative networks make it possible to draw
upon vital resources as needed, regardless of where they are physically and

regardless of who "owns" them—supplier or customer. "Collaborative networks deliver better products, higher quality, improved time-to-market, and higher returns to the bottom line," says Gordon Bridge, president of AT&T's messaging company. "They leverage the strengths of each link in the value chain, improve efficiencies, reduce expenses, and focus on the interoperability of processes and supporting systems."

"Virtual" Trends In the Marketplace

Several factors are driving businesses toward virtual enterprising.

- **Pace.** As Alvin Toffler predicted more than two decades ago, businesses now run at warp speeds, demanding immediate responses—anywhere, anytime. Today, "it's a survival of the fastest, not the fittest," he notes.
- **Cost.** The cost of market entry is often smaller than previously, especially in the information services and other technology-driven industries, where even undercapitalized startups can have an enormous impact on innovation.
- **Personalization.** Computerized manufacturing has made it economical to produce assembly-line product runs of a few dozen items instead of a few thousand. This has meant that corporations are now driven more by customer demands than by internal needs. Today, customers get what they want or go elsewhere.
- **Globalization.** Businesses no longer compete only with their nearest rivals, but internationally.

In the recent past, businesses could count on a steady stream of profit from a product line because a product's life cycle stretched ahead for years. Current product cycles have dropped to 18 months or less for some products. For example, the time it takes to conceive, design, manufacture, and sell 386-chip–based computers lasts maybe 18 months. If a company wants to recoup its *R&D* investments, it must truly be nimble.

As a result, large corporations are under pressure to drastically cut the time it takes to deliver a product from the engineer's workbench to the showroom floor. If they can't, they'll lose millions of dollars in investment to a faster competitor.

What has insulated many corporations from this reality, particularly in the United States, has partially been the high cost of entry into well-entrenched distribution networks. For years, U.S. car manufacturers could ignore consumer demands because it was too costly for a foreign competitor with a better idea or a better-made vehicle to enter the U.S. market.

All that changed when new technologies and political realities blurred national borders. GM, Ford, and Chrysler sprang to their feet when well-financed Japanese and German auto manufacturers started penetrating American barriers and delivering cheaper and better-designed cars.

Other industries besides car manufacturers are also getting the message. Giants like AT&T and IBM are *reengineering* themselves to be more agile. They are using their cash, extensive marketing machinery, and manufacturing might to form relationships with faster, less-encumbered companies—even startups.

Recently, the business news pages are bloated with reports of joint ventures between IBM and Apple, US West and Time Warner (to deliver new home entertainment services via fiber-optic cables), and AT&T and startups such as the Go Corporation, which develops pen-based operating software, and EO, which manufactures pen-based *palmtop* computers.

Many corporations are also motivated to form alliances by marketing and manufacturing considerations. Some form joint ventures with foreign partners (or even competitors) simply to gain better coverage of international markets or to take advantage of reduced labor and delivery charges in other countries.

As a result, business is no longer local or even national. It's global. For example, I know of a Spanish-speaking person who drives an "American" Ford designed in Europe, with a Japanese-built engine, assembled in Korea, and sold in Connecticut. Getting that car developed, assembled, delivered, and sold required important structural changes in business.

Mobile Knowledge Workers

Increasingly, the "office" is where the worker is—not the other way around. Today, 45 million U.S. workers now spend more of their time on the road than at their desks. This new mobile work force demands new tools that both *untether* them from the workplace and, at the same time, allow them to stay in touch anytime, anyplace, and (very importantly) in any way—via phone, computer, fax, pager, videoconference, and so on.

The new, ultra-mobile work force, nicknamed "road warriors," are message-intensive. They talk on the go and go where the action is. Road warriors need new tools as they go on their "infoquests" into the offices, factories, and homes of their clients.

As Intel's Andy Grove says, we are in the midst of a major paradigm shift in both the computer industry and the workplace itself. The new mobile work force doesn't so much need computer devices that communicate as they need communications devices that compute. We are at the brink of untethered communications. It is the dawn of a new era—the era of universal devices—when your pen-based palmtop PC becomes your personal communicator, serves as your mailbox, your fax machine, your notebook, and even your electronic secretary. This single device will manage and store your electronic communications, becoming, in essence, your "briefcase office."

Yet for this revolution in work and workplace to materialize, an invisible worldwide *infrastructure* of new hardware tools, wireless links, and land-based communications superhighways are needed for high-speed and broadband data transfer of high-definition documents, such as medical X-rays or multimedia presentations.

Increasingly, we will see a host of personal digital assistants (PDAs), also known as "pocket pals" or "personal communicators." These handy devices feature built-in wireless telephones and modems, voice-recognition and voice-synthesis capabilities, and have photographic-quality, touch-sensitive screens. Increasingly, companies will build their telecommunications operations around virtual networks, such as AT&T's Software Defined Network, which allows a company to piggyback on a private virtual network that has the intelligence and reach of AT&T's global public telephone network.

Once armed with these new tools, businesses will reengineer themselves. Powerful personal communicators are expected to trigger new applications in data collection so that, for example, an insurance claims adjuster can collect data in the field, complete an application or an accident report, and have it sent back to the office immediately.

Personal communicators will also allow vital information to be wirelessly downloaded to the field. For example, that same claims adjuster might need a diagram of an older-model car to be sent directly to his or her personal communicator for the accident report to be completed. Salespeople, too, can get immediate answers to customers' questions or price quotes downloaded wirelessly from headquarters and thus close a sale on the spot rather than having to postpone the sale until information is available.

With electronic messaging and wireless communications, the road warrior can now also have a universal mailbox. Colleagues need not follow his or her movements because they can deliver their communications—memos, faxes, spreadsheets, presentations—directly to the mobile worker anywhere by addressing his or her universal mailbox. And, wherever the worker is—on the road, on a plane, in a hotel, or at a client's office—those messages are waiting. And if there's no fax machine handy, the mobile worker can read messages on the computer through electronic messaging.

Unwiring Society

In the 1980s we noted proudly that we were a wired society. Soon we can proudly say we are an unwired society. It's the age of emancipation. Time and space will collapse, and the barriers to communications will fall away. It won't matter if you're in America and your trading partner is in Bulgaria. You will be truly connected—linked to one another by an invisible web of communications networks and intelligent, integrated appliances: the electronic virtual office.

Traditional offices, on the other hand, will shrink to mere landing sites, where mobile workers dock for an hour or so at a communal electronic desk. Here, you will plug in your personal communicator, or personal digital assistant, and download all the data you've collected into a single unit—an integrated intelligent document-processing and management appliance combining fax, copier, printer, and scanner all in a machine no larger than your current laser printer.

In the future, this intelligent peripheral will not only receive, store, and transmit data, but also manage your work flow. Truly an intelligent personal assistant, such a device will even turn your notes into desktop-published reports, including graphs, facts, and figures. It will sort through your files for the references you include and insert them where instructed.

It will also store and index information so that you can retrieve it instantly without intervention of a secretary. When you're on the road, it will receive your correspondence and, if the information is urgent enough, track you down and e-mail or fax your messages to you. Right now, several e-mail software developers are working on such intelligent assistants, including Lotus's *Notes* and Beyond's *Mail.*

Winning the Business War

Business is war. We *battle* our competition. We call our work force an *army.* We call our mobile work force road *warriors.* We *invade* markets. And, during crises, we call the conference room the *war room.* So what will make the virtual enterprise of tomorrow the most productive—that is, competitive—is *warware.* Computers without it will be little more than expensive paperweights.

Warware is strategic *simulation* software that allows executives to manage complexity, to create virtual realities (or virtual enterprises) on the computer screen, and to watch the results of their scenarios as they replay the parameters. It's not new. The Pentagon has been doing it for years. Even civilian PC users have been doing it. With *SimCity,* they play town manager; with *Gettysburg,* they fight again and again the famous American battle.

But we haven't gone far enough. When computers get smart enough, business executives will be charting reorganizations on computers, not on paper. They will make fewer mistakes and grow greater profits. They will assign project management to computers, not to line personnel. With warware, executives will open new markets, anticipate economic shifts, and play currency markets. They will have a strategic edge because they will be able to simulate business scenarios free of risk and will come away less bloodied when actions are taken later in the real world.

In addition to corporate warfare, however, there will also be personal software that increases an executive's capabilities. It's this sort of software that will cause executives to embrace hardware as never before. Contrary to popular myth, CEOs *do* use computers, but they're called vice presidents. The next generation of software will replace the VP as the CEO's intelligent assistant by mimicking the VP's activities. It will anticipate an executive's needs, learn from experience, conduct self-directed searches, synthesize data, provide analysis, and tailor-make reports.

Right now, the software isn't smart enough, and computers aren't powerful enough, so human vice presidents are still needed. But two developments will help change all that: parallel processing and fuzzy logic.

Parallel processing will allow software designers and systems experts to consider the workplace as a large number of independent processors acting in a coordinated fashion. By assigning rule-based operations to each processor and orchestrated actions to the whole, parallel processing will help more accurately simulate the corporation and anticipate the consequences of any corporate actions or policy changes.

To "think" like a person, however, computers must not only think faster, but differently. In many cases, the answer to a question or solution to a problem is not yes or no, but maybe; not good or bad, but okay; not hot or cold, but temperate. Fuzzy sets and fuzzy logic reject the binary notion that the world is entirely discrete and accepts a continuum of values. As a result, fuzzy logic will enable computers to think more like people do and to create real-world simulations.

Once we've accepted the preeminence of communication rather than location for winning enterprises, we will have come a long way toward reshaping corporations. Virtual enterprises will develop not in the image of the factory floor of 100 years ago, but as a new business ecosystem characterized by flexible relationships formed electronically at a moment's notice.

Reprinted by permission of the World Future Society.

• • • • • • • • • • • • • • • • • • •

Vocabulary

As you think about this essay, these definitions may be helpful to you:
1. **R&D**   research and development
2. **reengineer**   redesign completely to accommodate new purposes
3. **palmtop**   literally, computers that fit in your hand
4. **untether**   to free from a fastener
5. **infrastructure**   the underlying foundation of a system or organization
6. **simulation**   the act of imitating

Discussion Questions

1. According to Bleeker, how are corporations changing into "virtual organizations"?
2. What does Bleeker mean by by operating "without walls"?
3. What are the four virtual trends in the marketplace that Bleeker describes, and how do they encourage "virtual enterprising"?
4. How does the author describe "mobile knowledge worker"?
5. What is "warware," and what is its function?
6. Who is Alvin Toffler, and why is he mentioned in this essay?

How Can These Ideas Apply to You?

1. Would you like to be a "mobile knowledge worker"? Why or why not?
2. How can you prepare in college for the changes that the "virtual organization" will bring?
3. If you are not a business major, how might the changes that Bleeker describes affect your life?

Career Patterns for the 21st Century

Peggy Simonsen

Peggy Simonsen is president of Career Directions, Incorporated. She designs and implements career development and performance management systems and training for corporations. Simonsen is a nationally prominent speaker and frequent contributor to numerous journals and newsletters. In this essay she describes the career patterns that will emerge in the new century and how these will be different from old ways of thinking about career patterns.

Up is not the only way.
—Beverly Kaye

Managing your career strategically in the new century will require new ways of thinking.... A variety of career patterns are evolving. There may be flatter, team-based environments where expectations of upward progression are limited and limiting. A career pattern driven by internal choice rather than external structure will be the most valuable to individuals and will therefore add the most value to the employing organization. Newer employees in organizations today recognize this and aren't as likely as their predecessors to create careers based on incompatible structures or outdated expectations and reward systems. As one employee learning new ways to think about careers said, "You mean it's OK not to want to move up?"

Portfolio Careers

The career pattern most different from the traditional upward career path is that of the *portfolio* career, such as freelance writer. Not employed by a single organization, a freelance writer might have regular assignments with one publication, occasional articles published by others, and some consulting work creating PR campaigns or brochures. In addition, he or she might write and lay out a newsletter and perhaps take on a large one-time assignment to create a policy manual. This writer would be creating a portfolio of work he or she has done.

Today, portfolio careers have expanded to encompass more than one field. Sometimes used to build expertise while planning a career change, the portfolio career can give more autonomy, time, freedom, and opportunity for creativity and diverse activities. People with portfolio careers might be managing a traditional assignment in a large organization while building a small business on the side. An engineer might prefer to work for a job shop, taking on assignments that last from six months to two years, building a variety of experience, and having the freedom to leave when the project is completed or gets too routine. Someone with a love for a field that doesn't pay well might add another type of work to add more income, without giving up the work he or she loves. . . .

Portfolio careers might be driven by "*contingency* work"—that is, employment by a company as long as necessary, but not full-time, permanent employment. To remain flexible and avoid creating new bureaucracies, downsized companies are increasingly using contingency workforces. For a person wanting to hold on to the work patterns of the twentieth century, contingency work seems like a step down the ladder, with no chance for advancement and typically no company-paid benefits. However, for individuals who choose to build portfolio careers, the advantages are autonomy in selecting assignments, variety of work, time freedom, higher hourly pay than for the same work that is salaried, and the chance to build a greater *repertoire* of skills.

This career pattern requires individuals to recognize that they must market their capabilities. They need to be aware of the value of their skills in the marketplace and present themselves as people who can solve others' problems. While this may sound like the essentials of a job search, it must become a regular course of action for a successful portfolio career.

Lifestyle-Driven Careers

Women balancing family and work have been the primary practitioners of lifestyle-driven careers. Taking the primary responsibility for raising children, the wife and mother would work at a part-time job that wouldn't interfere with her home responsibilities. This career pattern is evolving and becoming a choice for men, too. With more two-career households, many couples are finding themselves with little time to build and enjoy their life together and with their families. Others have strong outside interests or *avocations,* so they want to balance their workloads to allow time for these. Still others find their lives out of balance because of excessive work demands after organizational downsizing. People are insisting that work be a subset of life, not all of it. So individuals are making choices about careers on the basis of life needs. The labor shortage gives individuals some leverage by causing employers to create more flexible policies and practices. Companies are recognizing the value of lifestyle-friendly policies, especially when retention of educated and skilled workers is a goal. But organizations are also recognizing that a culture of support for individuals—making work time more satisfying and less stressful—makes good business sense. . . .

Research on career motivation shows that lifestyle-driven careers are the fastest-growing pattern. People with this motivation say career is important, but more important for career decisions is having a balanced, fully satisfying life. The demands of many work environments make a lifestyle-driven career pattern difficult to implement.

Emerging workers, who may be willing to work eighty-hour weeks to meet critical deadlines, expect reciprocation and a break when the crisis passes. Without loyalty to an organization, they will pack up and leave when work demands become unreasonable.

Mature employees, who have lived through downsizing changes—and perhaps personal burnout from excessive time and work demands—often feel less commitment to their work and talk about leaving. Some are too risk-averse to take action to leave, but their work is likely to suffer. These are the people who need to take action, for their own good and that of their employers. Employers who don't recognize the validity of a lifestyle-driven career pattern will lose good people.

Linear Careers

Linear careers are the closest to the traditional career path. However, linear careers in the twenty-first century are not likely to be with only one organization. Rather than going to work for a good company and expecting to be employed for life, employees will avoid much of the frustration experienced upon reaching a level in the organization beyond which they cannot move. Individuals who expect to move up in responsibility and compensation in the future will change organizations when they reach a plateau or growth slows. People managing their careers strategically will not have the expectation that a linear career can happen in one organization. They will be more *proactive* to make it happen.

Organizations will still need leaders willing to take on greater responsibility. They will need to build commitment to the company's success. But they won't be able to take this commitment for granted, assuming loyalty at all costs. The mutual benefits of shared responsibility for organizational development and career success will be recognized by both organizations and employees.

Even today, after excessive downsizing, many organizations are recognizing the need for succession planning and workforce planning. They recognize the disruptive nature of constantly hiring from outside instead of developing from within. There is a growing trend to design systems to develop competencies in internal candidates for assignments as they become available.

Conversely, individuals cannot assume that length of service alone will determine career progression. They must constantly add value, build networks, and overcome barriers to their development. People who will build successful linear careers will take a broader, organizational perspective rather than a personally driven perspective. With flatter organizations, self-directed teams, and therefore fewer management positions, promotions will rarely occur through a person's being in the right place at the right time. They will more likely be based on proven ability to lead. People who fit this career pattern are motivated by achievement, power, and ambition and are willing to pay the dues necessary to achieve success the way they define it....

Expert Careers

Perhaps the only recognized alternative to moving up in the past was the role of individual contributor who chose not to become a manager. A career pattern that has existed forever but often was not valued in traditional organizations is that of the expert. I say "not valued" because rarely was a skilled expert compensated as well as a mediocre manager. The whole structure was designed to support linear careers, so people who turned down promotions because they preferred their technical tasks often felt like second-class citizens. As technology demanded expertise, some organizations created dual-ladder career paths to reward people who were individual contributors, not managers. However, most dual-ladder models still rewarded upward paths—for example, from junior engineer to senior engineer to group leader to project manager.

A few organizations whose success depended on superior individual contributions created rewards for exceptional outcomes, such as patents, scientific breakthroughs, journalistic awards, and record-breaking sales records. This latter pattern will continue into the next century. Led by young firms, without the baggage of the old corporations (especially compensation systems), the expert career pattern is coming into its own. People are rewarded with stock, profit sharing, or substantial bonuses when the project is completed successfully, not because it is the end of the year. Hard work and capability are not only valued, they drive the organization's success. As organizations require fewer managers but need all the state-of-the-art skill they can get, this career pattern may become predominant.

If an expert career pattern is right for you, it will require continuously developing your expertise. It will mean running fast to keep abreast of changes in your profession. The very traits that drive individuals to become experts might frustrate them when the work is changing so fast that it is impossible to maintain an expected level of expertise. It certainly is not a career pattern that allows one to slack off and trade on previous successes, as it might have been in an era of slow change. People whose career pattern is based on expertise need passion for their work, desire always to learn more, ambition to make significant contributions to their fields, and satisfaction from their technical competence. ("Technical" here means task specific, not necessarily electronic. An editor has technical competence in language use; a sales representative has technical competence in both the sales process and the products he or she sells.)

Like a linear career, an expert career probably will not happen in just one organization. It is up to individuals not only to manage their own growth in the field but also to be proactive about the environment in which the work is performed. The company might sell off the division that requires their particular set of skills and knowledge, so while the work doesn't change, the employer does. Technology might suddenly move a generation ahead, leaving experts' work obsolete or declining in value. Or the employer might not choose to move forward in technology, so experts might need to leave in order to continue growing in their areas of expertise. Organizational priorities might change in response to market demands, leaving a previously valued area of expertise now less important—and therefore with fewer resources to support the work. Expert employees might realize the unique nature of their expertise and decide to create their own organizations, to specialize in the work they have been paid to do as employees. While expertise may be seen as a career pattern out of the past, the circumstances in which it is applied will be more dynamic in the future. . . .

Managing your career strategically might mean recognizing the contribution you make and the satisfaction you derive from being an expert at what you do—and turning down a promotion. It is possible to take on management responsibilities and still maintain expertise, but the focus changes. In our fast-changing environments, it is hard enough to maintain expertise without having it be secondary to getting work done through others, but some highly competent individuals manage both roles well. . . .

Sequential Careers

A growing approach to managing your career strategically is the choice of a sequential career. Rather than involving simultaneous career activities, as in the portfolio career, in a sequential career one role ends before another is launched. As people retire from a primary career earlier in life, and as life expectancy is extended, the twenty-first century will see more sequential career patterns. In some cases, the second career is less demanding or not as well compensated as the first, but often it is just different.

We are seeing a substantial increase in the number of people choosing sequential careers because of the decline of the old career patterns. People who bought into the concept of a job for life—even if it was one they didn't choose or want to be in—are suddenly free to make other choices. Either because their job ended or because the paradigm changed and they are thinking about work differently, many are changing careers at midlife or beyond. Some have the opportunity for an early-retirement severance package, which leaves them with the financial base to make choices that are based on fit rather than compensation. Some who have been in the business environment are choosing new work in the not-for-profit sector, intentionally choosing to make income and lifestyle changes. . . .

Younger people are purposely building sequential careers because of the variety they allow. They work in one field for a while, building a level of competence or experience, and then when the challenge begins to wane they decide to pursue work in another area of interest. As long as they move from strength and not from unsatisfactory performance, the building of a sequential career is not seen as negative. Sometimes they move to completely different areas for the sake of new experience, which typically requires starting in a lower-paying job than the one they left. To avoid stepping back, sequential career builders often move to a related area where their background is valued, though not a direct contribution to the new field. For example, a financial analyst in a sales department who knows the company's products moves into a sales support position, then into marketing with another company, and finally into strategic planning, each time adding new skills and experience to her work history.

Sequential career builders may not stay long enough at one organization to build a strong reputation for expertise or to position themselves for promotions, but that isn't what's driving them. Change, variety, and challenge are their drivers, and they definitely don't want linear careers. However, it's important to distinguish between a successful sequential career and job-hopping. A sequential career is successful if the person attains some expertise, competence, and acknowledgment in each job. Young people, particularly, may go from one field to another without gaining any expertise. Then they find themselves at the age of thirty without a portfolio of well-honed skills and with an image of moving away from unsuccessful attempts. In some cases, they even turn down promotions, which might have been important for moving into higher-level situations. . . .

Entrepreneurial Careers

Some people seem to be born entrepreneurs. Creative, independent, driven by their own goals and passions, they need the autonomy of their own companies. These types have always existed, so what is different now? The career patterns we've discussed are enabling entrepreneurial types to start their own businesses in different ways:

- Portfolio careers, where people juggle paid employment with a fledgling business—perhaps in the same field, perhaps in a new area
- Lifestyle-driven careers, where some start their own businesses to get more time flexibility, or to reduce a commute, or to be less tied to a demanding environment
- Linear careers, when the move up has been derailed or a plateau has been reached; capable women who have hit the glass ceiling in a large organization often opt to start a business where their leadership skills can be maximized
- Expert careers, where people feel they can use their expertise better with fewer limitations in their own businesses, or where the expertise is no longer needed by an employer and so a former employee becomes self-employed to provide the same service or product to the market
- Sequential careers, where an entrepreneurial drive has been squelched for security reasons and now can emerge as the next career

Obviously, not all entrepreneurs are from the same mold—if they were they wouldn't be entrepreneurs. But there are some whose very nature is entrepreneurial. They are risk-taking, goal-oriented, creative, hard-driving, persevering, competitive, and challenge-driven. . . .

Not all entrepreneurs are driven to start more than one business. Some land at the helm by happenstance (as when they inherit a family business) and make a commitment to grow the business over many years. Some entrepreneurial people never start a business at all but become equity partners in small, already established operations, where they contribute to growth and success. These aren't people who need structure and a predictable paycheck; they can create their own systems and take financial risks because of the potential payoffs.

Many new companies in the field of technology are launched because their founders have the expertise and because they can be so much more responsive to market opportunities than old, bureaucratic organizations.

Increasingly, larger organizations are recognizing the value of entrepreneurial traits to innovation and creative problem solving inside the company.

Gifford Pinchot (1985)[1] calls this "intrapreneuring": the company provides the equivalent of venture capital, and a small group of employees creates a business plan for an innovative product or service to be developed in-house and brought to market.

Pluralistic Career Cultures

With the old "employment contract" an artifact of the twentieth century, something is needed to replace the way we define careers. Instead of shifting from the old, relatively stable structure to one of free-form *pandemonium,* organizations will need to recognize and support multiple career patterns. Brousseau, Driver, Eneroth, and Larsson[2] make a plea for organizations to adopt a pluralistic approach to career management and to develop a pluralistic career culture as a way to cope with change and the diverse needs of organizations and people. Encouraging and including a variety of career patterns can realign individuals and organizations.

We can hope that in the coming century, both individuals and organizations will value a variety of career patterns. Individuals will need to know which types of careers are appropriate for them at any point in time, and organizational practices will reward those patterns that serve their purposes and keep the company on track to achieve business goals. Today only slightly more than half of all work options are derivatives of traditional work arrangements (that is, full-time positions at the same workplace for a long time). The variety will expand as the new century grows. . . .

From Peggy Simonsen, *Career Patterns for the 21st Century.*

 Vocabulary

As you think about this essay, these definitions may be helpful to you:
1. **portfolio**   a selection of representative work
2. **contingency**   the state of happening by chance or unforeseen causes
3. **repertoire**   a supply of materials, skills, or devices
4. **avocation**   a hobby or occupation pursued for enjoyment
5. **proactive**   taking the initiative
6. **pandemonium**   wild disorder

[1] G. Pinchot III, *Intrapreneuring: Why You Don't Have to Leave the Corporation to Become an Entrepreneur* (New York: HarperCollins, 1985).
2 K. Brousseau et al. (1996), "Career Pandemonium: Realigning Organizations and Individuals," *Academy of Management Executives, 10*(4), 53.

Discussion Questions

1. In what ways do these new career patterns differ from the old, more traditional ones?
2. What, according to Simonsen, are the characteristics of the "lifestyle" career pattern?
3. How do modern linear careers differ from those in the past?
4. Why might an "expert" career pattern be difficult to maintain in work that changes rapidly?
5. Why are younger people purposely building sequential careers, according to Simonsen?

 ## How Can These Ideas Apply to You?

1. Would a portfolio career pattern fit your work values and goals? Why or why not?
2. Would you be willing to work without structure or a predictable paycheck for "potential payoffs," as the entrepreneur career pattern requires?
3. Which of the six career patterns that Simonsen outlines appeals to you the most? Why?
4. Do you personally believe you can "make a difference" in the world? Do you really want to? Why or why not?
5. Simonsen seems very optimistic in describing these various new kinds of careers. Do you agree with her? What drawbacks do you see to some of the types of careers she identifies?

UNIT SUMMARY

The readings in this unit provide a wide variety of opinions about work and workers. Reflect on your own ideas about your place in the work world and how these writers have added to your understanding of its complexities and challenges.

Summary Questions

1. Responding to a recent poll, younger workers indicated that they care more about job satisfaction than job security. How do you think that knowing this might influence what employers offer new workers?
2. Describe how you have searched for a job in the past and the differences a college degree might make.
3. Compare Thoreau's views on work with those of the "virtual organization" as described in the Bleecker reading.

Suggested Writing Assignments

1. The readings in this unit explore several beliefs, attitudes, and perspectives about work. Select one and write a brief essay on why the ideas in this reading agree or disagree with your own ideas about work.
2. Write a brief essay on what you want in your future career (e.g., independence, creativity, security, high salary) and why these work values are essential to you.
3. Write a brief essay about how you are currently approaching the choice of academic major and career field and what you still need to do in order to make an initial decision or confirm one you have already made.

Suggested Readings

Bolles, Richard. *What Color Is Your Parachute?* Berkeley, CA: Ten Speed Press, 2001.
Grantham, Charles. *The Future of Work.* New York: McGraw Hill, 2000.
Sears, Susan, and Virginia Gordon. *Building Your Career: A Guide to Your Future* (3rd ed.). Upper Saddle River, NJ: Prentice-Hall, 2001.
Terkel, Studs. *Working.* New York: Pantheon, 1974.

What Are My Rights and Responsibilities as a Student?

In many ways, the modern university forms its own community. Like a small town, a university or a college often has its own residential areas, business centers, spaces designed for sports and other recreation, food services including "fast food" options and some that are fancier, centers of government, a hospital or health service center, a security office, and so on. The resemblance is not limited to physical settings, because comparable lines of authority and responsibility can be found in both civil governments (as in villages or towns) and university structures. Like cities, colleges and universities have the authority to establish their own laws—codes of acceptable behavior—and penalties for violating those codes. As well, the state and federal laws apply both to cities and to colleges located within a given state or nation. Each of us is familiar with such laws—those against violence, theft of property, indecent or threatening behavior, excessive noise or other activities that constitute a public nuisance, and the like.

The freedom from work, from restraint, from accountability, wondrous in its inception, becomes banal and counterfeit. Without rules there is no way to say no, and worse, no way to say yes.

—THOMAS FARBER

Because many new college students are near or at the age when civil laws apply to them in a new way, they need to keep in mind that the older we are, the higher the level of responsibility for our actions the law is likely to expect of us. Some behavior that may be cute from a 2-year-old and merely annoying from a 10-year-old might well be illegal from someone 18 or older. Moreover, the cities and states we live in give us greater freedom when we reach 18 or 21, and with that freedom comes a higher degree of accountability. If you drove your parents' car illegally when you were 13, your parents were usually held responsible (though they may have, in turn, imposed their own regulations on you!), but if at 18 you drive illegally (under the influence of alcohol, for example, or faster than the speed limit allows), it is your own license that will be affected, and your own record that starts accumulating.

Other laws relate specifically to the people who make up the university community. These are generally developed, implemented, and enforced within the university itself. Such laws authorized by a university community usually include the expectation that students, faculty, and staff members will obey and respect the civil laws of their city, state, and nation, but they go further as well. Because a university has special characteristics, its code of prohibited behavior will take its special characteristics into account. We begin Unit 7 with an essay about the special characteristics that makes a university unique, "On Academic Freedom" by Halverson and Carter. With that essay to establish the context, the remaining essays in this unit take up the question of your rights and responsibilities as a student member of your college community. Krutch and Minnick each consider the ethical dimensions of your role as a student. Like many ethical questions, these essays raise issues that are perennially debatable, for which you may find only provisional answers. George Will suggests a change in the emphasis of discussions about these and other ethical issues. All of this is to be expected in a university setting, where the search for truth is constant and the searchers are continually hopeful of better, clearer, wiser answers to such age-old questions as "What is the best way to proceed?" and "How can we make a stronger community?"

On Academic Freedom

William H. Halverson and James R. Carter

William H. Halverson is associate dean emeritus of University College at The Ohio State University. After completing academic studies focused on philosophy, Halverson authored well-known textbooks for college philosophy classes. More recently, he has translated several books from Norwegian into English. James R. Carter, also a philosopher by education, is assistant dean of the College of Arts and Sciences at the University of Louisville, where he directs the Advising Center. In the following essay, Halverson and Carter define the notion of academic freedom, which is at the heart of a university as established and perpetuated in Western cultures.

People create institutions to serve a variety of purposes that they regard as important. They establish hospitals in order to care for the sick, retail stores to sell goods to consumers, banks to manage transactions involving the exchange of money, radio and TV stations to provide various sorts of program materials to the public, and so on. An institution is a means to an end, a way of doing something that society has decided needs to be done.

The Purpose of a University

What, then, is the purpose for which society has created universities? Why do people spend millions of dollars to build buildings—libraries, laboratories, classrooms, and the like—and additional millions to enable people like us (students, teachers) to occupy those buildings? What is a university for? What is its mission?

Try this: **the unique mission of a university is the discovery, preservation, and dissemination of truth.**

The discovery of truth: that is the heart and soul of the university. You must not think of professors and students as, respectively, those who already know the truth and those who do not. Professors have an edge on students by virtue of having been at the business of learning a bit longer than most students—but they would be the first to tell you, if they are candid, that even after many years of diligent study, their knowledge of the truth is limited, fragmentary, and mixed with error.

Our Common Ignorance

The professor's problem is the problem of human beings generally: we can rarely be certain that what we have learned, what we believe, is the *truth.* For many thousands of years, scholars believed that the earth was flat, and that it was stationary in the center of the universe, and that the sun, the planets, and the stars revolved around it. These beliefs, we now know with a high degree of certainty, were in error. We may be inclined to laugh at those silly people of yesterday who held such childish views. But let us not laugh too loudly, for it is highly likely that among the beliefs you and I hold today are some that will appear as foolish to future generations as the flat-earth theory does to us. Truth and error do not wear labels that enable us easily to distinguish between them.

Our situation, then, may be described as follows. We (that is, all people) hold many opinions, some of which are probably true and some of which are probably false. In addition, there are many matters about which we are totally ignorant, and about which we therefore have no opinions at all. Our task, if we wish to know the truth, is to rid ourselves so far as possible of both ignorance (no opinions) and error (false opinions), to exchange ignorance and error for the truth.

Seeking the Truth

How does one go about this? How does one attempt to determine the truth or falsity of any assertion? Clearly, one must look to the evidence that appears to be relevant to the truth or falsity of that assertion. *Paradoxically, the surest way to establish the truth of an assertion is to try to disprove it.* If there is some evidence in support of an assertion, and if nobody can find any evidence against it after making a reasonable effort to do so, then there is at least some reason to believe that the assertion may be true. Until, of course, some contrary evidence turns up, in which case one has to start all over again.

Thus we arrive at the following *axiom:* one who desires to know the truth concerning any matter must be persuaded by the evidence, and by the evidence alone. Anything or anybody who attempts to compel a conclusion based on anything other than the evidence is to that extent an enemy of truth.

Academic Freedom

Academic freedom is the opportunity to hold opinions based on the best evidence one has and to speak those opinions without fear of reprisal. Academic freedom means free and open discussion, a liberty to read what you want, to debate any issue, to defend new views and reinterpret or criticize old ones in an open forum.

Academic freedom can exist only when two conditions are met. First, it can exist only in a community of open and intelligent individuals who recognize that in principle every legitimate question deserves an answer, and that the legitimacy of question and answer cannot merely be assumed but must be shown capable of withstanding criticism. Second, academic freedom requires that this community make truth its common purpose, and free and open discussion the means to it. Unless both conditions are met, any freedom that there is will be purely accidental, and not very secure.

It is therefore an essential part of this idea to promote and provide for the intellectual development of every member of the academic community. In this community, it is not only those who have already cultivated a high degree of intellectual understanding who have a place. There must also be room for those who are just beginning their intellectual development. Students in each new generation must be allowed their skepticism; they must have time to examine and criticize even the most fundamental, most widely held views. But they in turn must be open to criticism and direction from their teachers and peers.

How does this notion of academic freedom affect your life? The university's need to maintain academic freedom means that *your* freedom to inquire is essential. You cannot be free if there is prejudice in the academic community. The idea of academic freedom requires that the individuals in the university actively help one another through the basic intellectual tactic of challenge and response. In his essay *On Liberty*, John Stuart Mill reminds us of this, and of the unique mission of an academic community, when he writes, "Complete liberty of contradicting and disproving our opinion, is the very condition which justifies us in assuming its truth...."

Enemies of Academic Freedom

Anyone or anything that tends to inhibit free inquiry and discussion concerning any matter, or that attempts to compel a conclusion based on anything other than the relevant evidence, is by definition an enemy of academic freedom. And there are, unfortunately, many such enemies.

Some of these enemies are purely internal, within the individual. They can be rooted out only by great effort on the part of that individual.

One of these is *fear.* The most comfortable opinions to hold are those that we have held the longest, and so we fear the discomfort of abandoning long-held opinions. The most comfortable opinions to hold are those that are widely held by those whose esteem we crave, and so we fear to adopt opinions that we know will be unpopular. A sage once said, "I never learned anything of importance without feeling a sense of loss because of the old and familiar but mistaken view that had to be abandoned." But we are human, and we fear such loss—even though it be for the sake of truth.

Sheer laziness is an enemy of academic freedom. It is easier, it takes less effort, simply to adopt a view that one has heard expressed by someone else than to study the evidence and draw one's own conclusion. But the easy way, unfortunately, is not the best way, for it gives us no basis for distinguishing between opinions that are true and those that are false.

Undue respect for tradition is yet another internal enemy of academic freedom. Indeed, the opinions of one's forebears deserve considerable respect, for they represent the accumulated wisdom of many generations. Still we must not be bound by them, and we must be willing to abandon them if the weight of the available evidence suggests that they are mistaken. For we, too, will pass on a fund of accumulated wisdom to the next generation, and those who receive it have a right to expect of us that it will contain relatively more truth and less error than that with which we began.

Perhaps the more obvious enemies of academic freedom are the external enemies. Every one of us is capable of being such an enemy and probably has in fact acted as one at one time or another. If in the course of a discussion one shouts down a would-be participant instead of allowing him or her to speak, one is playing the enemy. The same is true if one heckles, and so prevents from being heard, a speaker who holds views with which one disagrees. An instructor who uses the threat of a bad grade to compel agreement (or the *appearance* of agreement) with his or her own views is violating the academic freedom of students.

The administrator who denies promotion or *tenure* or a salary increase to an instructor because the instructor advocates views with which the administrator disagrees is violating the academic freedom of that instructor. A citizen who demands the ouster of a faculty member on the grounds that he or she holds views that are "dangerous" or "unorthodox" is asking (usually without realizing it) that academic freedom be abolished.

We repeat: anyone or anything that tends to inhibit free inquiry and discussion concerning any matter, or attempts to compel a conclusion based on anything other than the relevant evidence, is by definition an enemy of academic freedom. That academic freedom has so many enemies, both internal and external, underscores the important fact that the pathway to truth is not an easy one to find or to follow.

Academic freedom, then, is by no means a cloak for nonsense. It does not confer approval upon ideas that are *demonstrably* false, unsupported by evidence, or just downright silly. To the contrary: academic freedom makes it more likely that in due course such ideas will be shown up for what they are, and that views that are supported by the evidence—that is, truth—will prevail. In an institution whose business is the discovery, preservation, and *dissemination* of truth, academic freedom is the *sine qua non*—the "without which nothing," the essential condition in the absence of which it would cease to be a university.

Reprinted by permission of the authors.

● ●

 # Vocabulary

As you think about this essay, these definitions may be helpful to you:
1. **paradoxically**   in a manner seemingly contradictory to common sense and yet perhaps true.
2. **axiom**   a fundamental notion or idea that is assumed to be true
3. **tenure**   used within universities, this term denotes an earned privilege of assured continued employment following a long period—usually seven years—of probation during which a faculty member is evaluated on teaching ability, research productivity, and community service
4. **demonstrably**   capable of being proved, either logically or by reference to the real world
5. **dissemination**   dispersal; thus, universities are said here to exist for spreading the truth (by teaching and publishing, for example), not hiding it

Discussion Questions

1. Identify and explain the paradox in the statement, "the surest way to establish the truth of an assertion is to try to disprove it."
2. What, according to Halverson and Carter, are the two necessary conditions without which academic freedom cannot exist?
3. Halverson and Carter argue that "one who desires to know the truth concerning any matter must be persuaded by the evidence, and by the evidence alone." What else are people persuaded by?
4. What, according to Halverson and Carter, are the enemies of academic freedom?
5. How, according to Halverson and Carter, should we regard the opinions we have received from people we respect?

 # How Can These Ideas Apply to You?

1. What characteristics do you prefer in your friends: the willingness to disagree with you but remain quiet about it so that you don't get upset, or the willingness to tell you when they disagree with you and argue until discussion uncovers the truth? Why do you prefer the characteristics that you do?
2. How does a university differ from other institutions that seem to be, or ought to be, concerned about the truth—churches, for example, or the federal government?
3. Fear, laziness, and undue respect for tradition—have you ever struggled with these internal enemies of academic freedom? Be specific, and then describe how you resolved the struggle.
4. Academic freedom seems to be in conflict with the idea of majority rule. Is it?
5. Have you ever found yourself differing from the professor's opinion in class? How did you respond? How did the professor react to your difference of opinion?

The New Immorality

Joseph Wood Krutch

Joseph Wood Krutch was a distinguished professor of literature at Columbia University. The author of many books, Krutch was highly respected for his understanding of the ethical dimensions of literature. In the following essay, he comments on observations he made as a teacher and observer of students.

● ● ● ● ● ● ● ● ● ● ● ● ● ● ● ● ●

The provost of one of our largest and most honored institutions told me not long ago that a questionnaire was distributed to his undergraduates and that 40 percent refused to acknowledge that they believed cheating on examinations to be *reprehensible.*

Recently a reporter for a New York newspaper stopped six people on the street and asked them if they would consent to take part in a rigged television quiz for money. He reported that five of the six said yes. Yet most of these five, like most college cheaters, would probably profess a strong social consciousness. They may cheat, but they vote for foreign aid and for enlightened social measures.

These two examples exhibit a paradox of our age. It is often said, and my observation leads me to believe it true, that our seemingly great growth in social morality has oddly enough taken place in a world where private morality—a sense of the supreme importance of purely personal honor, honesty, and integrity—seems to be declining. *Beneficent* and benevolent social institutions are administered by people who all too frequently turn out to be accepting "gifts." The world of popular entertainment is rocked by scandals. College students, put on their honor, cheat on examinations. Candidates for the Ph.D. hire ghost writers to prepare their *theses.*

But, one may object, haven't all these things always been true? Is there really any evidence that personal dishonesty is more prevalent than it always was?

I have no way of making a historical measurement. Perhaps these things are not actually more prevalent. What I do know is that there is an increasing tendency to accept and take for granted such personal dishonesty. The bureaucrat and disk jockey say, "Well, yes, I took presents, but I assure you that I made just decisions anyway." The college student caught cheating does not even blush but shrugs his shoulders and comments: "Everybody does it, and besides, I can't see that it really hurts anybody."

Jonathan Swift once said: "I have never been surprised to find men wicked, but I have often been surprised to find them not ashamed." It is my conviction that though people may be no more wicked than they always have been, they seem less likely to be ashamed. If everybody does it, it must be right. Honest, moral, decent mean only what is usual. This is not really a wicked world, because morality means *mores* or manners and usual conduct is the only standard.

The second part of the defense, "It really doesn't hurt anybody," is equally revealing. "It doesn't hurt anybody" means it doesn't do that abstraction called society any harm. The harm it did the bribe-taker and the cheater isn't important; it is purely personal. And personal as opposed to social decency doesn't count for much. Sometimes I am inclined to blame sociology for part of this *paradox.* Sociology has tended too often to define good and evil as merely the "socially useful" or its reverse.

What social morality and social conscience leave out is the narrower but very significant concept of honor—as opposed to what is sometimes called merely "socially desirable conduct." The persons of honor are not content to ask merely whether this or that will hurt society, or whether it is what most people would permit themselves to do. They ask, and ask first of all, would it hurt them and their self-respect? Would it dishonor them personally?

It was a favorite and no doubt sound argument among early twentieth-century reformers that "playing the game" as the gentleman was supposed to play it was not enough to make a decent society. They were right; it is not enough. But the time has come to add that it is nevertheless indispensable. I hold that it is indeed inevitable that the so-called social conscience unsupported by the concept of personal honor will create a corrupt society. But suppose that it doesn't? Suppose that no one except the individual suffers from the fact that he sees nothing wrong in doing what everybody else does? Even so, I still insist that for the individual himself nothing is more important than this personal, interior sense of right and wrong and his determination to follow that—rather than to be guided by what everybody does or merely the criterion of "social usefulness." It is impossible for me to imagine a good society composed of persons without honor.

We hear it said frequently that what present-day people most desire is security. If that is so, then they have a wrong notion of what the real, the ultimate, security is. No one who is dependent on anything outside himself, upon money, power, fame, or whatnot, is or ever can be secure. Only he who possesses himself and is content with himself is actually secure. Too much is being said about the importance of adjustment and "participation in the group." Even cooperation, to give this thing its most favorable designation, is no more important than the ability to stand alone when the choice must be made between the sacrifice of one's own integrity and adjustment to or participation in group activity.

No matter how bad the world may become, no matter how much the mass man of the future may lose such of the virtues as he still has, one fact remains. If one person alone refuses to go along with him, if one person alone asserts his individual and inner right to believe in and be loyal to what his fellow men seem to have given up, then at least he will still retain what is perhaps the most important part of humanity.

Vocabulary

As you think about this essay, these definitions may be helpful to you:

1. **reprehensible**   deserving censure
2. **beneficent**   performing acts of kindness and charity
3. **theses**   long essays that incorporate the results of original thinking or research
4. **mores**   moral or ethical attitudes
5. **paradox**   a statement that is perhaps true, even though it seems to be contradictory

Discussion Questions

1. Define "honor" as you think Krutch means it.
2. What does Krutch mean by the sentence, "I hold that it is indeed inevitable that the so-called social conscience unsupported by the concept of personal honor will create a corrupt society"?
3. How might you attempt to answer the question "Is there really any evidence that personal dishonesty is more prevalent than it always was?" How does Krutch attempt to answer it?
4. Underlying Krutch's beliefs as expressed in this essay is the insistence that "for the individual himself nothing is more important than this personal, interior sense of right and wrong." Others might respond that such an internal sense is learned from those around us and therefore that different cultures are likely to result in different "personal, interior" senses of right and wrong. Which of these positions do you agree with? Why?
5. What does Krutch mean by the assertion that "Only he who possesses himself and is content with himself is actually secure"?

How Can These Ideas Apply to You?

1. What ethical standards would you violate if the price was right?
2. Do you agree that "what present-day people most desire is security"?
3. Take a survey among your contemporaries (people in one of your classes, members of an extracurricular group you belong to, or perhaps others who live in your campus dormitory) and find out how many would cheat on an assignment if they thought they could get away with it. Then interpret your results.

4. Why should you care if other people cheat?
5. Under the honor code systems of many colleges and universities, every student has an obligation to report knowledge of any student who cheats. If you had verifiable knowledge of cheating in any of its forms, would you report the fellow student who did it? Why?

Ideas as Property

Thomas L. Minnick

Thomas L. Minnick, an English teacher who admits to having graded more than 25,000 English composition papers, has served as an expert witness and researcher on issues relating to intellectual property and plagiarism in cases tried in New York, Ohio, and California. In this essay he emphasizes the positive value of ideas and other intellectual creations as property and draws attention to the fact that as property, under the law, ideas can be stolen or mistreated with serious consequences for the thief.

• • • • • • • • • • • • • • • • • •

The idea of "property"—that is, something owned by one person or group and therefore *not* owned by anyone else—is among the oldest, most widespread notions that humans share. Even cultures that believe that all things are owned jointly and equally by all members of the society (usually a tribe or clan) also believe that no single individual can claim ownership of those things. For example, because they believe that the land belongs to all, they also regard any individual who claims to own a part of it as violating the property rights of the group. The notions of "thieves" and "theft" depend on the idea of property, since stealing is defined as the act of taking something that does not belong to the thief. The ownership of property is also one of our most important ideas: many of our laws are based on the principle that three rights guaranteed to individuals living in a society are the right to life, the right to liberty, and the right to own property. Thomas Jefferson, writing the Declaration of Independence, paraphrased this already well-established principle when he identified "life, liberty, and the pursuit of happiness" as three *inalienable* rights of Americans.

We take for granted certain categories of property and, along with them, certain kinds of theft or other violations of property rights. For example, if you (or you and your local lending agency together) own a car, then a person who steals your car, drives it carelessly until the fuel is almost gone, then wrecks it, is unquestionably a thief, because he or she has taken your property without your permission and deprived you of it. Even if the car is returned to you no worse for wear, your rights have been violated, and no reasonable person would disagree that a theft has occurred. The same is true if someone takes your watch, your bookbag, your pet, or your Starter jacket identifying your favorite sports team. Furthermore, if someone takes your credit card and buys a substantial amount of merchandise in your name, even if the physical merchandise was never yours (and wouldn't fit you anyway), those items have been stolen from you since your property—in this example, your credit line and the dollars from it that will go to pay the bills—has been taken without your knowledge or approval.

Sometimes it may be less clear that *your ideas are your property,* but that is exactly what they are, and the courts recognize them as such. A specialization in legal studies is the field of intellectual property law, which is based on the premise that an idea belongs to the person who created it, and therefore that any profit, financial or otherwise, derived from that idea also belongs to the originator. The theft of ideas takes many forms. Suppose you design and *patent* an important new drug for the treatment of arthritis and, learning of your research, others market that drug under a different name. Unless you and they have entered into a prior agreement about distributing your drug and sharing the profits, their action violates your rights to your intellectual property. Or again, suppose you write a song, both words and music, and someone else, hearing it, decides the words are effective but that the music is not—then adapts your words to new music of their own. Given adequate evidence to establish your claim of prior ownership, you should be able to show that your intellectual property rights have been violated, and you should further be able to claim a monetary award for damages due to the violation of those rights.

Universities, whose defining reason to exist includes the development and teaching of ideas,[1] have a special stake in the principle that an idea belongs to the person who first conceived it. The integrity of a university depends on a strong belief in this principle, and so universities defend this principle in all they do. For what would a degree from your college or university be worth if students could be caught cheating and nevertheless receive credit for the courses where that offense took place? Undergraduates writing English compositions or research papers for courses in psychology or history, graduate students preparing their master's or doctoral theses, faculty members engaged in leading-edge research—all these participants in the university have a stake in preserving the principle of a creator's right to his or her ideas as property. If they misrepresent themselves as originating ideas that do not belong to them, they are violating the intellectual property rights of others. If they themselves are victims of plagiarists (people who copy their ideas, word-for-word or in paraphrases), then they are deprived of meaningful ownership of what they have created. Even if a particular idea is not worth much money on the open market, the theft of that idea means that the true originator may not receive the *intangible* credit or respect that that idea has earned. So it is essential to the credibility and integrity of a university, and therefore of the degrees that it confers, that it provide the best defense it can for the intellectual property of the members of its community. People who create new ideas should be respected for doing so, and people who claim as theirs those ideas that truly belong to others should be condemned.

Unfortunately, it is part of the nature of ideas that we find it harder to prove ownership of a new idea than, say, of a microwave oven. When someone has stolen your microwave oven, two statements are true: first, you no longer

---

[1]See the essay "On Academic Freedom" by William H. Halverson and James R. Carter earlier in this unit—ED.

have your microwave, and second, someone else probably does. Ideas are not like that: it is in the nature of ideas that I can tell you my idea, and then you and I both will have it. If I tell you my answer to the third question on our final examination in American history, I will know that answer and so will you. For that matter, I could tell my answer to everyone in our class and we all could produce the same answer on request. And so on: I could tell everyone at my college, or everyone in my state, or everyone in our country, or in the world—and yet I would still have the idea in the same way that I did before, while everyone else also now has it. Moreover, if someone steals your microwave oven, you will probably be able to identify it by brand, size, model number, and condition. If you have had the foresight to mark it as yours—by engraving it with your social security number, for example—then identifying it as your stolen property will be substantially easier. But it is very difficult to mark an idea as yours. Usually the proof of ownership for intellectual property takes the form of a patent or copyright, although it is possible to document prior ownership of an idea in other ways as well.

How can a university protect ideas from thieves? The first step is to make clear to every member of the university that ideas are a kind of property, and that the protection of those ideas really does matter to the well-being of the university. A second step is to teach students at all levels the conventions for acknowledging when they adopt or develop the ideas of someone else. The third is to deal seriously with instances of the theft of ideas, which in an academic setting commonly takes one of two forms—cheating (that is, copying someone else's answers during an examination) and *plagiarism,* the unacknowledged dependence on someone else's ideas in writing, usually in out-of-class assignments. That you are reading this essay is part of your university's effort to make clear that it values and protects ideas as property.

The second step, training in common academic procedures for acknowledging sources, involves learning the accepted forms for footnotes, bibliographies, and citations to other authors in the text of your work. If you have had to write a research paper as a composition exercise in high school or previous college work, then you have probably learned one of the many conventional systems available for acknowledging sources you have used and identifying the specific ideas and language from others that you cite in your own work.[2] What matters is that your reader should be able to tell what ideas are your own original work and what ideas you have adopted or adapted from others. If you quote a section of someone else's writing verbatim, you must enclose the quoted material within quotation marks *and* tell your reader where the original statement

---

[2]Perhaps the most widely used guide for authors using footnotes and bibliographies is "Turabian"—which is the shorthand way that writers refer to Kate L. Turabian, *A Manual for Writers of Term Papers, Theses, and Dissertations,* 6th ed. (Chicago: The University of Chicago Press, 1996). Other well-regarded guides of this sort include *MLA Handbook for Writers of Research Papers* (New York: Modern Language Association, 1999); *The Chicago Manual of Style* 14th ed. (Chicago: The University of Chicago Press, 1993); and *Publication Manual* 4th ed. (Washington, D.C.: American Psychological Association, 1994). Your instructor can help you decide among them.

appeared. If you rely on someone else's ideas, even if you do not quote them word for word, then a footnote identifying your source and indicating the extent of your indebtedness is appropriate.

The third step a college or university must take to ensure that ideas are credited to their true creators—namely, dealing seriously with instances of the theft of ideas—will be evident in the ways that instructors and the systems of the university react when a case of cheating or plagiarism is suspected. If an instructor suspects that a student has cheated on a test or copied someone else's essay, the easiest action to take will always be no action at all. But would such a lack of action be the right way to proceed? If cheating or plagiarism mean so little that they can be ignored, then the instructor is contributing to the institution's loss of integrity and the weakening of the degree—of *your* degree. Indeed, by such inaction an instructor would become an accessory to the theft. The right way to proceed is to put the investigation of the facts of the alleged case into the authority of a separate group of people—often called the Honor Board or the Committee on Academic Misconduct. By hearing many cases of this kind, such a group becomes familiar with the kinds of questions that should be pursued, the kinds of evidence that can be gathered, and the appropriate resolution of the incident. Since effective teachers make a commitment to put forth their own best efforts for their students, those teachers may feel a degree of betrayal when a student knowingly tries to misrepresent someone else's work as his or her own. Therefore, it is usually wiser for a neutral party or group to investigate and *adjudicate* a case of suspected misconduct.

Some schools automatically suspend a student who has been found in violation of the rules on cheating or plagiarizing. Such a suspension may be in effect for a term or several terms, and the student will not be permitted to re-enroll until that assigned time period has passed. Other schools dismiss a student permanently for violating the rules of proper academic conduct. The consequences of academic misconduct can be devastating: law schools, medical schools, and the other professional programs available to you may be permanently closed if your record contains a notation about academic misconduct. You need to know what your college considers to be academic misconduct, and you need to know what the penalties for committing such misconduct can be. At many colleges and universities, students are bound by an "honor code" that requires them to notify instructors of any cheating they may be aware of. In such places, the failure to notify an official about suspected misconduct also qualifies as a violation and is grounds for disciplinary action.

Know the relevant policies at your institution, but do not let the seriousness of those policies paralyze you when you start to write an essay or a research paper for one of your classes. Some students ask, with justification, "How can I be sure that my ideas are original? Surely someone else has had almost every idea before me at some time or another. How can I be safe from misconduct accusations?" When you are told to be original, your teacher does not expect that every idea in your essay will be unique in the history of human thought. But a teacher does have the right to expect that *when you knowingly depend* on the thinking of someone else, you will acknowledge that in the conventional way (using quotation marks, footnotes, and a bibliography). You can express your own original turn of thought by seeing an idea in a new light, or combining ideas that you have not read before in the same combination, or by modifying the acknowledged ideas of someone else with critical commentary or new emphasis, and so on. And just to be sure, if you really have any doubts about the originality of your work, talk to your instructor about them before you turn the work in for a grade.[3]

Reprinted by permission of the author.

• • • • • • • • • • • • • • • • • • • •

 # Vocabulary

As you think about this essay, these definitions may be helpful to you:
1. **inalienable**   incapable of being surrendered or transferred
2. **patent**   a license securing for an inventor for a term of years the exclusive right to make, use, or sell an invention
3. **intangible**   not capable of being precisely identified; abstract
4. **plagiarism**   stealing or passing off the ideas or words of another as one's own
5. **adjudicate**   to act as judge

 # Discussion Questions

1. What is the historical basis for "ownership of property"?
2. How does the author define "ideas as property"? How do ideas and material property differ?
3. Why is the concept of ideas as property so important in a university setting?
4. What steps can be taken by a university to ensure ideas as property are protected, according to the author?
5. What can happen to a student who is found to have cheated or plagiarized?

 # How Can These Ideas Apply to You?

1. Have you ever considered your ideas to be property? Explain.
2. The author indicates that the theft of ideas takes many forms; can you give an example of how an idea was stolen from you or someone you know?

[3] I am pleased to record my gratitude to my colleagues Professor Sara Garnes and Dean Virginia Gordon for their conversations with me about the topic of this essay.

3. Where are the policies of your college written about student violations of the theft of ideas (for example: cheating or plagiarism)? How familiar are you with them?
4. Do you know how to acknowledge other people's ideas when you write a research paper or composition (for instance, using footnotes and/or bibliographies)? If not, where on your campus can you find assistance to learn?
5. What is the procedure on your campus for adjudicating a case of suspected misconduct?

Please Stop This Talk About Values

George F. Will

George F. Will is a well-known and highly respected conservative columnist and
political analyst. In recent years he has been an articulate critic of higher education,
arguing on behalf of the "traditional" curriculum that has been under fire for at least
the last decade. In this essay, Will takes on a more general ethical issue, urging that
writers and teachers focus less on "values" and more on virtues.

H ere at Lafayette College in Easton, Pa., as elsewhere in our republic, the
birth of which was nobly assisted by the Frenchman for whom the university is named, today's peace and prosperity allow a preoccupation with the
problem of teaching what are nowadays called "values." Talk of values is a new,
and regrettable, vocabulary for discussing a recurring American concern.

When the Marquis de Lafayette returned to America in 1824, his tour cata-
lyzed the young republic's unease about what it sensed was a decline from the
pinnacle of virtue achieved by the Revolutionary generation that was then passing. Then, as now, the nation was feeling its oats economically, was feeling
queasy about whether its character was as strong as its economy and, thus, was
wondering about whether prosperity constituted progress.

Today it would be progress if everyone would stop talking about values.
Instead, let us talk, as the Founding Fathers did, about virtues.

Historian Gertrude Himmelfarb rightly says the ubiquity of talk about values causes us to forget how new such talk is. It began in Britain's 1983 election
campaign, when Prime Minister Margaret Thatcher embraced the accusation,
which is what it was, that she favored "Victorian values."

Time was, "value" was used mostly as a verb, meaning to esteem. It also was
a singular noun, as in "the value of the currency." In today's politics, it is primarily
a plural noun, denoting beliefs or attitudes. And Friedrich Nietzsche's *nihilistic*
intention—the demoralization of society—is advanced when the word "values"
supplants "virtues" in political and ethical discourse. When we move beyond
talk about good and evil, we are left with the thin gruel of values-talk.

How very democratic values-talk is: Unlike virtues, everyone has lots of
values, as many as they choose. Adolf Hitler had scads of values. George Washington had virtues. Who among those who knew him would have spoken of
Washington's "values"?

Values-talk comes naturally to a nonjudgmental age—an age judgmental
primarily about the cardinal sin of being judgmental. It is considered broad-
minded to say, "One person's values are as good as another's."

Values are an equal-opportunity business: They are mere choices. Virtues
are habits, difficult to develop and therefore not equally accessible to all. Speak-

ing of virtues rather than values is elitist, offensive to democracy's *egalitarian,* leveling ethos.

Which is why talk of virtues should be revived. Alexis de Tocqueville, who toured America not long after Lafayette did, noted that although much is gained by replacing aristocratic with democratic institutions and suppositions, something valuable is often lost: the ability to recognize, and the hunger to honor, *hierarchies* of achievement and character. So democracy requires the cultivation of certain tendencies of democracy.

So says Professor Harvey C. Mansfield, Harvard's conservative (who because of his opposition to grade inflation is known there as Harvey "C-minus" Mansfield). He notes that a theme of American literature, *writ large* in the works of Mark Twain, is the effect of democracy on the higher qualities of people. To counter democracy's leveling ethos, universities, Mansfield says, should teach students how to praise.

Students should learn to look up to the heroic—in thought and action, in politics and literature, in science and faith. After all, the few men and women who become heroes do so by looking up and being pulled up by a vision of nobility. Which makes a hero quite unlike a *role model.* A very democratic notion, role model: It is something anyone can successfully emulate.

Here, then, is higher education's special purpose in a democracy: It is to turn young people toward what is high.

A wit has said that in the 19th century, England's ruling class developed the system of elite secondary schools for the purpose of making sure that Byron and Shelley could never happen again. The proper purpose of American higher education is not to serve as a values cafeteria, where young people are encouraged to pick whatever strikes their fancies. Rather, the purpose of higher education for citizens of a democracy should be to help them identify that rarity, excellence in various realms.

These thoughts for commencement season are pertinent to the political season. Whenever you hear politicians speaking of "values," you are in the presence of America's problem, not its solution.

• • • • • • • • • • • • • • • • • • • •

 # Vocabulary

As you think about this essay, these definitions may be helpful to you:
1. **nihilism**   the belief that nothing has meaning or importance
2. **egalitarian**   the belief that all people should have equal social and political rights
3. **hierarchy**   a group of people arranged by rank or class, often related to political power

4. **writ large**   signified or expressed in a more prominent magnitude, or taken to a higher degree

 ## Discussion Questions

1. What is the fundamental difference that Will draws between values and virtues? What are his best examples of this difference, in your view? Can you suggest other examples?
2. Why does Will refer to Lafayette and Washington in this brief essay?
3. Did Hitler have "values," as Will claims? If so, what might they have been?

 ## How Can These Ideas Apply to You?

1. Before you read this essay, what would you have answered if someone asked, "What are your values?"
2. What virtues do you aspire to have?
3. Do you think the distinction that Will draws is important, or is it merely a matter of definitions?

UNIT SUMMARY

The essays in this unit focus on ethical values, especially those that relate to institutions of higher education. Halverson and Carter, Krutch, and Minnick discuss aspects of intellectual honesty as they relate to academic study, and Will encourages readers to substitute "virtues" for "values" in talk about ethics.

Summary Questions

1. Do you agree with the essentially intellectual picture of the university that the authors in this unit share? What are some alternative views of the purpose of a university or college education? Can your alternatives fit compatibly with the views these authors offer?
2. An important qualification in most ethical theories is the belief that "ought implies can"—that is, that we cannot be expected to measure up to impossible standards. In the essays in this unit, do any of the authors ask you to do what you cannot reasonably be expected to do?
3. What university courses might you take to further explore the kinds of moral and ethical issues discussed in these essays?

Suggested Writing Assignments

1. Write a short essay connecting your ethical beliefs to those given in one of the essays in this unit. Show how your beliefs significantly differ or coincide with those expressed here.
2. The authors in this unit agree that acts of intellectual dishonesty, like cheating on tests and plagiarizing, are not acceptable at a university. Write a short essay identifying some other forms of behavior that are inappropriate at a university. Suggest a plan for limiting such inappropriate activities.
3. Might you expect your sense of values or virtues to change as you complete an undergraduate degree? Why? How?

Suggested Readings

Emmons, M. L., and R. E. Alberti. *Your Perfect Right.* San Luis Obispo, CA: Impact, 1974.
Lewis, H. *A Question of Values.* New York: Harper & Row, 1990.
Pojman, L. P. *Ethics: Discovering Right and Wrong.* Belmont, CA: Wadsworth, 1990.

UNIT 8

What Is Diversity and Why Is It Important to Me?

J ust about anyone interested in American higher education can start an argument these days by bringing up the topic of "political correctness." The phrase is highly specific to our times and became important largely because of changes in the way that educators think about how to design a college curriculum.

Before 1980, the question of what to include in a well-designed college program of studies would have had different answers from different scholars, but most of them would have differed only in matters of degree. The questions people asked were "How much science should be required? How many courses of European, English, or American literature should be expected? Should Faulkner receive as much emphasis as Melville?" More recently, debates on the appropriate content of a required curriculum in general studies have grown louder, more political, and nastier. The questions people now tend to raise include "Why have you omitted literature by women and people of color? How can you prefer courses

We reason deeply when we forcibly feel.

—MARY WOLLSTONECRAFT

about the European cultural tradition when students will increasingly need to deal with Asian, African, and Hispanic cultures in their daily lives in the 21st century? Do the courses you propose to require prepare students to improve the world, or just to describe it?" The "gentleman's agreement" (to use a phrase that some would argue expresses the problem) about what to include in a college degree program and how to talk about it is no longer in effect.

Detachment from political considerations used to be thought of, among scholars, as an ideal to be cultivated by educated people. Now many regard such detachment as an illusion and say that every author, teacher, and speaker should begin by identifying his or her political assumptions. So let us say up front that without abandoning the rich history of Western thought, we value diversity and believe that the free expression of diverse points of view is essential to the well-being of a university.

We do not regard that as a predominantly political point of view, though it certainly is a notion with political consequences. On this principle, for example, we oppose all intellectual straitjackets—such as those the Nazis imposed on German universities in the period from their rise to power until the end of World War II, a time when faculty members and students alike suffered imprisonment and death for expressing ideas that were politically incorrect according to the ruling powers of the time. Further, we believe that argument and dissent need to proceed within a civilized framework—that there are reasonable constraints on behavior that all members of a community need to observe and respect. But the essential nature of a university cannot long survive in the presence of restraints on thinking and expressing ideas.

We value diversity of opinions and cultures because the free exchange of ideas is the surest way to expose bad thinking and to find the good. The essay on academic freedom by Halverson and Carter in Unit 7 provides the rationale for this belief.

We also value diversity on the fundamental ground of our shared nature as human beings: We all want to be treated fairly, and we all object to unearned punishments and rewards. So Unit 8 continues with essays in which many individuals speak about why the fact that they are different from the majority—in race, religion, gender, looks, sexual preference—should not disqualify them from the respect accorded to us all in a civilized environment, especially in a free democratic nation. Erickson and Strommer talk about how much a sense of "fitting in," that feeling of belonging at the university, really matters to new students. In the subsequent essays, students talk about the ways that thoughtless or premeditated comments or other forms of behavior have affected them and made them feel like outsiders. This feeling of alienation is often the motivation that opens the dialogue among diverse groups, a dialogue that is most evident on our campuses perhaps because no other class of institutions is better suited for carrying on just such a dialogue.

Defining dialogue is not an easy task. The sort of dialogue we mean is not merely a conversation. Rather, we intend this term in the way that thinkers such as the 19th-century Catholic philosopher John Henry, Cardinal Newman, and the early 20th-century Jewish teacher Martin Buber have meant it: one person speaking to another, heart to heart, and listening. Universities and colleges offer unequaled opportunities for students to meet others who are different from themselves and to enter into dialogue with them. The goal of dialogue is understanding and connecting with another person, and the result of dialogue is often to understand oneself better through understanding someone else. International students, students from different religions and cultures, students who share your goals in education but may differ from you in almost every other way—these are people worth seeking out for what they can teach you about themselves and about yourself. Dialogue is the means by which we discover and evaluate truth, and diversity is the starting point for dialogue.

Among the most powerful statements of the reasons that America—and especially American universities—needs to keep this dialogue alive will be found in the selection that closes this unit: the speech, "I Have a Dream," that Reverend Martin Luther King, Jr., delivered shortly before his assassination. His vision of a society free at last from judgments based narrowly on the accidents of birth joins in perpetuity such other classic statements of the need for freedom of expression as "Areopagitica," the poet John Milton's defense of a free press, and "On Liberty," philosopher John Stuart Mill's reasoned explanation of the essential character of a free society.

Fitting In

Betty LaSere Erickson and Diane Weltner Strommer

Betty LaSere Erickson is an instructional development specialist at the University of
Rhode Island and conducts workshops and seminars on college campuses nationwide.
Diane Weltner Strommer is former dean of University College and Special Academic
Programs at the University of Rhode Island and frequently consults on programs to
improve new students' first year. In this essay they draw on their own studies and
experience, as well as important research about college students, to point out the
importance of "fitting in" to the college environment. They explore the role that a
sense of belonging can play for students as they adjust to university life and work.

It's easy to veg out in your room. I know you can't expect people and activities to
come to you, but it's hard to be independent and assertive. I want to be involved
in the school, but I don't know how.— Freshman

How freshmen elect to spend their time suggests the kind and extent of
involvement they have with the college, how well they are fitting in. While
more than 80 percent of college-bound seniors still graduate from public high
schools enrolling fewer than 500 students,[1] since 1950 most colleges and universities have grown steadily larger, with the average enrollment of all institutions expanding by about 25 percent in the fifteen years between 1970 and
1984.[2] As colleges have grown and become more bureaucratic and complex,
freshmen accustomed to a smaller scale find it more difficult to locate a niche,
to feel they fit in. Although some schools have instituted strong systems of support for freshmen, on most campuses freshmen are expected to assimilate themselves to the ongoing system as quickly as possible. Nothing much has changed
since the Hazen Report of 1968. Then as now colleges can be criticized for doing little, if anything, to maintain the curiosity of freshmen, to stimulate their interest, to expose them to intellectual experiences, or to involve them in college
activities.[3]

Although freshmen clearly understand the need to find their place academically as well as socially, the first priority of most is to make new friends with
whom to "hang out." Most do so surprisingly quickly, and engaging in "friendly

---

[1]The College Board. *College Bound Seniors National Report: 1988, Profile of SAT and Achievement
Test Takers.* New York: College Entrance Examination Board, 1988.
[2]National Institute of Education. *Involvement in Learning: Realizing the Potential of American
Higher Education.* Washington, D.C.: U.S. Department of Education, 1984.
[3]Hazen Foundation, The Committee on the Student in Higher Education. *The Student in Higher
Education.* New Haven, Conn.: Hazen Foundation, 1968.

fun"...occupies much of their time outside class. Most colleges report a distinct decline in participation in more formalized extracurricular activities. On our campus at the University of Rhode Island, for instance, only 8 percent of the freshmen reported some degree of participation in student clubs or student government in an informal survey taken in 1989. Although freshmen often mention the need to take part in extracurricular activities with great earnestness, as if it were a faintly pleasant duty, their preference during nonworking hours is clearly for more private and casual fun with their peers—parties, pickup games or intramural sports, rock concerts.

Finding a circle of friends and becoming accepted can be particularly difficult for students who do not quite match the campus norm; disabled, minority, international, gay, and older freshmen may all feel particularly alienated and isolated. For minority students and many international students, the painful *disparity* between their college life and home life may increase their sense of isolation. Trying to live in two worlds can be exceedingly difficult. As Marcus Mabry, a black student from New York attending Stanford, writes, "The ache of knowing [my family's] suffering is always there. It has to be kept deep down, or I can't find the logic in studying and partying while people, my people, are being killed by poverty. Ironically, success drives me away from those I most want to help by getting an education."[4]

For minority students, particularly those from disadvantaged backgrounds, the connection to college is often tenuous. They are less likely than majority students to have successful graduates in their immediate or extended families, less likely to have heard that they were expected to be successful in college from others or to have had strong, long-term expectations for themselves, have fewer previous on-campus experiences, and have fewer peers to help them in exploring and adjusting to their new environment or in fitting in.[5]

Although Moffatt reports that during his association with the dorm at Rutgers, blacks and Puerto Ricans "lived reasonably *amiably* among their white peers all year long," he also notes that the minority students did all the adjusting. "They were swamped," he comments, "by the white majority on an 'integrated' floor" and they "lived on the floor in terms of the white majority. None of them were 'threatening.' None of them made much of her or his black or Puerto Rican identity."[6] Another study reports that "the social environments of the large, predominantly white, public universities ... were problematic even for well-prepared minority students."[7] Minority freshmen may find social support only off campus. Institutions that expect all adjustment to be on the side of freshmen

[4]Mabry, M. "Living in Two Worlds." *Newsweek on Campus*, April 1988, 52.
[5]Attinasi, L. C., Jr. "Getting In: Mexican Americans' Perceptions of University Attendance and the Implications for Freshman Year Persistence." *Journal of Higher Education*, 1989, *60* (3), 247–277.
[6]Moffatt, M. *Coming of Age in New Jersey.* New Brunswick, N.J.: Rutgers University Press, 1989.
[7]Skinner, E. R., and Richardson, R. C. "Making It in a Majority University." *Change*, May/June, 1988, 37–42.

"limit the range of minority students they can serve responsibly to those who . . . resemble traditional college-goers."[8]

Along with this ever-present assumption that minority students can and will conform to the majority, the past several years have seen a disturbing *resurgence* of racially and ethnically motivated violence and conflict on a number of campuses, demanding that colleges pay serious attention to the climate for minority groups. While middle-class white students usually know they ought to appreciate diversity, they are in fact often frightened by it, a fear especially apparent as it relates to homosexuality, since being openly *homophobic* is more socially acceptable to peers than is fear of blacks, Hispanics, or Asians.

Typically, therefore, minority freshmen experience an unusual degree of stress as they attempt to fit in, to accommodate: the gay student concealing his or her homosexuality, the black student acting white. In the classroom, faculty create the climate. We know, for instance, not only that overt faculty prejudice "can result in inappropriate racial or ethnic remarks in class or in lowering the performance of alienated or discouraged minority students," but also that "unconscious assumptions that minority students are unable to perform up to par may become self-fulfilling prophecies."[9] Subtle behaviors or different treatment—like calling on students more or less frequently, not asking students the same kinds of questions, not paying the same attention—can create what Hall and Sandler first identified as a "chilly classroom climate" for members of minority groups and women.[10]

Older students, too, need sensitive understanding. As one observes, "Faculty could be more tuned in to the fact that it's not that easy; you're balancing a lot of responsibilities. With age some people find it particularly difficult to admit they need help. Faculty could ask if they need help. And not make up impossible rules. I had one professor who said from the beginning that there would be absolutely no excuses for missing an exam. If you miss an exam, you get a zero. I hardly ever miss a class. But my initial reaction was, what if something happens at home?"

The classroom may be key not only to the successful academic *assimilation* of freshmen, but, interestingly, to their personal growth as well. One somewhat surprising finding of a study designed to determine the benefits of college attendance was that "academic integration" had both direct and indirect effects on freshman-year reports of personal growth.[11] Finding a niche academically, fitting into and succeeding in classes, may have more influence on personal

---

[8]Green, M. F. (ed.). *Minorities on Campus: A Handbook for Enhancing Diversity.* Washington, D.C.: American Council on Education, 1989.

[9]Hall, R. M., and Sandler, B. R. *The Classroom Climate: A Chilly One for Women?* Washington, D.C.: Association of American Colleges, Project on the Status and Education of Women, 1982.

[10]Hall, R. M., and Sandler, B. R. *Out of the Classroom: A Chilly Campus Climate for Women?* Washington, D.C.: Association of American Colleges, Project on the Status and Education of Women, 1984.

[11]Terenzini, P. T., and Wright, T. M. "Students' Personal Growth During the First Two Years of College." *The Review of Higher Education,* 1987, *10* (3), 259–271.

growth, this study suggests, than does fitting in socially. Authors Terenzini and Wright conclude, "Students' integration into the academic systems of an institution may be as important to their personal growth as to their academic and intellectual development. These findings suggest a potential need to rethink campus and departmental orientation programs, many of which focus on introducing students to social, rather than academic, aspects of the collegiate experience. The results also have important implications for faculty members who foster academic integration as they advise students. . . . Finally, the results suggest a coherence and integrity in the developmental process: experiences that promote students' academic or intellectual development also appear to influence students' personal growth."[12]

Vocabulary

As you think about this essay, these definitions may be helpful to you:
1. **disparity**   fundamental difference
2. **amiably**   in a friendly, agreeable manner
3. **resurgence**   state of rising again into life or prominence
4. **homophobic**   irrationally fearing homosexuality
5. **assimilation**   absorbtion into the cultural tradition of a group

Discussion Questions

1. Adapting to a new environment can mean learning to "fit in" to many new situations. Identify some of these situations that are common to most first-year students.
2. Many people regard a new environment as unsettling, but a better way may be to think of each new environment as a new opportunity. How can these different points of view affect students' behavior as they attempt to "fit in"?
3. According to Erickson and Strommer, what special problems do new minority students face when they attempt to fit in at college?
4. In general, what is the role of faculty members in helping students to fit in? Does this have specific implications for minority students?
5. Why do Erikson and Strommer consider the results of the study by Terenzini and Wright to be "somewhat surprising"?

[12]Ibid., pp. 268, 270.

How Can These Ideas Apply to You?

1. Have you found it easy or difficult to fit in to college life? Why? What are you doing to fit in?

2. In your judgment, are Erickson and Strommer correct when they write: "While middle-class white students usually know they ought to appreciate diversity, they are in fact often frightened by it, a fear especially apparent as it relates to homosexuality, since being openly homophobic is more socially acceptable to peers than is fear of blacks, Hispanics, or Asians."? What factors—other than fear—might contribute to students' unwillingness to "appreciate diversity"?

3. Compare your feelings on your first day in college with your feelings today. In what ways have they changed? How did those changes occur?

4. Some adaptations are easier than others. In adjusting to college life, what did you find easiest? Most difficult?

5. Suppose that Terenzini and Wright are correct in their conclusion that learning to fit in academically at college is more important than learning to fit in socially. What steps should you take in order to fit in academically?

How Discrimination Works and Why It Matters: Five Personal Statements

Chana Schoenberger, from Bethesda, Maryland, was a high school student when she wrote her comments and published them in *Newsweek*. Joy Weeber was a graduate student in a doctoral program in Psychology at North Carolina State in Raleigh. Edward Delgado-Romero is a psychologist at the University of Florida Counseling Center in Gainesville. Donna Talbot coordinates the student affairs graduate programs in the Department of Counselor Education and Counseling Psychology at Western Michigan University, Kalamazoo. And Lisa J. Brandyberry is a senior psychologist and director of adult outpatient and emergency services at Piedmont Behavioral Health Care in Albemarle, North Carolina.

Getting to Know About You and Me

Chana Schoenberger

A religious holiday approaches; students at my high school who will be celebrating the holiday prepare a presentation on it for an assembly. The Diversity Committee, which sponsors the assemblies to increase religious awareness, asked me last spring if I would help with the presentation on Passover, the Jewish holiday that *commemorates* the Exodus from Egypt. I was too busy with other things, and I never got around to helping. I didn't realize then how important those presentations really are, or I definitely would have done something.

This summer I was one of 20 teens who spent five weeks at the University of Wisconsin at Superior studying acid rain with a National Science Foundation Young Scholars program. With such a small group in such a small town, we soon became close friends and had a good deal of fun together. We learned about the science of acid rain, went on field trips, found the best and cheapest restaurants in Superior and ate in them frequently to escape the lousy cafeteria food. We were a happy, bonded group.

Represented among us were eight religions: Jewish, Roman Catholic, Muslim, Hindu, Methodist, Mormon, Jehovah's Witness, and Lutheran. It was amazing, given the variety of backgrounds, to see the ignorance of some of the smartest young scholars on the subject of other religions.

On the first day, one girl mentioned that she had nine brothers and sisters. "Oh, are you Mormon?" asked another girl, who I knew was a Mormon herself.

The first girl, shocked, replied, "No, I dress normal!" She thought Mormon was the same as Mennonite, and the only thing she knew about either religion was that Mennonites don't, in her opinion, "dress normal."

My friends, ever curious about Judaism, asked me about everything from our basic theology to food preferences. "How come, if Jesus was a Jew, Jews aren't Christian?" my Catholic roommate asked me in all seriousness. Brought up in a small Wisconsin town, she had never met a Jew before, nor had she met people from most of the other "strange" religions (anything but Catholic or main-stream Protestant). Many of the other kids were the same way.

"Do you all still practice animal sacrifices?" a girl from a small town in Min-nesota asked me once. I said no, laughed, and pointed out that this was the 20th century, but she had been absolutely serious. The only Jews she knew were the ones from the Bible.

Nobody was deliberately rude or *anti-Semitic*, but I got the feeling that I was representing the entire Jewish people through my actions. I realized that many of my friends would go back to their small towns thinking that all Jews liked Dairy Queen Blizzards and grilled cheese sandwiches. After all, that was true of all the Jews they knew (in most cases, me and the only other Jewish young scholar, period).

The most awful thing for me, however, was not the *benign* ignorance of my friends. Our biology professor had taken us on a field trip to the EPA field site where he worked, and he was telling us about the project he was working on. He said that they had to make sure the EPA got its money's worth from the study—he "wouldn't want them to get Jewed."

I was astounded. The professor had a doctorate, various other degrees and seemed to be a very intelligent man. He apparently had no idea that he had just made an anti-Semitic remark. The other Jewish girl in the group and I debated whether or not to say something to him about it, and although we agreed we would, neither of us ever did. Personally, it made me feel uncomfortable. For a high-school student to tell a professor who taught her class that he was a *bigot* seemed out of place to me, even if he was one.

What scares me about that experience, in fact about my whole visit to Wis-consin, was that I never met a really vicious anti-Semite or a *malignantly* preju-diced person. Many of the people I met had been brought up to think that Jews (or Mormons or any other religion that's not mainstream Christian) were differ-ent and that difference was not good.

Difference, in America, is supposed to be good. We are expected—at least, I always thought we were expected—to respect each other's traditions. Respect requires some knowledge about people's backgrounds. Singing Christmas car-ols as a kid in school did not make me Christian, but it taught me to appreciate beautiful music and someone else's holiday. It's not necessary or desirable for all ethnic groups in America to assimilate into one traditionless mass. Rather, we all need to learn about other cultures so that we can understand one another and not feel threatened by others.

In the little multicultural universe that I live in, it's safe not to worry about explaining the story of Passover because if people don't hear it from me, they'll hear it some other way. Now I realize that's not true everywhere.

Ignorance was the problem I faced this summer. By itself, ignorance is not always a problem, but it leads to misunderstandings, prejudice and hatred. Many of today's problems involve hatred. If there weren't so much ignorance about other people's backgrounds, would people still hate each other as badly as they do now? Maybe so, but at least that hatred would be based on facts and not flawed beliefs.

I'm now back at school, and I plan to apply for the Diversity Committee. I'm going to get up and tell the whole school about my religion and the tradition I'm proud of. I see now how important it is to celebrate your heritage and to educate others about it. I can no longer take for granted that everyone knows about my religion, or that I know about theirs. People who are suspicious when they find out I'm Jewish usually don't know much about Judaism. I would much prefer them to hate or distrust me because of something I've done, instead of them hating me on the basis of prejudice.

• •

 # Vocabulary

As you think about this essay, these definitions may be helpful to you:
1. **commemorate**   to mark by some ceremony or observation
2. **anti-Semitic**   discriminating against Jews as a religious or racial group
3. **benign**   mild or harmless disposition
4. **bigot**   one who is intolerantly devoted to one's own opinions or prejudices
5. **malignantly**   injuriously, intentionally harmful

What Could I Know of Racism?

Joy E. Weeber

• • • • • • • • • • • • • • • • • • •

What could I know of racism, being a middle-class, college-educated White woman. What could I know of the pain of being rendered invisible because of a single characteristic? What could I know of having the complexity of myself, a Dutch American from a large extended family living around the world, reduced to that feature which marks me as "different" from the dominant culture? What could I know of being denied entrance to public facilities or required to sit in segregated places because of that characteristic? What could I know of being forced to use a back service entrance, like a second-class citizen? What could I know about being told that if I "work hard enough" I could make it, although getting in the front door for an interview seems an impossibility? What could I know about having to endure painful procedures to make my appearance more acceptable? What could I know of being charged a higher price for services because of the way I look? What could I know about not being able to ride a bus with dignity? What could I know of having a hard time finding a place to live because of housing discrimination or being unable to visit in the homes of my classmates? What could I know of growing up in a society that never portrays my people with positive images in the media, except for those exceptional, inspirational heroes who have more than made it? What could I know of being viewed as less intelligent simply because of the way I look? What could I know of being educated in a segregated school setting, not expected to amount to much and denied opportunities because of it? What could I know of being thought of as less than acceptable because of the way that I speak? What could I know of having to work twice as hard as others just to prove I am as good as they are? What could I know of being viewed as a charity case, rather than one who possesses civil rights?

I can know the pain of all of these things because I am disabled. My disabled brothers and sisters and I experience such acts of discrimination on a daily basis, and the pain these encounters cause is the same pain that racism causes people of color. It is the pain caused by the unconscious beliefs of a society that assumes everyone is, or should be, "normal" (i.e., White and very able-bodied). It is the pain caused by the assumption that everyone should be capable of total independence and "pulling themselves up by their own bootstraps." It is a belief in the superiority of being nondisabled that assumes everyone who is disabled wishes they could be nondisabled—at any cost. In the disability community, we call this "ableism," a form of prejudice and bigotry that marks us as less than those who are nondisabled. In this narrative, I use language the disability community claims in naming its own lived experience. And although it may not be "politically correct," it is meant as a true reflection of how many of us view ourselves and our lives as members of the disability community.

Ableism causes pain because it convinces us that there is something fundamentally wrong with us, that we are not acceptable just as we are. After all, we are the ones who are "defective," with bodies, speech, hearing, vision and emotional or cognitive functioning to be fixed by doctors and therapists. Ableism also causes pain to nondisabled people who are unprepared to deal with their own vulnerability and mortality when accidents and aging require that they do so. I did not understand the pain these attitudes had caused me until I was 35, despite having lived with the effects of polio since I was an infant. Until then, I did not know that I had spent my entire life trying to prove how I had "overcome" my polio, which is no more possible than overcoming being female or African American! I did not understand that these ableist attitudes and acts devalued my body and denied an essential element of who I am.

I only began to understand all of this when I read an essay, "The Myth of the Perfect Body," by Roberta Galler (1984),[1] who also had polio as a child. I felt as if I were reading my own diary! I was not an alien; I had a disability! I was the "supercrip" she wrote about, the defiant opposite of the pathetic cripple I had been made so deathly afraid of being. I had spent enormous amounts of my energy proving how "able" I was, to counter society's belief that I am "unable." I thought I had "passed" as normal in my nondisabled world (despite my crutches and braces), because I was often "complimented" by strangers and friends who "did not think of me as handicapped." Only when I read this woman's words did I begin to understand how my life had been shaped by living with a disability, even though my family and I had not been able to acknowledge that it existed! Only then did I begin to understand how my sense of self had been constructed by how my body had been touched, treated, and talked about by those who had been my "caregivers." Only then did I begin to understand how my life had been lived as an outsider, struggling unconsciously for acceptance.

Throughout my childhood, I had successfully resisted sincerely religious strangers' urgings for me to get "healed," people who thought of me as sick and infirm. Although these encounters left me feeling violated and nauseated, I knew I was fine and intact the way I was! Why did they think I was sick? I lived in a tight-knit community that accepted me as a whole person; they did not see me as sick. Not once had I been stopped from living life fully by anyone's low expectations, fear, or lack of imagination in how to change the world to meet my needs. I had been allowed to participate on my terms and discover my own physical limitations. My parents understood the stigma that society places on people with disabilities and were determined to nurture a sense of self that could deflect such negativity.

And yet, at the age of 10, I was marked as "other" by a diagnosis of scoliosis, found to be "defective" with a curving spine and weak leg muscles, and in need

---

[1] R. Galler, "The Myth of the Perfect Body," in C. Vance (ed.), *Pleasure and Danger: Exploring Female Sexuality* (Boston: Routledge and Kegan Paul, 1984), pp. 165–172.

of "corrective" surgery. Thus began my searing journey into a medical world that would teach me well what it really means to be disabled in this society! It was a world that taught me I was invisible, a defective body part to be talked about as if not connected to a lonely, hurting child. It was a world that taught me I had to be tough to survive, cut off from the emotional support of my family for all but 2-hour visits a week. It was a world that taught me that it was okay for others to inflict pain on me—if their goal was to make me more "normal." This world taught me that what I felt or wanted had nothing to do with what happened to my body, that it was okay to publicly strip children and parade their defects in front of strangers. The result of seven surgeries and innumerable scars was a girl who was numb, disconnected from both body and soul. I was fragmented and lost to a family who had no clue of my inner devastation. The emotional isolation of the hospital followed me home, as I heard in my family's lack of understanding that something was "wrong" with how I responded to life—emotionally, psychologically, spiritually, and politically!

My response to the horror of those years was to make myself outdo everyone, need help from no one, and take care of everyone else's needs. I was constantly proving I was the "exception," not one of those dependent cripples society cannot tolerate. Never mind that I spent my entire adult life struggling with devastating bouts of exhaustion-induced depression—although others only ever saw my bright, cheerful self. Never mind that I was alone, unable to sustain any vital romantic relationships, ever untouchable and independent. I became the angry one who spoke out against social injustice and felt the sexism in our community and family. I was the one who felt the arrogance and violence of racism. I was the one who felt the fragmentation of only seeking spiritual and physical sustenance, while psychological and emotional needs went unacknowledged. Being alone in the hospital, and the thought of seeking the company of those who might share them never crossed my mind.

At no time did I connect my different ways of perceiving and responding to the world with my experience of living with a disability. I couldn't. There was no disabled person in my world to help me understand that my empathy for those who suffered from injustice or were devalued because of race was rooted in my own experience of being devalued because of my disability. In the 7 years since my first encounter with a disabled person who understood, I have never felt alone. I have come to know the healing of belonging, of being understood without a word in a community of people who validate my feelings. I did not know how fragmented I was, and I needed other disabled people to teach me to love myself wholly! I had needed them to teach me how to embrace that part of myself that society so devalues. I needed them to show me the commonalities between our experiences of ableism and others' experiences of racism. I needed them to give words to the feelings I had never had reflected back to my self in my nondisabled world.

Most of us with disabilities learn to survive alone and silently in our nondisabled families and worlds, never knowing a disability community exists. I was the only disabled person in my family, my community, schools, and my adult social world. As a child, I had learned an aversion to the company of other disabled people because they were associated with being "defective" and stigmatized, and I was neither of those! My only experiences with other disabled people had been in situations in which nondisabled professionals "medicalized" our lives, defining us negatively. I even had my own turn at working in such settings, "helping" others in sheltered workshops and group homes, although always quitting for emotional reasons I only now understand. I had never been in an environment in which disabled people defined themselves in their own terms and celebrated their uniqueness. And now, in the written words and in the company of disabled people, I have found brothers and sisters who are teaching me that there are powerful ways of dealing with the pain of being "other." They are helping me find the words to express what I have always "known" in my body, but had no language to express.

James Baldwin (1972) wrote that "to be liberated from the stigma of blackness by embracing it, is to cease, forever, one's interior argument and collaboration with the authors of one's degradation (p. 190)."[2] It has been my experience that learning to embrace my whole self, disability and all, was not a task I could do alone. I needed the support and guidance of others who not only had lived my experience but also had ceased their internal collaboration with the negative voices of society. It is the same process that bell hooks (1989) speaks of in *Talking Back: Thinking Feminist, Thinking Black,*[3] as the need to "decolonialize" one's mind by rooting out all that does not honor one's own experience. I have found that in addition to decolonializing my mind, I have also needed to decolonialize my body. I have had to cease my interior argument with society's negative messages that I am not as good as everybody else by no longer pushing my body beyond its limits. As I have learned to listen to my body's limits, honoring them as a source of wisdom and strength, I have experienced the healing and liberation of the embrace, and I have begun to thrive.

A most profound way that I have begun to thrive is that I no longer require that I spend most of my energy walking to get around—I have begun to use a scooter for mobility. What an act of liberation—and resistance—this has been! I felt like a bird let out of a cage, the first time I used one! I could go and go and not be exhausted! I was able to fully participate in the conference I was attending, rather that just be dully present. To choose to use a scooter, when I can still walk, flies in the face of all the "wisdom" of those without disabilities. We are taught that to walk, no matter how distorted or exhausting it is, is far more virtuous than using a chair—because it is closer to "normal." Never mind that my galumphing polio-gait twists my muscles into iron-like sinew that only the hardiest of masseuses can "unknot." Never mind that my shoulders and hands, never meant for walking, have their future usefulness limited by 40 years of misuse on crutches. To choose to use a scooter also places me squarely in that stigmatized group of "pitiful unfortunates" who are "confined" to their chairs. It removes me

---

[2]J. Baldwin, *No Name in the Street* (New York: Doubleday, 1972).
[3]b. hooks, *Talking Back: Thinking Feminist, Thinking Black* (Boston, MA: South End Press, 1989).

from the ranks of "overcomers," such as Franklin Delano Roosevelt, Wilma Rudolph, or Helen Keller, whom society mistakenly believes actually "got over" their disabilities. My using a scooter is an act that scares my family. They are afraid that somehow giving up walking will make me give up—period! It makes them think that I am losing ground, becoming dependent on the scooter, when they and society need me to act as if I am strong and virile. Only now that I am embracing my limitations do I know how I spent much life-energy protecting my family from them. I rarely slowed them down or burdened them with feelings they could not understand. Only now can I celebrate my unavoidable need for interdependence in a society that oppresses everyone with its unattainable standard of independence!

Traditionally, families are taught by professionals that their child's disability is an individual functional problem that can only be remedied by individualized medical interventions. And so it remains the focus of many families to adapt their child to a society that needs them to be "normal." The larger social and cultural oppression that some of those interventions represent is only now being raised by those of us, former disabled children who question the extreme and painful measures taken to "fix" us, measures that went beyond what may have been truly needed to ensure our full, unique development. In my scooter, I am choosing now to live by other values—the values of the disability community that require society to adapt to our needs rather than vice versa.

In using my scooter, I experience the full range of the disability experience, including those aspects I avoided when I thought I was "passing" as normal. In my scooter, I experience being denied access to places walking people enter without a thought, because they are inaccessible. In my scooter, I am eligible to use service entrances near stinking dumpsters and seating at public events that is segregated from my walking companions. Seated in my scooter, I am even more invisible to those who could never look the walking-me in the eye—an averted gaze not even required to obliterate my presence. In my scooter, I cannot visit some friends' homes because of stairs or use their bathrooms because of narrow doors. The very cost of my scooter includes a sizable "crip tax"—as the sum of its component parts is far less costly than its hefty price tag in the inflated (and captive) medical equipment market. In my scooter, I don't have full assurance that I will even be able to get on public transportation, much less treated with dignity when I do. In my scooter I feel the insult of those telethon hosts who want to paint my life as pathetic, not livable, unless I am cured. In my scooter, I know that I am viewed as far less able, needing public assistance rather than ramps and power doors to get into job interviews. Although my speech was not affected by polio, my scooter provides further reason to dismiss me, as society dismisses my brothers and sisters who use voice synthesizers to communicate their artistic vision of the world. In my scooter, I am inextricably and unavoidably a member of the disability community, with all the pain and privileges associated with that membership.

I am proud to have found my way home to the disability community. I am now able to "hang out on the porch" and hear stories from the elders of how their visions of equal justice for all took shape, how legislation acknowledging our civil rights was passed. And although it is true that we continue to struggle to define our own lives and live it on our own terms, we have also begun to create a culture that brings us together and celebrates our unique ways of being in the world. I am moved when I hear poetry that speaks my truth and read books that truly reflect my life experiences. I am healed when I see unflinchingly honest performances dealing with the reality and pain caused by ableism. I now know that I have indeed experienced the pain of ableism and I know why I felt the pain of racism when I had words for neither. I now also know the liberating power of embracing my disability and of celebrating who I am because of it.

Reprinted by permission of the American Counseling Association.

The Face of Racism

Edward A. Delgado-Romero

• • • • • • • • • • • • • • • • • •

When thinking of racism, people might imagine the vision of a hooded Ku Klux Klan member lighting a cross, a "skinhead" wearing swastikas, or an angry lynch mob. However, when I think of racism, one image is clear. I learned about racism in the face of my father. I learned hatred, prejudice, and contempt, and, most important, I learned how to turn that racism inward. After many years of self-reflection and healing, I have just begun to understand how deeply racism has affected my attitudes toward others and toward myself. I have begun to understand that racism works on two fronts. One is the overt and obvious racism of the Klan member. The other is the covert and subtle racism that the victim of overt racism begins to internalize, the racism my father taught me.

My father came to this country seeking to escape the personal demons that had haunted him throughout his life. He saw the United States and New York City as a new opportunity, a new beginning. Part of that beginning was rejecting all the things that he had been. My father sought to reinvent himself as an American. In those days, being an American meant being White (some people might argue that this is still true). My father felt he *was* White, because part of his family was descended from Spaniards. Somehow my father thought being Spanish (and therefore European) was better and of higher status than being a South American or a Colombian, and it was certainly better than being *Indio* or native. Our ancestral records show that the Delgado family was a virtuous family with a long tradition in Spain. However, the only records that remain of my ancestors who were native (South) Americans are a few photographs and some of their physical features that were passed along through "blood."

The United States of America taught my father to hate anyone who was not White. Richard Pryor once observed that the first English word that an immigrant is taught is "nigger." Always a quick learner, my father learned to hate "niggers," "gooks," "spics," "wetbacks," and any other "damn immigrant." However, my father soon found out that he was not excluded from the hatred. After days filled with jokes about "green cards" and "drug dealing," my father would return home to his wife and children, full of pent-up rage. We lived in fear of his anger and his explosiveness. My father tried to transform himself yet felt ambivalent about losing his security. Therefore, we were not allowed to speak Spanish to my father, and my mother was not allowed to learn English. By attempting to separate his children from their culture while denying his wife the chance to acculturate, my father replicated his divided psyche. My mother was forced to be the keeper of the culture and language, which she did with incredible bravery and pride. It was through the courage of my mother that I was eventually able to reconnect with my Latino heritage.

My father's drive to be accepted and to be acceptable knew no bounds. I remember one time as a child, we were driving a long distance to go to a restaurant (which was unusual for us). We sat and ate fried chicken and blueberry pie as my father anxiously waited for the owner of the restaurant to come over and acknowledge him. The owner finally did come over, and I remember how proud my father was to meet "a great American." It was only when I was older that I realized that this man was Georgia politician Lester Maddox. Maddox was one of the fiercest opponents of integration during the civil rights era. He was made infamous by keeping a bucket of ax handles by the door of his restaurant as a reminder of the violence that he had threatened to use against any Black person who would try to integrate his home or business. It shocks me to realize how racism had blinded my father to the fact that his fate as an immigrant and a minority group member in the United States was tied to the fate of other minorities.

As hard as he tried to fit in, my father never really succeeded. Often his physical features, his accent, or his clothes would give him away as being different. My father would react violently when confronted with his failure to become one hundred percent American. For example, during an interview for a promotion, the interviewer asked my father about the "good pot" grown in Colombia. At the time my father laughed it off. However, when he returned home he exploded in rage. These explosions became a daily event. My brother, sister, and I were a captive audience. We had no choice but to listen as he would berate us for being worthless. The angrier he became, the more pressure my father would put on us to "be American." We were wildly successful at being American, which only made my father angrier. As I became a teenager, my father became increasingly competitive with and abusive toward me. The fact that I physically resembled him only made things worse. He saw in me things he could never achieve: I spoke English without an accent, was headed toward college, and I dated Caucasian women exclusively.

I learned racism from my father, and just as he had done, I turned it inward. I came to hate the fact that I was Latino, that my parents spoke with an accent, that my skin, although light for a Latino, was darker than it should be. I wanted to be a White Anglo-American, and for many years, I actually thought I was. During my high school and college years I was in deep denial that I was Latino. I believed that America was a "color blind" society that rewarded people solely on the basis of hard work. I remember my Caucasian high school guidance counselor steering me away from minority scholarships for college and telling me "Ed, you want to get in on your own merit." At the time I believed her, and my "own merit" led to my status as a "token" at a predominantly Caucasian college, thousands of dollars in student loans, and 4 more years of denial.

I remember being deeply embarrassed by Latino music, food, customs, and history. My mother would often talk about her home country with pride and fondness. I used to get angry with her because she was being so "un-American." One time, in an attempt to share her culture with me, my mother gave me an expensive recording of Colombian music. I actually had the nerve to give it back to her because I was ashamed of everything Latino. I was particularly ashamed of my Spanish surname because of the way that my peers could mispronounce it in demeaning ways. I became so used to being called names that often I would participate in using ethnic slurs against myself and other minorities. I remember vividly a Latino varsity football player who was proud that his nickname was "Spic." Having a racial slur as a nickname was a badge of honor; it meant he was accepted. As an enthusiastic participant in the ethnic name-calling, I could continue to deny that I was different. The height of my own denial was when I told a Mexican joke to a priest, who was Mexican. The priest laughed, more out of shock than humor. The joke was, quite literally, on both of us. He confronted me, and pointed out that he was Mexican. As I stood in awkward silence, having offended someone I cared about, something began to awaken within me.

I began to realize that I was an impostor and that there was another side of me that I was denying. Although I felt intimidated and uncomfortable around people of color, there was a depth of connection that was missing in most of my relationships. I struggled to make sense of what I was feeling. My longing for connection with other minorities was first manifested in college through my participation in a fraternity. When I joined the fraternity, the membership was almost exclusively White. However, as I was able to influence member selection, the membership became increasingly diverse. I began to surround myself with other people who could understand what it felt like to be of two worlds and never fully at peace in either one. These were my first steps toward healing the racism that I felt inside.

My cultural explorations coincided with the divorce of my parents. My father eventually left our home and emotionally and financially disowned his family. This split helped me to continue the self-exploration and reclamation of my heritage that had begun in college. I learned about my ancestors, their names, and their lives. I learned my full name and the proper way to pronounce it. I was able to become friends with Latino men and Latina women. I asked my mother to give me back the recording of Colombian music I had refused to take from her and asked her to teach me about her culture. My mother saved up her money and took me on a trip to Colombia. I wish that I could say that I found my "home" in Columbia. I wish that I could say that I reconnected with my ancestors on some deep level. However, in Colombia I felt every bit the foreigner that I was. What I gained from my trip to Colombia was an understanding and appreciation for the enormous sacrifice that my mother had made for her children. In Colombia I realized that I was neither fully Colombian nor fully American. I had to find a way to make sense of my divided identity.

Many of my colleagues in psychology say that therapists enter the profession motivated in part by a need to deal with their own issues. As much as I used to argue that I was the exception to the rule, obviously I was not. In an effort to somehow identify, understand, and deal with my issues, I was drawn to graduate study in counseling psychology. I was offered a lucrative fellowship at a major university. However, only one professor (who later became my adviser and mentor) was honest enough to tell me that it was a minority fellowship.

Many of the faculty and students saw the minority fellowship as a way for me to cheat the system because they did not think I was "really" a minority. One student explained his belief that I was not a real minority because I did not speak "broken English." The pressure to fit in and deny that I was different was enormous. I was faced with a choice that reminded me of dealing with my father: stay quiet and accept the status quo of the University and the program (basically "pass" as Caucasian) or assert myself and challenge a culturally oppressive system. I wish I could say that I chose to try to change the system simply because it was the moral or just thing to do. However, I think I chose to fight the system because I was tired of being quiet. Multicultural psychology became my passion and the focus of my career. I have my doubts as to how much I was able to change a deeply entrenched racist, sexist, and homophobic system, but I have no doubt that I underwent tremendous personal and professional growth.

As I progressed through my graduate training and into internship, I found that I surrounded myself with other people who could understand what it was like to face overt and covert racism. I formed a supportive network of friends and colleagues of all colors. At first I felt some animosity toward Caucasian people, but a Caucasian friend once pointed out that all people would benefit from being liberated from racism. I found that the term *liberation* captured the essence of what I was searching for: liberation from hatred and racism and, personally, a liberation from the past. I realized that liberation meant letting go of the intense anger and resentment I felt toward my father. My anger toward my father was like wearing a shrinking suit of armor: Although the anger could make me feel powerful and protected, the anger was not letting me grow and, in fact, was starting to choke me. However, I was concerned that, stripped of my armor, I would lose my motivation to fight racism. I was surprised to find that by liberating myself from my father's legacy, I was able to find peace and that from this peace I could generate more energy and motivation to face racism than I had imagined possible.

As I grow older and consider having my own children, I find myself looking in the mirror to see if I can see my father's face. There have been times when I have been both shocked and disappointed to hear his voice angrily coming out of my mouth or have seen my face contorted with his rage. I was surprised to find out that liberation did not mean I could change the facts of my past or get rid of any influence from my father. However, I gained something even more valuable: I learned that because of my experiences, I can understand why someone would be racist. I can understand what it is like to be both a perpetrator and a victim of racism. I have also come to understand that the answer to fighting racism begins with a moral inventory, a fearless look at oneself. I have come to the conclusion that I can never afford myself the luxury of asking the question "Am I racist?" Rather, I need to continually ask myself, "How racist am I?" As I struggle to deal with the reality of racism in my personal and professional life, I will continue to check my mirror and look for the face of racism.

Personal Narrative of an Asian American's Experience with Racism

Donna M. Talbot

• • • • • • • • • • • • • • • • • • • •

Growing up in New England during the '60s and '70s had its benefits and difficulties. Although the northeast region of the country had larger pockets of people of color and immigrants than most other parts of the United States, the stiffness and arrogance of old money and elitist educational institutions created some inevitable friction among people with greatly diverse cultural backgrounds. It is in this environment (less than 5 miles from a large Air Force base) that I began my identity development, although unknowingly, as a person of color—as an Asian American.

My parents are both naturalized citizens; they were thankful to be in the United States, the land of opportunity and upward mobility. My father is French Canadian and Huron Indian and my mother is 100 percent Japanese. Although my two brothers and I were clearly raised with Japanese values and culture, my mother, our primary caretaker, insisted that we should grow up to be "good American citizens." This was driven by her pride in being a U.S. citizen and her fear of racist acts against us. What she didn't realize was that, despite her wishes, she couldn't help but raise good Japanese American citizens....

Many of my most vivid memories of what I believe to be acts of racism, sexism, and oppression took pace in "American institutions," such as schools, social organizations (Moose and Elks Clubs), and church. This fact has largely influenced my decision to become an educator, student affairs practitioner, and counselor; unfortunately, I think these experiences have also influenced my decision to move away from Christianity and to explore other forms of spirituality. In my professional roles, I address my agenda openly—to advocate for oppressed and marginalized populations so that they may not have to be subjected to the same negative experiences that I was.

My first overt experience of racism and recognition that I was "different" took place in school around the third grade. I remember waiting with my classmates in the hallway to go into social studies class. As I was standing there, several boys started to circle me while chanting that their fathers, uncles, and other male relatives had bombed my people. Then, they proceeded to pull up the corners of their eyes with their fingers, so they appeared slanted, and made funny noises like "ching," "chang," and so forth. For me this was extremely confusing because we had all grown up in the same neighborhood; but as I cried in the bathroom and looked in the mirror, it was the first time I cognitively realized that my eyes were different from theirs. Probably the most embarrassing part of this experience for me was that the teacher just stood in the doorway and laughed at the boys taunting me; he never tried to stop them or indicate that they were wrong. From that time on, through most of grade school, I hated myself and my mother for looking and being different.

A few years later, I learned how to be angry toward bias and ignorance. My older brother wanted to play baseball with his friends during the summer. To do that, my parents had to join the local Moose Club so that he could play in their leagues. Because my family would have been classified as "working class poor," this was a major commitment of which my parents were very proud. My father went to the club, completed the paperwork, and paid the application and membership fee. Everything seemed fine for about 2 weeks until we received a call from the membership person at the Moose Club; he explained to my father that the Moose, and other similar clubs, had a policy that prohibited interracial members from joining. The only apology he made was for not catching it sooner!

It wasn't until high school that I started to realize that there were benefits to being different—although I still resented being Asian. Teachers remembered me because I looked so different from my classmates, and the boys liked my long, black, straight hair and clear, olive complexion. Even colleges were interested and pursued this "high achieving" minority student. Although I was encouraged (actually, I was tracked) to take honors math and science courses, I had a strong interest in the social sciences and education. Most people were surprised, even shocked, when I turned down large scholarships from institutions with well-known engineering and computer science programs to go to a small liberal arts college. This marked the second most significant racist, or "classist," event in my educational experience. Early in my senior year, I was the first person in my local public high school ever to be accepted (early decision) to a very prestigious, liberal arts college—Amherst College. Soon, after the word was out that this had happened, I was summoned to the vice principal's office. Being the arrogant young "scholar" I thought I was, I assumed that the vice principal was calling me to give me "strokes" for my accomplishment. Several minutes into the discussion, a dark haze started to crowd my mind as I realized that this was an entirely different conversation than I had anticipated. Very confused and angry, I finally asked the vice principal what, exactly, she was trying to say to me. Her words rang loudly, almost deafeningly, in my ears, "Frankly, Donna, we're not sure you come from the *right kind of family* to be the first to represent our high school at Amherst College." At that point, I remember standing up and announcing that this meeting was over; however, as I was walking out, I suggested that this was a conversation she needed to have with my father. Although there were several other minor attempts to block my efforts to attend Amherst College, they were unsuccessful. I don't think I ever mentioned these incidents to my parents because I didn't want them ever to feel the humiliation that I had. Needless to say, the vice principal never called to have that conversation with my father.

College was an amazing experience for me—every day was a challenge to grow (personally and academically). Toward the end of my sophomore year, I was suspended, with many other Amherst students, for participating in demonstrations and a lock-out of the administration building. During that time, we had an African American dean who believed that the damage from slavery was over and that it was time to eliminate the programs and services that were created in the '60s to assist African American students. Naturally, we just labeled him an "Uncle Tom" and protested these decisions as well as demanded that the college divest its stocks in South Africa. My parents, especially my mother, were very angry with me; they were embarrassed that I would show such blatant disrespect for "authorities" and that I could jeopardize my education. During one of the many scoldings I received for this inappropriate behavior, my mother asked why I always had to be the one to stand up and challenge things, even the issues that didn't apply to me. My response to her was that I had to object twice as loud and twice as often because she wouldn't; either she was going to ride in the boat of change or she would be left behind on the shores of oppression and discontent. This response startled her and, though I didn't know until years later, pushed her into thinking about the role of "activism" and her own multicultural journey.

My faculty adviser at Amherst was a Returned Peace Corps Volunteer (RPCV-Micronesia). As well as turning me on to liberation theology through Freir's (1970) *Pedagogy of the Oppressed*,[1] he also taught me about the "toughest job I ever loved." Three weeks after graduation, despite my parents' hope that I would go to law school, I was on a plane to Ghana, West Africa. Before [I left] for the Peace Corps, friends and family would ask me what I thought about moving to an "uncivilized" country. I thought I knew what they meant, though I had no answers. After several months in my small village in Ghana, my host country friends and colleagues finally felt comfortable enough to ask me what it was like to live in an "uncivilized" country—they were referring to the United States. It suddenly became clear to me that often times we speak the same language, use the same words, and we assume that we all mean the same thing. When my family and friends in the United States used the term "uncivilized" to describe Ghana, they were making comments about the less industrialized nature of the country; when my Ghanaian friends and colleagues called the United States uncivilized, they were referring to the need to lock our doors and to never walk alone at night for fear of our personal safety. This taught me to resist assuming that I understand another person's experience well enough to casually ascribe meaning to his or her words.

When I entered the Peace Corps, I had lofty goals; these idealistic plans soon took a backseat to survival, literally and figuratively. It struck me as humorous, at some point in my service, that I felt less like an outsider here (in Ghana) than I did in my own home country. On one of my many travels across the country, I was stranded on the road without food or shelter as nighttime approached. A young Ghanaian man saw me standing by the road and realized my situation. He invited me home to his village where his family gave me a place to sleep,

[1] P. Freire, *Pedagogy of the Oppressed* (New York: Continuum, 1970).

shared what little food they had, and fetched me drinking and bathing water from a well nearly a mile away. When I was leaving in the morning, I asked if I could give them something for their troubles. They refused my offer, indicating that they did what anyone would do. With this comment, I became extremely embarrassed and uncomfortable as I imagined how this young "Black man" would be treated in the United States if he were stranded by the road. Stimulated by this incident and many other experiences, my time in Ghana was a time of deep introspection and what I now refer to as my "rebirth." Though returning to the States was more traumatic and painful than moving to Ghana, I knew that I had to return because there was work to do here in the United States....

Reprinted by permission of the American Counseling Association.

• •

Pain and Perseverance:
Perspectives from an Ally

Lisa J. Brandyberry

● ● ● ● ● ● ● ● ● ● ● ● ● ● ● ● ● ●

I grew up as "poor, White, trash" in the middle of the Midwest. The city I lived in was an industrial one—mostly union workers—and always smelled like french fries or rubber. It was mostly White, but there were a fair number of African Americans and Latinos living in various monoracial communities throughout the city. From beginning to end, the schools I went to were integrated, so there is no time I can remember that I didn't know any Black (the term I grew up with) people.

During grade school one of my best friends was Garth, a Black child in my class. We hung around a lot together during lunch hours. I don't remember being upset about the fact that when he and I played together none of my White friends would join us. Some other Black children would come over and join us from time to time. I couldn't have both his friendship and the other White kids' friendships simultaneously.

I felt good around Garth and many of the other Black children. I felt all right around most of the other White children. I was one of few working-class Whites in that particular school. I never had the right clothes because my family shopped at Kmart and hoped for blue-light specials while we were there. My mother gave me haircuts; unfortunately, it wasn't her talent. I was often too loud in my laughter, too crude in my language.

I was also fat, an automatic object of ridicule and harassment for other children. Between being too poor and too fat, there was a lot about me to pick on and many reasons to ostracize me. But, I was never totally rejected. Somehow, something in me was enough to compensate for my "failings," so I always had friends. But with most, if not all, of my White friends, I always knew I was inferior. After the sixth grade, Garth and I were shuffled to different schools, and I didn't think I'd ever see him again.

By my senior year in high school, I had become painfully aware of what made me "inferior" to my classmates. As do many people struggling with internalized oppression, I worked hard to compensate for my failings because I had grown to believe that there was something wrong with me. I worked hard at my classes and did very well; I was always smiling, always willing to do more for others, to laugh at myself when the ridicule would come my way.

My senior year the city closed down one of the other high schools, and the students were bused to different schools. Garth ended up at mine. I saw him one day walking down the hall near my locker, and I started laughing and walking toward him, remembering how good it had felt to have him for a friend. Initially, I thought he didn't recognize me, but he did. He was uncomfortable; he didn't want to be found talking to me. I tried for a few more minutes to talk with him, to find out about what had happened to him. Then I gave up, maybe too soon. After so many years of rejection from others, I was pretty aware of what it felt like to be with someone who didn't want to be with me. We ended with a "see you around" after about 2 minutes of awkwardness. That's the last time I ever spoke to him.

Being a White female, I had learned that my weight was a primary reason for rejection from others, especially males. When Garth seemed not to want to be seen with me, I assumed it was for that reason. I was too fat, too ugly. Who knows? Maybe that was part of it. But now, looking back, I believe it was probably more about race than weight. He had spent the previous 5 years in a predominantly Black school. Who knows how White people had treated him, a Black male adolescent, during those years?

My college life intensified my feelings of being an outsider. I received a scholarship to a small, private liberal arts college where the majority of the students were wealthy and White. There were a few of us paying for school through scholarships, jobs, and loans. There were even fewer Black students on campus, but they were there. All the pain I felt growing up being poor and fat was multiplied at this college, but it was there that I got angry about it. Angry about the privileges of wealthy people who seemed to believe that it was normal to have more than enough money to go to Europe on vacations, to shop for new clothes every weekend, to have cars at their disposal, to have plenty of leisure time because they weren't trying to fit in a job on top of classes and studying.

I tried reaching out to some of the few Black students on campus and became close with one woman, Doris. I cannot begin to imagine what it was like for a young Black woman from Chicago to have to survive in that small Iowa town. After we had struck up a friendship, she started pushing me to go to Black dance clubs in a nearby city. I initially refused—I didn't even go to White dance clubs. But, eventually, I agreed to go. She took charge of what I was going to wear because I couldn't dress like those "White folks," who dressed down to go out. This was time to go all out with jewelry, makeup, and hairstyles. I remember being very nervous on the long drive to the city, scared about being the only White person in the club. I was too embarrassed by this to tell my friend.

Through this experience I got my first taste of being a racial minority. Although this was unpleasant, it was vital in my development. I felt what it was like to have people be angry that I had merely walked into their place, to feel cautious about what I said and how I said it, to feel like a complete outsider, to imagine that everyone in the room must hate me because of my skin color. I am thankful that Doris didn't allow me to disappear into a corner. She pushed me out on the dance floor and pulled me around introducing me to people she knew. By the end of the night I had had a great time, and we went back together several times during the next year.

Graduate school pushed me more than any other experience to really examine myself. I was fortunate to end up in a program that emphasized diversity issues. There were many times it was painful and frightening, because I was challenged to look beyond my "liberal" attitudes to honestly examine myself. I had to go deeper than focusing on all the positive experiences I had had with people of color. I had to examine all the negative messages I had absorbed and determine how much they were still affecting me. I had to learn to see myself as part of the White race, whether I liked it or not.

My family, church, and the media were major influences on me. I went to a church that was entirely White and remember watching how any Black families that would come to visit would have it made clear to them that they weren't welcome. They were treated much like I was when I went to the Black dance club, except they didn't end up having fun and meeting nice people. The stares and whispers didn't end; the shared laughter never started.

I was affected by hearing my brothers talk about "niggers," or more often about "Black bitches." I remember my parents not allowing one of my brothers to go play basketball at a certain court because it wasn't safe around "those" people. I remember my father pointing out what we thought was a garishly painted house and saying "colored" people have no taste. I also remember him making it clear that he didn't want me ever to bring home a Black man. As much as I want to believe I never accepted these attitudes, I know they influenced me and what I believed. I came to believe that "they" were different from "us."

The process of acknowledging what was meant by "us," of owning my own racial heritage, included owning all the history that goes with being White. During this process, the only part of that history I could see was its shame: slavery and genocide of Africans, American Indians, Asians, and Mexicans. There didn't seem to be any horror that wasn't committed in the name of the "manifest destiny" and superiority of European Whites. My reaction was to feel an incredible amount of guilt and shame; I didn't want to be White, didn't want to belong to this group, didn't want to be part of this "us."

Even more painful than that was having to examine how I had benefited from racism. I had to question how I could hold so much anger toward those who were wealthy (or male) because they didn't recognize their privileges but had never acknowledged the privileges I enjoyed from my skin color. It had never crossed my mind that there was a way in which I was privileged. I didn't come from money, I wasn't born beautiful, my family life had been far from perfect, and I had struggled to get where I was.

It wasn't easy to look at the probability that I had struggled less than if I were a person of color. That maybe my White skin had allowed me access to the upper-level college preparatory classes despite being working class, which, in turn, probably increased my test scores, which opened doors to receive academic scholarships and, basically, gave me the opportunity to achieve a level beyond where I was born. I'd like to think that I earned everything I have, but I can no longer tell myself that. I earned some of it, and some of it was very likely given to me because of being White. I have grown to recognize the privileges I receive every day for being White.

It was during this time of feeling overwhelmed with guilt and shame about my race that I worked for a year as the only White person in an all-African American agency. It was not a job I had applied for or wanted; it was a job I was requested (and eventually forced) to accept. I didn't want the job because I was afraid the staff would hate me. I remember talking with my boss about my fears. He was an African American man with whom I'd worked before and who had requested my placement in the position. He never denied that hostility was possible, but he never let me off the hook regarding my responsibility. He made it clear that it was my place to deal with any prejudice directed at me and that he would support me in that process, but that it was something I would have to face. He also reminded me that it was something minorities face on a daily basis. Again, in having to walk through my fear, I enjoyed a wonderful experience. There was only one person who made it clear she didn't want me there, and even she taught me a valuable lesson. She taught me how subtle sabotage can be. I would miss meetings because I never received the memorandum informing me of them. I wouldn't receive phone messages. I'd receive paperwork late or not at all, and I could *feel* her dislike emanating from her. It was through this experience that I learned to be very hesitant to question the experiences of persons of color who feel they are being discriminated against but can't name anything grossly inappropriate.

My professional life has moved me farther in my journey to overcome racism. A large part of that has come from my close work and friendship with an African American lesbian, Jan. We connected immediately when I came to interview and quickly became friends. We have done numerous programs together focusing in general on oppression issues and, often, specifically on race. We have had to struggle together with issues of race more so than any other issue. What has saved our relationship is our willingness to talk about race, to put our "raggedy selves" on the table.

Many of these struggles have come from my desire not to have race separate us and Jan's desire to keep part of her personal space monoracial; that is, sometimes she just wants to hang with the Black folks. Intellectually, I understand this. I sometimes don't want men around because there is a comfort in groups of women that doesn't exist with men present. It has nothing to do with disliking men; it's simply a different vibe that exists. But on a personal level, it continues to hurt. I struggle with feeling rejected, separated because of my skin color, not seen as the person who is Jan's friend but as a representative of the White race. She knows this because we've talked about it at length. She struggles with it as well because she knows it hurts me, but she wants to have her needs met too.

I now understand why I sometimes feel closer to, and more connected with, some people of color than with many White people. My understanding came through viewing oppression as encompassing all the different groups experiencing it. Having been born into a working-class family, I share many cultural dynamics with people of color also born into this economic sphere. It is often difficult for me, and apparently others, to figure out how to separate race from class. My sensitivity to how I've experienced oppression personally, through class, body size, and gender issues, has allowed me to have some sense of perspective on the pain of racism. Finally, my willingness to admit to and name privileges that I experience because of my race seems to afford me some credibility with people of color....

My conclusion, sadly, is that most people of color simply don't expect much from White people. They don't expect us to be open, to have thought about these issues, to have thought about ourselves (rather than them) in terms of these issues, to be working against racism inside and outside of the therapy room. I believe it is my responsibility, as a member of the majority group, to fight racism. As I benefit and derive increased societal rewards from racism's existence, perhaps my voice may reach other White ears that refuse to listen to the voices of people of color. I believe this as passionately as I believe that men must speak to other men about sexism, that heterosexuals must speak to members of their own group about homophobia, and so on.

Those of us committed to being allies must be willing to persevere in this struggle. People of color do not have the option of ignoring racism and its effects; therefore, we must not ignore it either. We must choose to persevere in the face of rejection, criticism, and suspicion from members of majority and minority groups. Not everyone wants Whites to be involved in this struggle, and I understand this lack of trust. But racism is the problem of the racists, not those who are oppressed by it. As a part of the problem group, I must be involved in eliminating the problem itself.

Some say that no one willingly gives up power, and while members of majority groups refuse to see any benefit to themselves for changing the system (personal and institutional), progress will be slow and painful. But when majority group members can see that *their* lives will improve, *their* accomplishments will be seen as more completely due to merit rather than privilege, that the quality of life will improve for all of us, then, perhaps, change will be possible.

Reprinted by permission of the American Counseling Association.

 Discussion Questions

1. What do these five personal statements have in common?
2. Each of these essays considers diversity from a different kind of concern. Are they equally important concerns? If you had to rank them, how would you select the one or two that truly matter? If you find you cannot rank them in importance, why not?
3. Do these authors raise issues of political correctness? Or is that too narrow a way of viewing their experiences?
4. What other groups—minority or majority—might put forward similar experiences and draw similar conclusions from them?

5. Federal, state, and local laws now identify specific groups of people as "protected classes." These usually include groups defined by characteristics shared in common such as religion, race, gender, physical disability, and Vietnam-era veteran status. Should these be legally "protected" classes? Explain.

 ## How Can These Ideas Apply to You?

1. What group or groups of people do you identify with? Fraternity or sorority members? Athletes? Nationality group? Religion? Have these groups been the target of discrimination? Have you suffered discrimination based on your being a member of a group?
2. Most prejudiced beliefs originate in early training or experience. Examine your own attitudes and behavior seriously and objectively. Do you make judgments *in advance* about people who are members of any minority group? If you answered yes, can you identify the source of your attitudes? What would it take to change them?
3. What expectations about fair treatment do you have for yourself—both in how you want to be treated and how you want to treat others? What does the Golden Rule—"Do unto others as you would have others do unto you"—mean to you?
4. A university is a specialized kind of institution. Does the nature of a university have implications for issues related to discrimination?
5. How should your college or university foster a just environment for all its students? What about for faculty and staff?

Race and Racism in America

Jesse L. Jackson Sr.

The Reverend Jesse Jackson Sr. is known worldwide as one of the most politically active and sometimes controversial private citizens in the United States. A native of South Carolina, he was ordained a Baptist minister in 1968, having already worked for several years beside Martin Luther King Jr. in the American protest movement for civil rights. A candidate for president in 1984 and 1988, he formed the Rainbow Coalition, an association of many groups that support civil rights, which he continues to lead. In this essay, he argues that the civil rights movement has benefited Americans of every race and color.

● ● ● ● ● ● ● ● ● ● ● ● ● ● ● ● ● ●

I began to participate in the movement against racial discrimination as a young man in Greenville, South Carolina, who sought to do normal things such as using the public library; the library, after all, was funded by the taxes paid by my parents and other black people. For this, I experienced my first arrest. I went on to become involved with the Civil Rights Movement directed by the Southern Christian Leadership Council as a staffer to its head, Dr. Martin Luther King, Jr. It is important to understand that the movement for civil rights, which took place primarily in the 1960s, was not the product of one man or one organization, but was a people's movement. From the time when Martin Luther King, Jr., led the Montgomery bus boycott in 1955, until today, the Civil Rights Movement lives and is a product of every person who will not bow down to the dehumanization of another person or group of people.

Some of the most dramatic events that the popular history of the movement has not captured were the individual acts of courage by persons who simply made up their minds to act because freedom was a precious thing that could not be obtained as a gift from someone else. They came to understand how deeply it depended upon their own personal commitment to do something that would bring about change.

The results of this movement were concrete: the 1964 Civil Rights Act, the 1965 Voting Rights Act, the 1968 Fair Housing Act, and Affirmative Action. Through these laws, many people of all colors have been able to achieve upward mobility in society. Blacks have benefited from laws that made it illegal to discriminate in hiring and promotion, or selling a house, or voting and holding office, or providing higher education. As a result, the black middle class has grown, achieving ever-greater break-throughs in every field of employment; black elected officials have grown from 250 at the time that the Voting Rights Act was passed to nearly 9,000 today. Currently there are thirty-eight black members of Congress. Also, 1.1 million blacks are now attending America's colleges and universities.

Women of all colors have benefited from Title IX, which has equalized their opportunities to participate in sports activities as both amateurs and professionals, and to make substantial salaries in the process. Indeed, more than any other group white females have benefited from Affirmative Action with their pace of achieving employment and starting businesses for themselves. Also, whites as a whole have benefited more than blacks from laws passed in the 1980s that have prohibited discrimination against the elderly and the disabled. Therefore, laws that protected disadvantaged groups from discrimination and promoted the ability of people of color also have helped to create the conditions that have allowed all disadvantaged groups in society to compete on a more level playing field.

Backlash Against Civil Rights Laws

Nevertheless, great disparities in opportunity still remain today between the white majority and disadvantaged groups; yet, rather than accept advances we have made as a sign of the movement of society toward a truly democratic system, some in the majority have felt threatened enough to launch a counter-movement to eliminate the laws and to use public policy to exact more severe punishment of offenders. This has led to challenges to Affirmative Action and to its elimination in the states of California, Washington, and more recently Florida. In addition, the Supreme Court has invalidated Affirmative Action in higher education in Texas. In California and Texas, the results have shown a tendency toward the segregation of higher education by class, as more selective institutions such as Berkeley and the University of Texas Law School have reported a reduction in the numbers of black and Hispanic students. Also, just as there are over one million blacks in college, there are more than one million in prison.

Much of the negative reaction has been launched because of the new competition among racial groups in society and because of the perception among many in the majority that there is no longer any need for such protections for the disadvantaged, that racism no longer exists. There has arisen the so-called "angry white male" phenomenon where, surveys show, a segment of the population of white males has constituted the leading edge of the resistance to the social progress of many peoples of color, both in terms of politics and in social attitudes.

Racism Still Exists

However, racism not only still exists; it has come to be an informal term for describing the many kinds of racial discrimination that are still very much a part of American life. Here are a few examples:

- Studies by the Federal Reserve System show that housing discrimination is still rampant in the granting of home and business loans by banks.
- The U. S. Department of Housing and Urban Development issued a 1999 study showing the persistence of racial discrimination in housing.
- A 1989 study by the *Harvard Business Review* revealed persistent consumer discrimination against blacks.

- Studies by many groups have shown that blacks receive poorer medical care, a fact which has been traced to racism in the delivery of various services.

And one could go on.

The most dramatic reminder of the evils of racism has been those high-profile incidents that occasionally publicly expose the cultural divide among Americans on race. Examples are the O.J. Simpson trial, the Los Angeles Riots, the lynching of James Byrd, the shooting of Amadou Diallo, and the like. These incidents suggest that race is still one of the most vexing problems we face as a society, but they do not automatically tell us how to cope in a way that shares justice. Justice is too often viewed as a zero-sum game, where one race loses and one wins. The biggest winner recognizes that race is not the issue, but that injustice is, and that for racism to stop, the injustices perpetrated by one side or the other must end.

I learned in the Civil Rights Movement that although everyone has a responsibility to help eliminate racism, a special responsibility rests with those who hold effective power. It is their moral obligation to share power to the point that it is used to bind up the wounds of the nation caused by racial injustice. And so it is today. This means the election of officials who will fight for public policies that build a material foundation under disadvantaged people aimed at eliminating misery; the use of private capital in responsible ways that employs people regardless of color, that shares technology with less fortunate groups, and that invests and builds in poor communities; and the cultivation of a spiritual center that sees the expansion of color in America as a good, human thing and a filling out of the meaning of democracy, rather than as a threat.

Therefore, regardless of the persistence of racism, America must get ready for the new reality of a multicultural society. In this sense, while the black/white paradigm has established the processes for achieving racial justice, the fight for inclusion by more cultural groups will bring to that paradigm a different content. It will bring to the table of our American humanity issues of new languages and cultures that will affect education, neighborhood composition, and political power. The combination of new immigration and births of children to foreign-born adults already in this country is changing the face of the country from one that is overwhelmingly white to one where minorities will account for 90 percent of the nation's population growth in the first half of the twenty-first century. Census projections tell us that by 2050, non-Hispanic whites, who were 87 percent of the population in 1950, will be 53 percent, creating a true "Rainbow nation," as Bishop Desmond Tutu says of South Africa today. Asians and Pacific Islanders are the fastest growing group, having increased by 189 percent since 1980, and will constitute 9 percent in 2050; Hispanics, less than 3 percent of the population in 1950, will be 24 percent of Americans by 2050; and blacks, now 12 percent of the population, will grow to 15 percent by 2050.

In 1984, I founded the Rainbow Coalition on a concept of cultural diversity as the basis of my presidential campaign. It reflected not only the way I see America, but more importantly, the way I think that the struggle for justice has to unfold among those who have suffered from many forms of disadvantage. This concept, therefore, reflects my continuing commitment to the progressive agenda of the Rainbow/Push Coalition. I learned in the Civil Rights Movement that the most powerful manifestation of the struggle for justice occurred when peoples of all colors came together to pool their power, with the same purpose of ridding the country of the scourge of racism and forging a new concept of freedom for everyone. I say "everyone" meaning those who also manage the system of oppression, a position taken in the Civil Rights Movement by Dr. Martin Luther King, Jr., and reinforced by Nelson Mandela when he emerged into the sunlight of freedom, after having been jailed for twenty-seven years, holding the hand of his white jailer. This view reflected the understanding of our movement that in order to hold a man down in a ditch, you must get into the ditch with him. So, if the oppressed is able to free herself, she also frees her oppressor from the indignity of that situation.

Finally, I believe that racial progress has been good for America. If there had been no Civil Rights Movement in the South, there would be no "New South" that attracted the Olympics to Atlanta, Georgia; no sports franchises would have placed racially mixed teams in highly segregated cities; no companies would have settled in metropolitan areas where they could not benefit from the free flow of skilled labor of all colors; and the same Southern cities would have been no Mecca for international trade and investment. This is the real story of race and the "flip side" of racism, and this lesson must be promoted vigorously if America is to survive in the global competition of this century, where economic markets depend on sophistication in the knowledge and use of other cultures as the key to survival. The dignity of race and the richness of its legacy to America is a fundamental reason for our social progress since the encounter of the European and the Native American. We must recognize that this fact is the way to the future and that racism is the path to the past.

Reprinted by permission.

Discussion Questions

1. Explain why Jackson can claim that "more than any other group white females have benefited from Affirmative Action . . . " Does this claim surprise you?
2. Jackson cites several examples to show that "racial progress has been good for America." Do you agree that these are examples that support his generalization? Are there others you can suggest from your experience in your hometown or on campus?
3. Do you know the following names that Jackson cites: Desmond Tutu, Nelson Mandela, James Byrd, Amadou Diallo? If not, use your Internet search engine to learn something about each of them. What are they known for?

How Can These Ideas Apply to You?

1. Jackson correctly points out that higher education has been at the center of much discussion about affirmative action. What is the current state of affirmative action laws in your state? Does race or other minority status have a place in admissions or other policies of your college? Should it?
2. Do you consider yourself to be a member of a minority? If so, have you benefited from the civil rights movement in any way that you are aware of? Ask your parents or older friends to comment on this question, and check to see if your answer agrees with theirs.
3. Jackson points to a demographic fact that is widely acknowledged—namely, that within your lifetime there will be no majority population in the United States. How will this affect your life in the future? How should you plan for that now?

I Have a Dream

Martin Luther King Jr.

On August 28, 1963, Dr. Martin Luther King Jr., the preeminent civil rights leader in America during the 1950s and 1960s, delivered this speech as the keynote address of the March on Washington for Civil Rights. His widow, Coretta Scott King, has said of that occasion: "At that moment, it seemed as if the kingdom of God appeared. But it lasted for only a moment." This speech is one of the enduring documents of 20th-century American history.

⬤ ⬤ ⬤ ⬤ ⬤ ⬤ ⬤ ⬤ ⬤ ⬤ ⬤ ⬤ ⬤ ⬤ ⬤ ⬤

I am happy to join with you today in what will go down in history as the greatest demonstration for freedom in the history of our nation.

Fivescore years ago, a great American, in whose symbolic shadow we stand today, signed the *Emancipation Proclamation*. This momentous decree came as a great beacon light of hope to millions of Negro slaves who had been seared in the flames of withering injustice. It came as a joyous daybreak to end the long night of their captivity.

But one hundred years later, the Negro still is not free; one hundred years later, the life of the Negro is still sadly crippled by the manacles of segregation and the chains of discrimination; one hundred years later, the Negro lives on a lonely island of poverty in the midst of a vast ocean of material prosperity; one hundred years later, the Negro is still *languished* in the corners of American society and finds himself in exile in his own land.

So we've come here today to dramatize a shameful condition. In a sense we've come to our nation's capital to cash a check. When the architects of our republic wrote the magnificent words of the Constitution and the Declaration of Independence, they were signing a *promissory note* to which every American was to fall heir. This note was the promise that all men, yes, black men as well as white men, would be guaranteed the *unalienable* rights of life, liberty, and the pursuit of happiness.

It is obvious today that America has defaulted on this promissory note insofar as her citizens of color are concerned. Instead of honoring this sacred obligation, America has given the Negro people a bad check; a check that has come back marked "insufficient funds in the great vaults of opportunity of this nation." And so we've come to cash this check, a check that will give us upon demand the riches of freedom and the security of justice.

We have also come to this hallowed spot to remind America of the fierce urgency of now. This is no time to engage in the luxury of cooling off or to take the tranquilizing drug of gradualism. Now is the time to make real the promises of democracy; now is the time to rise from the dark and desolate valley of segregation to the sunlit path of racial justice; now is the time to lift our nation from the quicksands of racial injustice to the solid rock of brotherhood; now is the time to make justice a reality for all God's children. It would be fatal for the nation to overlook the urgency of the moment. This sweltering summer of the Negro's legitimate discontent will not pass until there is an invigorating autumn of freedom and equality.

Nineteen sixty-three is not an end, but a beginning. And those who hope that the Negro needed to blow off steam and will now be content, will have a rude awakening if the nation returns to business as usual.

There will be neither rest nor tranquillity in America until the Negro is granted his citizenship rights. The whirlwinds of revolt will continue to shake the foundations of our nation until the bright day of justice emerges.

But there is something that I must say to my people who stand on the warm threshold that leads into the palace of justice. In the process of gaining our rightful place we must not be guilty of wrongful deeds.

Let us not seek to satisfy our thirst for freedom by drinking from the cup of bitterness and hatred. We must forever conduct our struggle on the high plane of dignity and discipline. We must not allow our creative protest to degenerate into physical violence. Again and again we must rise to the majestic heights of meeting physical force with soul force.

The marvelous new militancy that has engulfed the Negro community must not lead us to a distrust of all white people, for many of our white brothers, as evidenced by their presence here today, have come to realize that their destiny is tied up with our destiny and they have come to realize that their freedom is inextricably bound to our freedom. This offense we share mounted to storm the *battlements* of injustice must be carried forth by a biracial army. We cannot walk alone.

And as we walk, we must make the pledge that we shall always march ahead. We cannot turn back. There are those who are asking the devotees of civil rights, "When will you be satisfied?" We can never be satisfied as long as the Negro is the victim of the unspeakable horrors of police brutality.

We can never be satisfied as long as our bodies, heavy with fatigue of travel, cannot gain lodging in the motels of the highways and the hotels of the cities. We cannot be satisfied as long as the Negro's basic mobility is from a smaller ghetto to a larger one.

We can never be satisfied as long as our children are stripped of their selfhood and robbed of their dignity by signs stating "for whites only." We cannot be satisfied as long as a Negro in Mississippi cannot vote and a Negro in New York believes he has nothing for which to vote. No, we are not satisfied, and we will not be satisfied until justice rolls down like waters and righteousness like a mighty stream.

I am not unmindful that some of you have come here out of excessive trials and tribulation. Some of you have come fresh from narrow jail cells. Some of you have come from areas where your quest for freedom left you battered by the storms of persecution and staggered by the winds of police brutality. You have been the veterans of creative suffering. Continue to work with the faith that unearned suffering is redemptive.

Go back to Mississippi; go back to Alabama; go back to South Carolina; go back to Georgia; go back to Louisiana; go back to the slums and ghettos of the northern cities, knowing that somehow this situation can, and will be changed. Let us not wallow in the valley of despair.

So I say to you, my friends, that even though we must face the difficulties of today and tomorrow, I still have a dream. It is a dream deeply rooted in the American dream that one day this nation will rise up and live out the true meaning of its creed—we hold these truths to be self-evident, that all men are created equal.

I have a dream that one day on the red hills of Georgia, sons of former slaves and sons of former slave-owners will be able to sit down together at the table of brotherhood.

I have a dream that one day, down in Alabama, with its vicious racists, with its governor having his lips dripping with the words of interposition and nullification, that one day, right there in Alabama, little black boys and black girls will be able to join hands with little white boys and white girls as sisters and brothers. I have a dream today!

I have a dream that one day every valley shall be exalted, every hill and mountain shall be made low, the rough places shall be made plain, and the crooked places will be made straight and the glory of the Lord will be revealed and all flesh shall see it together.

This is our hope. This is the faith that I go back to the South with.

With this faith we will be able to bear out of the mountain of despair a stone of hope. With this faith we will be able to transform the jangling discords of our nation into a beautiful symphony of brotherhood.

With this faith we will be able to work together, to pray together, to struggle together, to go to jail together, to stand up for freedom together, knowing that we will be free one day. This will be the day when all of God's children will be able to sing with new meaning—"my country 'tis of thee; sweet land of liberty; of thee I sing; land where my father died, land of the pilgrim's pride; from every mountain side, let freedom ring"—and if America is to be a great nation, this must become true.

So let freedom ring from the prodigious hilltops of New Hampshire.

Let freedom ring from the mighty mountains of New York.

Let freedom ring from the heightening Alleghenies of Pennsylvania.

Let freedom ring from the snow-capped Rockies of Colorado.

Let freedom ring from the curvaceous slopes of California.

But not only that.

Let freedom ring from Stone Mountain in Georgia.

Let freedom ring from Lookout Mountain in Tennessee.

Let freedom ring from every hill and molehill of Mississippi, from every mountainside, let freedom ring.

And when we allow freedom to ring, when we let it ring from every village and hamlet, from every state and city, we will be able to speed up that day when all of God's children—black men and white men, Jews and Gentiles, Catholics and Protestants—will be able to join hands and to sing in the words of the old Negro spiritual,"Free at last, free at last; thank God Almighty, we are free at last."

• •

Vocabulary

As you think about this essay, these definitions may be helpful to you:
1. **Emancipation Proclamation**   issued by President Abraham Lincoln in 1862 freeing all slaves in all territory still at war with the Union
2. **languished**   suffering neglect
3. **promissory note**   a pledge to pay a debt, an "I.O.U."
4. **unalienable**   incapable of being surrendered or transferred
5. **battlements**   fortified walls, behind which soldiers are protected while they attack

Discussion Questions

1. What does King mean by the phrase "the tranquilizing drug of gradualism"?
2. King argues that physical force must be countered by "soul force." What does he mean?
3. Using the language of his own time, King speaks of "the Negro." Today's authors would probably not use this word. Why?
4. Discuss the ways in which repetition of key words and phrases plays a part in making this an effective speech.
5. As a Christian minister, King drew heavily on the language of the Bible, which was natural to him. What effect does including such language ("we will not be satisfied until justice rolls down like waters and righteousness like a mighty stream,""every valley shall be exalted, every hill and mountain shall be made low") add to this speech?

How Can These Ideas Apply to You?

1. Do you agree with King that "the marvelous new militancy that has engulfed the Negro community must not lead us to a distrust of all white people, for many of our white brothers, as evidenced by their presence here today, have

come to realize that their destiny is tied up with our destiny and they have come to realize that their freedom is inextricably bound to our freedom"?

2. The phrase most often used to describe King's political methods is "militant nonviolence," which reminds us of his admiration of Mahatma Gandhi, the great moral leader of India in the first half of this century. King expressed this admiration by arguing: "We must forever conduct our struggle on the high plane of dignity and discipline. We must not allow our creative protest to degenerate into physical violence." Was he right?

3. What kind of America does King describe in his speech? Has this nation changed for better or worse since the 1960s that King describes?

4. For what social or political cause would you be willing to demonstrate in a public way?

5. History and morality are separate, though often related, areas of inquiry. Are you interested in either? In one more than the other? In neither? Why?

UNIT SUMMARY

The essays in this unit discuss some of the conditions necessary to ensure that the pursuit of truth, identified in Unit 7 as the defining characteristic of a university, can be carried out by all participants in the university community without interference. Some observers believe that university faculty and students are just trying to be "politically correct" when they acknowledge and try to protect diversity. However, the essays in this unit are not grounded in the relatively recent notion of "political correctness." Instead, these essays address contemporary topics of concern within the framework of a vision of all individuals exercising their freedom to express ideas—a freedom that is essential to, and therefore precious within, the university.

Summary Questions

1. Were you surprised with any of the conclusions that these writers defended? How do they differ from your own current, or previous, beliefs?
2. Can you give examples of finding value in diversity—examples that have made a difference in the way you think or behave?
3. Many people would comment that such visions of the future like that presented by Martin Luther King Jr. are attractive and useful as a goal but too idealistic to be realized in a complex society. Do you agree? How might we go about preparing the kind of world that King envisioned in his dream?

Suggested Writing Assignments

1. Do you tend to make judgments about any group of people (for example, a nationality group, a fraternity or sorority, or a religious group) based on membership in that group? If so, write a short essay explaining why you do this. Are there any times when *group* characteristics appropriately outweigh individual character?
2. Have you ever been the object of bigotry? Write an essay describing how you were singled out and suggest a plan for responding to such behavior.
3. Whose job is it to ensure that within a university, people are judged only on the basis of their ability? Write an essay identifying those who need to act on this matter and specify the most important steps they should take.

Suggested Readings

Fisk, E. B. "The Undergraduate Hispanic Experience." *Change* (May/June 1988), 29–33.
Haley, Alex, and Malcolm X. *The Autobiography of Malcolm X.* New York: Grove Press, 1976.
Halpern, J. M., and L. Nguyen-Hong-Nhiem, eds. *The Far East Comes Near: Autobiographical Accounts of Southeast Asian Students in America.* Amherst: University of Massachusetts Press, 1989.

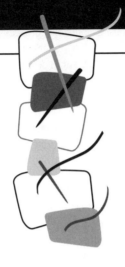

Life After College: Future Success or Future Shock?

Imagine the day you will be wearing a cap and gown and receiving the diploma that attests to your status as a college graduate. What does the future hold for you? Several readings in previous units offered visions of the future from different perspectives. These can stimulate your thinking about what you might hope to accomplish during your college years so that your college education can prepare you both for the workplace and for your leisure hours.

In Unit 1, several authors described the value of a college education and emphasized the importance of taking advantage of the opportunities offered through the experience of higher education. You were asked to examine your reasons for being in college and how these might affect your initial goals for the college experience itself. The beginning of your college life is a good time to set some tentative goals to reach by the day you are ordained a college graduate. Through your college career, you will want to broaden those goals to

Climb high

Climb far

Your goal the sky

Your aim the star.

—INSCRIPTION ON JOHNS HOPKINS MEMORIAL STEPS

include specific actions to prepare for the future lifestyle you desire. Some of your ideas might change very much.

You will also want to set goals related to the type of work you want to do and the type of worker you want to become. These should take into account both the type of job you hope to obtain after college and the quality of your work life. Thoughtful planning now can also improve your effectiveness as a worker later in life.

A commission established by the Secretary of Labor in 1990—the Secretary's Commission on Achieving Necessary Skills (SCANS)—defined the skills that young people need in order to succeed in the workplace of the future. The SCANS report outlined five competencies and other basic skills and personal qualities essential for future workers. Among these are the abilities to use resources productively, to acquire and use a wide variety of interpersonal skills, to learn to use information effectively, and to use technological and organizational systems. Future workers will also be expected to demonstrate such critical basic skills as effective reading, clear writing, and computational expertise. Oral communication skills will also be important. Computer literacy will be an absolutely required skill in the future workplace. Certain personal qualities such as integrity, effective self-management, responsibility, and sociability were also named as essential for success in the future workplace.

It is during the college years that many of these foundational skills and personal competencies can be acquired and practiced, usually in a nonthreatening environment. The quality of your life after college will depend on how well you take advantage of the opportunities presented to you during your college years.

The essay by Pellegrino was commencement address in which the speaker distinguishes between receiving a baccalaureate degree and being educated. The reading by Wells is a reminder of how difficult it is to predict the future and how important it is, as Orville Wright declares, to "think big thoughts." Levine and Cureton compare the current generation of college students with those of the past and suggest four attributes today's students need to possess to live successfully in the new century. The last reading, by Carter, offers some perspectives on the workplace itself and the importance of setting your own standards and ethical principles as you are engaged in productive work.

In addition to discussing these issues in class, you might want to talk to family, friends, and others to whom you look for guidance. Examining what is important to you now and in the future is a first step in setting thoughtful, realistic goals for your life after college. Don't wait until the day you march down the graduation aisle to consider who you are and where you want to be when that day arrives.

Having a Degree and Being Educated

Edmund D. Pellegrino, M.D.

Edmund D. Pellegrino is the director of the Center for Clinical Bioethics at Georgetown University where he is the John Carroll Professor. This essay was a commencement address given by Dr. Pellegrino at Wilkes College.

• • • • • • • • • • • • • • • • •

Few humans live completely free of illusions. Reality is sometimes just too harsh to bear without them. But comforting as they can be, some illusions are too dangerous to be harbored for very long. Eventually they must meet the test of reality—or we slip into psychosis.

I want to examine a prevalent illusion with you today—one to which you are most susceptible at this moment, namely, that *having* a degree is the same as *being* educated. It is a bit *gauche,* I admit, to ask embarrassing questions at a time of celebration. But your personal happiness and the world you create depend on how well your illusion is brought into focus. And this *emboldens* me to intrude briefly on the satisfaction you justly feel with your academic accomplishment.

The degree you receive today is only a certificate of exposure, not a guarantee of infection. Some may have caught the virus of education, others only a mild case, and still others may be totally immune. To which category do you belong? Should you care? How can you tell?

The illusion of an education has always plagued the honest person. It is particularly seductive in a technological society like ours. We intermingle education with training, and liberal with professional studies, so intimately that they are hard to disentangle. We reward specific skills in politics, sports, business, and academia. We exalt those who can *do* something—those who are experts.

It becomes easy to forget that free and civilized societies are not built on information alone. Primitive and despotic societies have their experts too! Computers and animals can be trained to store and retrieve information, to learn, and even to out-perform us. What they can never do is direct the wise use of their information. They are imprisoned by their programmers and their own expertise. The more intensive that expertise, the more it cages them; the less they can they function outside its restricted perimeter.

In a technological society experts proliferate like toadstools on a damp lawn. Some are genuine. Others are quick studies specializing in the predigestion of other people's thoughts. They crowd the TV screens, the radio waves, the printed page, eager to tell us what to believe and how to live—from sex and politics to religion and international affairs. They manufacture our culture, give us our opinions and our conversational *gambits.*

Now that you have a degree in something, you are in danger of stepping quietly into the cage of your own expertise—leaving everything else to the other experts. Whether they are genuine or phony makes little difference. If you do, you sacrifice the most precious endowment of an education—the freedom to make up your own mind—to be an authentic person. Knowledge, as Santayana said, is recognition of something absent. It is a salutation—not an embrace—a beginning, not an end.

You cannot predict when you will be brutally confronted by the falsity of your illusion like the juror who was interviewed following a recent murder trial. He was responding to one of those puerile how-does-it-feel questions that is the trademark of the telecaster's *vacuity.* "Being a juror was a terrible thing," he said. "I had to think like I never thought before. . . . I had to understand words like justice and truth. . . . Why do they make people like us judges?"

This is the pathetic lament of a sincere, sympathetic, but uneducated man. He was surely an expert in something but he could not grapple with the kind of question that separates humans from animals and computers. Justice and truth are awesome questions indeed. But who should answer those questions? Is being a juror another specialty? Do we need a degree in justice and truth? Does not a civilized and democratic society depend upon some common comprehension of what these words mean?

These same questions underlie every important public and private decision—from genetic engineering to nuclear proliferation, from prolonging human life to industrial pollution. They determine *how* we should use our expert knowledge, *whether* we should use it, and *for what* purposes. The welfare of the nation and the world depend on our capacity to think straight and act rightly—not on the amount of information we have amassed.

To be a juror, to be a person, to live with satisfaction, requires more than a trained mind—it requires an educated one, a mind that does not parrot other men's opinions or values but frames its own, a mind that can resist the potential tyranny of experts, one that can read, write, speak, manipulate symbols, argue, and judge, and whose imagination is as free as its reason.

These attributes are not synonymous with simple exposure to what is *euphemistically* called an education in the humanities or liberal arts, even when these are genuine—as often they are not. That belief only piles one illusion upon another. Rather than courses taken, or degrees conferred, the true tests of an educated mind are in its operations. Let me suggest some questions that indicate whether your mind operates like an educated one—no matter what your major may have been.

First, have you learned how to learn without your teacher? Can you work up a new subject, find the information, separate the relevant from the trivial, and express it in your own language? Can you discern which are your teacher's thoughts and which are your own? Your first freedom must be from the subtle despotism of even a great teacher's ideas.

Second, can you ask critical questions, no matter what subject is before you—those questions that expose a line of argument, evaluate the claims being made upon you, the evidence adduced, the logic employed? Can you sift fact from opinion, the plausible from the proven, the rhetorical from the logical? Can you use skepticism as a constructive tool and not as a refuge for intellectual sloth? Do you apply the same critical rigor to your own thoughts and actions? Or are you merely rearranging your prejudices when you think you are thinking?

Third, do you really understand what you are reading, what people are saying, what words they are using? Is your own language clear, concrete, and concise? Are you acquainted with the literature of your own language—with its structure and nuance?

Fourth, are your actions your own—based in an understanding and commitment to values you can defend? Can you discern the value conflicts underlying personal and public choices and distinguish what is a compromise to principle and what is not? Is your approach to moral judgments reasoned or emotional? When all the facts are in, when the facts are doubtful and action must be taken, can you choose wisely, prudently, and reasonably?

Fifth, can you form your own reasoned judgments about works of art—whether a novel, sonata, sculpture, or painting? Or are you enslaved by the critic, the book reviewer, and the "opinion makers" vacillating with their fads and pretentiousness? Artists try to evoke experiences in us, to transform us as humans. Is your imagination free enough to respond sensitively, or are you among the multitude of those who demand the explicitness of violence, pornography, dialogue—that is the sure sign of a dead imagination and an impoverished creativity?

Sixth, are your political opinions of the same order as your school and athletic loyalties—rooting for your side and ignoring the issues and ideas your side propounds? Free societies need independent voters who look at issues and not labels, who will be loyal to their ideals, not just to parties and factions. Do you make your insight as an expert the measure of social need? There is no illusion more fatal to good government!

If you can answer yes to some of these indicators, then you have imbibed the essence of a liberal education, one which assures that your actions are under the direction of your thought, that you are your own person, no matter what courses you took and what degree you receive today. You will also have achieved what is hoped for you:

> Education is thought of as not just imparting the knowledge of a professional discipline, but also as demonstrating a certain way of life—a way of life which is humane and thoughtful, yet also critical and above all rational.

If your answers are mostly negative (and I hope they are not), then you are in danger of harboring an illusion—one that is dangerous to you and society. The paradox is that the expert too has need of an educated mind. Professional and technical people make value decisions daily. To protect those whose values they affect, to counter the distorted pride of mere information, to use their capabilities for humane ends, experts too must reflect critically on what they do. The liberal arts, precisely because they are not specialties, are the indispensable accoutrements of any mind that claims to be human.

There are two kinds of freedom without which we cannot lead truly human lives. One kind is political and it is guaranteed by the Bill of Rights. The other is intellectual and spiritual and is guaranteed by an education that liberates the mind. Political freedom assures that we can express our opinions freely; a liberal education assures that the opinions we express are free. Each depends so much on the other that to threaten one is to threaten the other.

This is why I vex you with such a serious topic on this very happy occasion. The matter is too important for indifference or comfortable illusions. My hope is that by nettling you a bit I can prevent what is now a harmless illusion from becoming a delusion—firm, fixed belief, impervious either to experience or reason.

May I remind you in closing that the people who made our nation, who endowed it with the practical wisdom that distinguished its history, were people without formal degrees. One of the best among them, Abraham Lincoln, went so far as to say: "No policy that does not rest upon philosophical public opinion can be permanently maintained." Philosophical public opinion is not the work of information or expertise but of an educated mind, one that matches the aim of Wilkes to impart a way of life that is "...humane and thoughtful, yet also critical and above all rational."

T. S. Eliot, in his poem "The Dry Salvages," said: "We have had the experience of an education—I hope you have not missed the meaning." You have had the experience of an education—I hope you have not missed the meaning.

Reprinted by permission of the author.

· · · · · · · · · · · · · · · · · · ·

Vocabulary

As you think about this essay, these definitions may be helpful to you:
1. **gauche**   (pronounced gōsh) lacking social experience or grace
2. **embolden**   to instill with boldness or courage
3. **gambits**   in this essay, remarks intended to start a conversation or make a telling point
4. **vacuity**   the state of being empty or lacking content
5. **euphemistically**   substituting an agreeable or inoffensive expression for one that may offend or suggest something unpleasant

Discussion Questions

1. Why does Dr. Pellegrino think it is an illusion that having a degree and being educated are the same?
2. What is an uneducated person, according to Pellegrino?

3. How does Pellegrino define "knowledge"?
4. List six ways that, according to Pellegrino, the mind works. Why?
5. What are the two kinds of freedom needed to live "truly human lives," according to Pellegrino?

 ## How Can These Ideas Apply to You?

1. What is your definition of being educated?
2. What is your understanding of justice and truth?
3. Do you think it is helpful for first-year students to think about how an educated mind works? Why?
4. What are some specific actions you can take to master the six ways the mind of an educated person operates during your college career?
5. When you graduate, do you think your perception of "being educated" will be different from your view today? How?

Peering into the Future with Wilbur and Orville Wright

Malcolm Wells

Malcolm Wells is an architect specializing in environmentally friendly designs. Using a real quotation from Wilbur Wright, Wells creates an imaginary conversation in which Wilbur and his brother Orville talk about the future of flight. Wells uses irony to point out that, as we face the future, we need to maintain an open and creative way of thinking.

* * *

Wilbur: Orville, when you get that strut repaired, I want to talk to you about the commercial value of these machines. What I mean to say is aside from putting on demonstrations at fairgrounds, do you really think there's any money to be made from flying?

Orville: Are you serious? Airplanes are going to carry millions of passengers someday. And thousands of wagonloads of freight, too.

Wilbur: Come on, now, Orville, talk sense. Even a flying machine 10 times bigger than ours wouldn't carry more than 20 people. And I doubt that they'd even be willing to sit out here. Imagine women and children traveling that way.

Orville: Not on the wings, Wilbur; inside. There'll be enclosed cabins with soft seats and carpet on the floor.

Wilbur: And electric lights, too, I suppose. You really are a crackpot.

Orville: Flying machines will be big enough to carry hundreds of people at a time, seven or eight miles above the earth, at speeds we never thought possible.

Wilbur: And feed them, too, no doubt. Will those future flying machines of yours have uniformed waiters serving dinner up there in the clouds?

Orville: You think you're joking, Wilbur, but that's just the way it's going to be. Giant airplanes will streak through the skies at more than 500 miles an hour, crossing the country without stopping, and crossing the ocean too.

Wilbur: Dream on, Orville! How are you going to move your giant machines that fast? A propeller would spin itself to matchsticks at those speeds.

Orville: No propellers will be involved. Huge engines burning thousands of gallons of kerosene will blow out torrents of hot air to push the machines through the sky.

Wilbur: Do you know how much one of those things would weigh? It would need a ton of wood and fabric.

Orville: Metal.

Wilbur: Metal? You're dreaming about flying machines made of metal? Do you know how heavy metal is? Do you know how many blacksmiths—and blacksmith shops—it would take to build one of those giants? And how many horses it would take to pull it out to a field big enough for flying? Don't you see, Orville, your ideas couldn't possibly come true.

Orville: I predict that in the future it won't be uncommon for a flying machine to weigh over 100 tons.

Wilbur: Certainly. And where are you going to get those thousands of gallons of kerosene you mentioned? Look at the trouble we have trying to find gasoline for this thing.

Orville: By then there'll be great petroleum works all over the world, producing millions of gallons of fuel, enough kerosene to keep thousands of airplanes aloft everywhere on earth.

Wilbur: I see. And how will they launch themselves into the sky? Won't you need some huge meadows? I can just imagine all the burnt fields your air-blast engines will create. And in the winter—they will fly in the winter, won't they?

Orville: Don't laugh. They'll not only fly in the winter, but at night as well, and even in rain and snowstorms. Inside, the temperature will be as comfortable as it is around the kitchen stove. Think big thoughts, Wilbur.

They won't use grass fields. The flying machines of the future will leave from giant terminals paved all around with cement. They'll roll on rollways two or three miles long to get up to flying speed.

Wilbur: Two or three miles! Orville, you are crazy. Can you imagine the hundreds of horses and carriages your big air terminals would have to accommodate? And the stampedes you'd see every time one of those huge air blowers started to roar? Have you thought of all that?

Orville: I have thought of those things, and for the moment they have me stumped. Carriages obviously couldn't handle crowds like that. Maybe railways could take passengers to the terminals. I'll have to give it more thought.

Wilbur: Well, while you're at it, think about how to keep your aerial *leviathans* from crashing into each other up there. No doubt you'll supply them with signal lanterns. But at those speeds ...

Orville: You won't believe the kinds of warning lights they'll have. But lights won't be the main protection against collisions. Wireless warnings will be sent from one machine to the next. The drivers will not only be able to talk to each other that way, they'll be able to see all the flying machines in their vicinities on lighted glass plates right there by the steering bars.

And the drivers won't even have to steer if they don't want to. They'll be able to turn on electrical control boxes to guide the machines to their destinations thousands of miles away. Think of it, Wilbur! It's all going to happen.

Wilbur: Yes, Orv.

Now, why don't you get back to that broken strut. I think I've got the whole picture in my mind now: flying machines made of metal, and weighing tons, will roll for miles on beds of cement in order to get off the ground while carrying hundreds of passengers and thousands of gallons of fuel. The passengers will sit indoors—not out—eating dinners served by uniformed waiters while the machines streak through storms and darkness guided by electric brains. And millions of passengers each year will somehow get to the giant air terminals even though there aren't enough horses, and the roads are too muddy, to get them there.

Ah, Orville, you always were the family dreamer, and I guess that's a good thing, up to a point. But can't you see what an awful world you'd create? People traveling at rifle-bullet speeds just to go faster than a train . . . drums of kerosene piled by the thousands at air-meadows . . . throngs of people getting in the way of the air-planes . . . Is that the kind of world you'd like to see?

Now that we've proved it possible to fly, I think people will lose interest in the subject. All the excitement and challenge are going out of it. I think we should turn to some sort of practical invention—not one based on all those pie-in-the-sky predictions.

Reprinted by permission of the World Future Society.

• •

Vocabulary

As you think about this essay, this definition may be helpful to you:
leviathan   a large and formidable animal

Discussion Questions

1. How does the author use humor to help you think about the future?
2. Can you imagine such a conversation actually taking place in the Wright Brothers' era? Why or why not? Could it take place now, but related to some other miracle of modern engineering? Why or why not?
3. Wilbur insists on viewing the future based on what he knows in his own time. How does this affect his ability to imagine the future and its possibilities?
4. In this brief selection, Orville proves himself to be a futurist. What characteristics do you think are necessary for being a futurist?

How Can These Ideas Apply to You?

1. Is it difficult for you to adapt to the technology that is now emerging? Do you have trouble visualizing where technology may take us 100 years from now? Why or why not?
2. Do you really want to know what technology may become available in 10 or 20 years? Why? How would you use such knowledge if you had it?
3. Think about today's technology that you take for granted. Was it once as absurd as the picture that Wilbur makes Orville's vision out to be?

A Time of Discontinuity

Arthur Levine and Jeanette S. Cureton

- Arthur Levine is president and professor of education at Teachers College, Columbia
- University. Jeanette Cureton is an academic researcher, formerly of the Harvard
- Graduate School of Education. This reading is taken from the authors' recent book,
- *When Hope and Fear Collide: A Portrait of Today's College Student.*

• • • • • • • • • • • • • • • • • •

There are rare times in the history of a society in which rapid and profound change occurs. The change is so broad and so deep that the routine and ordinary cycles of readjustment cease. There is a sharp break between the old and the new. It is a time of *discontinuity*. In the history of this country, there have been two such break points.

The first was the Industrial Revolution, which began in earnest in the first decades of the nineteenth century. It brought about a transformation in the United States from an agricultural to an industrial society. For those who lived through it, everything appeared to be in flux. The nation's economy was turbulent and uncertain, with wide swings both up and down. New technologies with the capacity to remake the nation's daily life, ranging from steamboats and canals to railroads and mechanized factories, were burgeoning. Old industries were dying, and new industries were being born. Demographics were shifting dramatically as the population moved west and south, from rural to urban areas. Large numbers of immigrants, with relatively little formal education, were coming to America. All of the country's major social institutions—church, family, government, work, and media—were being transformed. Reflecting on the vastness of the changes, Henry Adams concluded that "the old universe was thrown into the ash heap and a new one created."

Adam's assessment was very close to the mark. The effects of industrialization have been well documented. Among the consequences are family disorganization, *attenuation* of kinship ties, and a splintering of connections between generations. Mate selection and marital patterns are retarded. Gender roles change. Homogeneity gives way to heterogeneity. Apathy and alienation grow. New and higher literacy levels are required to function in society, causing sharp differentiation in the wealth and status of the populace. Mass communication expands, and isolation within society declines. Interest groups and associations multiply....

The second break point or time of discontinuity is occurring now. The United States is currently undergoing profound demographic, economic, global, and technological change. Demographically, the U.S. population is aging, changing color, coming from other countries, and redistributing itself across the country at astounding rates....

For today's college students, this world of change dominates their lives. The cycles of community and individualism have given way to a world of unceasing, unknowable change.

This reality is compounded by the enormous size of the population attending college today. As a consequence, the benefit of a college education has diminished. When only a small proportion of an age group graduates from college, they are virtually guaranteed the best jobs a society offers. When the majority attend college, this is no longer possible. The guarantee of the best jobs expires along with the guarantee of any job. In short, the students who attended college at the turn of the century were shopping at the educational equivalent of Tiffany's. Today's undergraduates are at something much more akin to Kmart. The multiplication in size of the college student population means they are subject to exactly the same social forces as the rest of the nation's population. A smaller, more *elite* group might have been protected from the waves of change crashing upon the rest of the country. The college *cohort* is simply too large today to be sheltered in any fashion....

The consequence of rapid social change and shifting conditions in higher education today is a generation straddling two worlds, one dying and another being born. Each makes competing and conflicting demands on today's college generation; they are torn between both. A dying world makes them want security, and a world being born makes urgent their call for change. In the same fashion, pragmatism wrestles with idealism, doing well with doing good, and fear with hope. They are, above all else, a transitional generation, not unlike the young people of Henry Adams's day, and they are experiencing the same symptoms as did those who lived through the Industrial Revolution.

Education for a Transitional Generation

As a group, current undergraduates might be described as having the following characteristics. They are

- Frightened
- Demanding of change
- Desirous of security
- Disenchanted with politics and the nation's social institutions
- Bifurcated in political attitudes between left and right; the middle is shrinking
- Liberal in social attitudes
- Socially conscious and active
- Consumer oriented
- Locally rather than globally focused
- Sexually active, but socially isolated
- Heavy users of alcohol
- Hardworking
- Tired
- Diverse and divided
- Weak in basic skills and able to learn best in ways different from how their professors teach

- Pragmatic, career oriented, and committed to doing well
- Idealistic, altruistic, and committed to doing good
- Optimistic about their personal futures
- Optimistic about our collective future
- Desperately committed to preserving the American dream

This generation is no better and no worse than any other generation, but, like every other generation before, it is unique. As a result, this generation requires a unique brand of education that will enable it to attain its personal dreams and to serve the society it must lead. The education we offered to previous generations, whether successful or not, will not work for these students. They are different, and their times are different. Above all, current undergraduates are in need of an education that provides them with four things.

Hope

The first is hope. When we speak about hope, we do not mean the flabby or groundless, rosy-eyed, Pollyannaish brand. Rather, we mean the kind of conviction that allows a person to rise each morning and face the new day. It is the stuff Shakespeare talked of when he wrote, "True hope is swift and flies with swallow's wings; / Kings it makes gods, and meaner creatures kings" (*Richard III* 5.2.23). Current students profess to being optimistic about the future; but that optimism is frail.

By way of example, in the course of our research we talked with a student who told us she was majoring in business. We asked how she liked it. She said she hated it. We asked what she would rather be majoring in. She said dance. We asked, Why not major in dance? She looked at us the way one would look at a dumb younger sibling and said, "Rich is nice. Poor is not nice. I want nice," and she walked off. We had no answer that day, but over time we have thought about that student a lot. She gave up all of her dreams to study a subject she hated. If she follows a career that flows from her major, she will probably dislike that too. The saddest, saddest part of the story is that she did not have to make the choice she did. This student may not have become a professional dancer, but she could manage a dance company, or be a dance teacher, or a critic, or perhaps operate a store selling dance equipment. The tragedy of the story is not that she made a bad selection. It is that the young woman gave up her hope. It was so tenuous that she dared not hold onto it....

Responsibility

The second *attribute* is responsibility. Despite all we said about the adversities this generation is facing, current college students are still among the most fortunate people in the world. They owe something to others. Indeed, they are more involved in service activities than their predecessors, but at the same time they are not convinced that they can both do good and do well. Many feel that when it comes to security and responsibility, a choice must be made.

At a New England liberal arts college, all first-year students were required to participate in an exercise called "Freshman Inquiry." Students were required to prepare an essay talking about what they had learned and not learned in college so far, their hopes and aspirations for the future, and how they planned to use the remainder of their college education. After the essay was written, each student met with a panel composed of a faculty member, an administrator, and a fellow student to discuss it. One student submitted an essay to a panel, saying when she grew up she wanted to be CEO of a multinational corporation, become a U.S. senator, head a foundation that provided scholarships for college students, and work for nuclear disarmament. The student was asked what she needed out of college to accomplish all this. After a little thought, she answered, "A killer instinct." Her listeners sought clarification. She said this meant the ability to step on people or walk over them when necessary to get what she wanted. She was asked about altruism. This time she asked for clarification, and the word was defined for her. She said that was not part of her game plan. The panel reminded her of her desire to work for nuclear arms control. Surely that was altruistic. She told the panel they did not get it: "If there were a nuclear war, I would not get to be CEO of a multinational corporation." Three years later, the student graduated, plans and opinions intact. Her grades were high, and several years later she was attending one of the nation's better business schools. All of her dreams may come true, but one is forced to conclude that her college experience was inadequate. It never taught her about responsibility, what she had an obligation to do for others.

Appreciation of Differences

The third attribute is understanding and appreciation of differences. Today's undergraduates are living in a world in which differences are multiplying and change is the norm, but they attend colleges that are often segregated on the basis of differences and where relationships between diverse populations are strained.... It is imperative that college students learn to recognize, respect, and accept their differences.

Efficacy

The final attribute is efficacy, that is, a sense that one can make a difference. Here again, current undergraduates affirmed this belief at the highest rates recorded in a quarter-century.... It brings to mind a group we met at a well-known liberal arts college. The college had created a special program for its most outstanding seniors to prepare them for the nation's most prestigious graduate fellowships. Levine [a co-author of this essay] was asked to talk to the students about leadership. After a few minutes of watching the students squirming in their seats, looking out the windows, and staring at their watches, he concluded the talk was not going well.

He told the group what he suspected; they agreed. They traded hypotheses back and forth about what had gone wrong. Finally, one student said, "Life is short. This leadership stuff is bullshit. We could not make a difference even if we wanted to." Levine took a quick poll of the group to see how many agreed with the student. Twenty-two out of twenty-five hands went up.

Today's students need to believe that they can make a difference. Not every one of them will become president of the United States, but each of them will touch scores of lives far more directly and tangibly—family, friends, neighbors, and coworkers. For ill or for good, in each of those lives students will make a difference. They need to be convinced that making a difference is the birthright. They should not give it away. No one can take it away....

Reprinted by permission of Jossey-Bass, Inc., a subsidiary of John Wiley & Sons, Inc.

● ●

 # Vocabulary

As you think about this essay, these definitions may be helpful to you:
1. **discontinuity**   lack of continuity or cohesion
2. **attenuation**   weakening
3. **elite**   a powerful minority group
4. **cohort**   in statistics, a group of individuals having a great deal in common
5. **attribute**   an inherent characteristic

 # Discussion Questions

1. According to the authors, what are the two periods in history when profound change occurred? What do these two periods have in common?
2. Why do the authors claim the benefit of a college education has diminished?
3. Do you agree with the author's description of current undergraduates? Why or why not?
4. What four attributes must a college education provide? Do you agree these are the most important for the future? Why or why not?
5. What can college students do to make sure they will "make a difference"?

 # How Can These Ideas Apply to You?

1. Are you feeling the "time of discontinuity" that the authors describe? If so, in what way?
2. Do you think you are getting a Tiffany or a Kmart education? Why?
3. What would you add to or subtract from the authors' list of characteristics they attribute to current undergraduates?

4. Do you agree that current college students "owe something to others"? Why or why not?

5. Do you personally believe you can "make a difference" in the world? Do you really want to? Why or why not?

Outlooks and Insights:
Succeeding on the Job and in Life

Carol Carter

Carol Carter received her education from the University of Arizona. She is assistant vice president and director of college marketing for Prentice-Hall publishers. This essay appears in her book *Majoring in the Rest of Your Life* and discusses what might happen after you obtain your first job. Her latest book *Keys to Effective Learning* focuses on effective learning techniques that can serve for a lifetime.

• • • • • • • • • • • • • • • • •

No matter what your first job after college happens to be, it is a first step. But it is also a point of departure. If you started with the company and the position of your dreams, great. Your job might also be less than terrific. But you have to start somewhere, building your skills, meeting people and developing work habits. That's a positive, exciting challenge.

You'll go from there to a string of promotions, to a better job with another company, to a smaller company, back to graduate school or to begin your own company. Your first job is like a blank page. You fill it in as you go. And your options are limitless as long as you pursue them.

Games People Play

In the real world, people measure themselves by all kinds of things—how much money they make, what their job is, how many people they know, how many dates they have, what kind of clothes they wear or what kind of car they drive.

Many of these things have to do with *appearances,* not reality. They reflect what people want others to think, not necessarily what they really are. Know the difference between the two and be true to yourself and your values. The best job in the world isn't worth much if you are not happy. Similarly, no amount of money or possessions you can buy will satisfy you if you aren't content with who you are.

[You need to define] those things that are important to *you,* and you alone. So resist comparing yourself with those around you. That's a game you'll never win. There will always be people who are better and worse off than you. In college and in life, it's important to do what you believe and what you feel is right.

People may not always agree with you, especially if they feel threatened by your abilities. That's okay. Preserve your *integrity* and don't let someone get the better of you. Your satisfaction will come from knowing that you took the high road.

President John F. Kennedy said it best in his inaugural address: "For of those to whom much is given, much is required. And when at some future date the high court of history sits in judgment on each of us, recording whether in our brief span of service we fulfilled our responsibilities to the state, our success or failure, in whatever office we hold, will be measured by four questions: First, were we truly men of courage? . . . Second, were we truly men of judgment? . . . Third, were we truly men of integrity? . . . Finally, were we truly men of dedication?"

Is It Ethical?

Ask yourself these questions: Would others approve of my behavior if they knew about it? Would I want someone else to behave similarly? Is what I'm doing right for the company? Is what the company is doing right? If not, how do I handle it? What are my own personal standards and how do I define them?

In journalism, the accepted rule for quotes is that if someone says something to you and then says, "Don't print that," only *after* he made the statement, you are allowed to print it. But several journalists I've talked to said they would not print the quote if it was made by a "civilian," a nonpolitician or anyone not familiar with the rules of the press. The reason? Plain fairness.

On Being Happy

Once you've landed your job, take pride in what you do. Concentrate not just on job success but on overall happiness. If there is any one point that this book makes, it's the importance of balancing several goals—personal and professional. Your job is only one aspect of your life.

It takes a strong commitment and hard work to maintain a healthy balance on the job and off. Being happy won't just happen. Like anything else, you have to work at it.

In a graduation speech to students at his alma mater, MIT, Kenneth Olsen, CEO of Digital Equipment Corporation, reflected on his thirty years of work since graduating from college: "Running a business is not the important thing. Making a commitment to do a good job, to improve things, to influence the world is where it's at. I would also suggest that one of the most satisfying things is to help others to be creative and take responsibility. These are the important things."

"Your most precious *commodity* is not material," says Charles S. Sanford, Jr., CEO of Bankers Trust New York Corporation. "It is and always will be your time." If you keep work in balance with other things in your life, Sanford says, you can accomplish even more on the job. "Read a little poetry, enjoy friends, and most of all, don't take yourself too seriously. In the final analysis, whatever you have accomplished won't be worth much unless you've had fun."

Okay, so the *cynic* in you cries: How much time did these CEOs spend working in their twenties and thirties? Good point. They probably spent a lot of time, but you have to ask yourself: Do you want to be a CEO? Most people would say, "No, thanks." You have to carefully weigh the trade-offs of your long-term goals against what you are doing—and enjoying—in the short term. The majority of the population thrive quite happily between entry-level positions and the top of the heap. They enjoy their work and still have the time to be with their friends and raise a family.

Maybe you won't have all the money in the world, but you will have had time to enjoy those things that count the most when you're ninety—a job you liked, a lifestyle you enjoyed and the opportunity to contribute to your own growth and that of others.

Thoughts for the Journey

I'd like to tell you a personal anecdote. It has to do with becoming discouraged.

About three months before I finished this manuscript, I was exhausted. My job was quite *tedious*—not because the work itself had changed, but because my approach to it had. I made little time to see my friends, and at night I just wanted to go to sleep early. Boring. In short, I was doing all those things I have said never to do. Realizing that I wasn't being myself, and knowing for a fact that I wasn't having a good time, I decided to take a break to get back the *perspective* I knew was missing.

Egypt was the place for perspective. Why Egypt? It was exotic, distant and vastly different from life as I knew it. Moreover, one of my interests is travel, and after my junior year in Spain, I made a personal promise to visit as many countries as I could. So off I went for the first time on a vacation by myself, leaving my "normal" life and my work behind me.

When I saw the pyramids at dusk, a renewed energy and inspiration filled me. The 4,500-year-old pyramids symbolize balance, perfection, human achievement and teamwork. (Fortunately, today we can work in teams in business and organizations; the Egyptians dictated to slaves in the most oppressive style.) Witnessing the achievements of an ancient culture that survived 4,500 years left me with a feeling of great awe and real humility. I wondered how many American monuments would survive 450 years, let alone into the year 6500.

Clearly, the Egyptians saw no limits to what they could accomplish. They saw things not in terms of what they were in the moment, but in terms of what they could become in time. They made dreams into realities.

Well, bully for Tut, you say, but what has this got to do with college and careers and human potential? The pyramids helped me to recover my "edge," my own potential. The tensions loosened inside of me and confidence took over.

My perspective restored, I was free to concentrate on challenges, including work, the book and my personal life, with confidence and energy.

Throughout your life, the inspirations that motivate you will ebb and flow. You won't always feel inspired and you won't always perform at peak. The important thing to remember when you reach an impasse is not to panic. Remove yourself from the ordinary—through reading *Don Quixote* or going to a concert or exhibit or taking a day trip by yourself. Maybe your most relaxing time is spent watching a football game or a weekly sitcom. That's fine. Just allow yourself time to unwind and replenish your own central energy source.

The Blue Sky Ahead

You have a lot to be proud of. If you are reading this book for the first time as a freshman, you get credit for getting this far and for committing yourself to making college and your career pursuit everything they can be. Good for you.

When you graduate and you are wondering how four years could come and go so fast, take time to pat yourself on the back. Look down from where you are now, realize how far you've come and be proud of your accomplishments. The next peak you scale, your first job, is very similar to what you've learned in the last few years. Accept the challenges that are before you. And in addition to doing a good or a great job, give to the world something of what it has given to you through your family, your friends, your activities and your actions. Don't be typical. You are unique. Show the world the special gifts and contributions that only you have to offer.

And so here's to your unique success story. Here's to the ability that you have to dream the dream and make it real. Go change the world.

 Vocabulary

As you think about this essay, these definitions may be helpful to you:
1. **integrity**   firm adherence to a code of moral or artistic values
2. **commodity**   something useful or valuable
3. **cynic**   a faultfinding critic who believes that human conduct is motivated wholly by self-interest
4. **tedious**   tiresome because of length or dullness
5. **perspective**   point of view

 Discussion Questions

1. How is your first job like a blank page, according to Carter?
2. Do you agree that many measurements of success that people use only have to do with "appearances"? Explain.
3. What are some "games people play"?
4. Why is ethical behavior so important in the workplace?
5. Why is it important to balance your personal and professional life?

How Can These Ideas Apply to You?

1. How will you measure success in the "real world"?
2. List three work values that are important to you. Why are they important?
3. How do you define your personal standards as they relate to ethical behavior?
4. How do you "unwind and replenish your central energy source"?
5. What can you do now while still in school to facilitate a better personal transition into the workplace?

UNIT SUMMARY

In Unit 9 you have read several authors' perceptions of how life after college might be different, along with some of their suggestions for preparing for the day after graduation. The following questions and writing assignments may help you clarify your aspirations for what you want in the future and how you might begin to prepare for it now.

Summary Questions

1. How important is having a degree to you? Do you think it is important to be educated when you graduate? How might your response affect your future career and life?
2. Levine and Cureton describe four attributes that an education must provide. Of these (hope, responsibility, appreciation of differences, and efficacy), which will be the most difficult for you to acquire? Why? The easiest? Why?
3. As you look forward to your years in college, do you expect them to be easy or difficult? In what ways?

Suggested Writing Assignments

1. If you wrote an essay in Unit 1 about your reasons for being in college, reexamine these reasons. Are they still the same? Have they changed? Have you added any? What has influenced your thinking the most?
2. How has the prospect of finding a job after college influenced your initial choice of major? Have your experiences so far confirmed that decision? In what way? If you are considering a change, discuss some possible alternatives and why you are considering them.
3. Discuss how you intend to prepare yourself to become an effective worker in tomorrow's workplace. Describe specific ways, such as work and volunteer opportunities, campus involvement, and academic and other experiences, that will help you acquire the general competencies and skills necessary to be effective.

Suggested Readings

Carter, Carol. *Keys to Effective Learning.* Upper Saddle River, NJ: Prentice-Hall, 1999.
Covey, Stephen. *The Seven Habits of Highly Effective People.* New York: Simon and Schuster, 1989.
Mitchell, S. *American Generations: Who They Are, How They Live, What They Think.* New York: New Strategist, 1998.

Author Index

Subject Index